KT-473-823

UNIVER... OF
ER

THE LIFE
OF
THE DRAMA

KA 0250729 3

WITHDRAWN FROM

ERIC BENTLEY

THE LIFE
OF
THE DRAMA

ATHENEUM

NEW YORK

1975

809.2
BEN

02507293

Copyright © 1964 by Eric Bentley
All rights reserved
Library of Congress catalog card number 64-14930
ISBN 0-689-70011-3
Manufactured in the United States of America by
Halliday Lithograph Corporation,
West Hanover, Massachusetts
Published in Canada by McClelland & Stewart Ltd.
First Atheneum Printing December 1966
Second Printing December 1967
Third Printing April 1970
Fourth Printing January 1972
Fifth Printing January 1974
Sixth Printing April 1975

TO THE MEMORY OF MY FRIEND

PERRY MILLER

CONTENTS

PART TWO: DIFFERENT KINDS OF PLAYS

Auf die ewige Lebendigkeit kommt es an, nicht auf das ewige Leben.

NIETZSCHE

. . . ce principe certain de l'art, qu'il n'y a ni moralité ni intérêt au théâtre sans un secret rapport du sujet dramatique à nous.

BEAUMARCHAIS

Our descent into the elements of our being is then justified by our subsequent freer ascent toward its goal: we revert to sense only to find food for reason. . . .

SANTAYANA

Part One

ASPECTS OF
A PLAY

1

PLOT

THE RAW MATERIAL OF PLOT

THE LIVING EXPERIENCE of a play, as of a novel, or a piece of music, is a river of feeling within us which flows, now fast, now slow, now placidly between broad banks, now in a torrent between narrow ones, now down a slope, now over rapids, now cascading in a waterfall, now halted by a dam, now debouching into an ocean. With this, the immediate experience, scholarship and criticism and pedagogy are amazingly little concerned. The professionals have theories about *Hamlet* and are sure these are correct. But ask them why they go to a show or a movie on Saturday night and you will find them much less certain. Now there would seem to be something a little suspect in claiming to solve the advanced problems if you haven't solved the elementary ones. But have you ever solved the elementary ones? The easiest questions are the hardest. And you can only broach them as you broach the hardest: by breaking them down into their component parts, tackling the cruder components, and working your way through to the less crude.

What is plot? The finished product that comes to mind is nothing if not intricate and subtle. From what raw materials was the product made? From life, we may confidently venture, life in its diversity and not excluding its seamy side. But there can be no answers, even tentative ones, while the questions remain so broad. The analysis of the material of plot can begin only when some smaller unit than "life" is isolated, preferably—since our subject is plot in drama—a unit characteristic of drama in particular. In finding such a unit, I take a hint from a remark of George Santayana's to the effect that, while the novelist may see events through the medium of other men's minds, the dramatist "allows us to see other men's minds through the medium of events." If plot is an edifice, the bricks from which it is built are events, occurrences, happenings, incidents.

Events are not dramatic in themselves. Drama requires the eye of the beholder. To see drama in something is both *to perceive elements of conflict* and *to respond emotionally to these elements of conflict.* This emotional response consists in being thrilled, in being struck with wonder, at the conflict. Even conflict is not dramatic in itself. Should we all perish in a nuclear war, there will continue to be conflict—in the realm of physics and chemistry. That is not a drama, but only a process. If drama is a thing one sees, there has to be a *one* to see. Drama is human.

How dramatic is this life of ours? The opinion certainly exists that the dramatic elements are rare, and that everyday experience is boring, lacking in conflict. That things go on and on in an endless round might be said,

4

and has been said, of life in general. It has also been said of particular epochs and places.

But if drama is a matter not only of the happenings themselves but of our emotional response, then the question: how dramatic is life? is in part a subjective matter. What one person feels to be boring, another experiences as thrilling. Even a man who thinks life in general to be undramatic will notice exceptions.

> A banker who flees in an airplane, gangsters who make away with the child of a national hero, a girl who turns into a boy, a house painter who becomes Caesar, we can put a name to all these novelistic episodes which have been composed by an indefatigable journalist who doesn't much care about verisimilitude.

These lines were written in the nineteen thirties by Robert Brasillach, and it would be very easy to match such "dramas" from the newspapers of the forties, fifties and sixties. Life, as reported in the newspapers, is dramatic. What else keeps the newspapers going?

But still, it may be argued, Lindbergh was exceptional in being a national hero, and the gangsters were exceptional in being gangsters. The newspapers are directed at the others, who can dream of being national heroes, and sigh with relief at not having their babies kidnaped. For better or worse, the life of the others—of the millions— is conventionally taken to be undramatic, and the conventional opinion, as befits convention, corresponds to the externals of the case. We only dream of being national heroes. But this is another way of saying that we are national heroes in our dreams. Once we realize that we dream most of the time, we have to reverse the conventional view and declare that our lives are dramatic after all.

Freud wrote a revealing book called *The Psychopathology of Everyday Life,* in which he showed that verbal activities which had no apparent content actually covered a wealth of meaning. Beneath a trivial intellectual surface lurked strong emotional conflicts. May we not speak, in a similar sense, of *the drama of everyday life,* even where drama seems totally lacking?

I have been using the word *dreams* loosely. I mean both daydreams and dreams during sleep. I mean all our fantasies—which was one of the things our ancestors meant when they said, as they so often did, that life was a dream. These fantasies are the direct or indirect expression of wishes, wishing being the fuel in the human engine. It is not just that life seems dramatic to us. We wish it to be dramatic; therefore, it is; this particular wish being insistent and imperious. Even our constant complaint that life is boring testifies chiefly to our refusal to be bored. We insist that every twenty-four hours be a drama in twenty-four acts. Even the rejection of life—as human beings reject it—is a drama. One finds in any case of suicide an element of revenge and a last pathetic spasm of exhibitionism. What is undramatic in human behavior—as in Anglo-Saxon manners—is a trick of emphasis by understatement. Anglo-Saxons are so arrogant they shout in whispers. The undramatic is their peculiar drama.

The conventional view is that life is undramatic until a journalist or a playwright "dramatizes" the issues. This is to omit to mention what the journalist and the playwright chiefly count on: our insatiable appetite for drama. Consider the activity known as doing nothing. Think of being too tired even for daydreams. You doze off in your chair. Perhaps you feel relatively serene as you do so. No sooner are you asleep than, as we say, "hell breaks loose." Gigantic struggles, terrible pursuits, agonizing frustrations come before the inner eye of your dreams.

If only they ended after you woke up! But the mood of your dream persists, as well it might, considering that it embodies your principal anxieties. You take it out on your wife. A Strindberg play! Your irritation is the same size as your nightmare. The phone rings. A small problem has arisen in the office. But at this moment, small is large. The office problem takes on the proportions of an aerial bombardment. You hang up in a rage. A social drama!

On the one hand, the big dramas of the Lindberghs and the Hitlers; on the other, the little dramas of each one of us each day. But these little dramas, to the imagination, are big, and are cast in the likeness of precisely the big dramas described in the newspaper. Thus it is that plays are generally about the big people, though what they say applies to the little people. And there is a converse to this proposition: that when a great playwright, such as Chekhov, presents the littleness of everyday life, he manages to suggest—as indeed he must—the largeness of everyday life, the size of those fantasies which range from the secret life of Walter Mitty to the chivalric musings of Don Quixote.

Virginia Woolf once spoke of the novel as an extension of the range of our gossip. The drama, being in general a more violent phenomenon, could be regarded as an extension of the range of scandal. Both genres testify to the human love of information about other human beings, particularly of the kind of information that is normally withheld, and the dramatist is an extremist about this as about many things, a man who otherwise might have been a Peeping Tom or a police spy. If this much is not granted at the outset, we shall only be baffled later on, as I think some otherwise very fine critics have been—Edwin Muir, for example, who wrote in his book on the novel:

> Irresponsible delight in vigorous events is what charms us in the novel of action. Why a mere description of violent actions should please us is a question for the psychologists.

The second sentence incidentally provides a bit of evidence that a literary man may wish to avoid the more elementary facts of literary experience. For surely Mr. Muir couldn't have meant that the appeal of violent actions is far to seek. Why does even a bad description of violent actions please us? How could it fail to? We tend to feel our lives are lacking in violence, and we like to see what we are missing. We tend to be bored, and we like to be caught up in someone else's excitement. We are aggressive, and we enjoy watching aggression. (If we don't know we are aggressive, we enjoy watching aggression even more.) We never had it so bad, and we like others to be having it worse. And even if there's a war on, and we are in fact leading a violent life, murdering "the enemy" or stabbing our "comrades" in the back when our officers aren't looking, at twilight when the lights are low we like to turn on the TV and see Americans nonchalantly killing each other in some jolly Western. In this way we can insure that the violence in our lives be absolutely uninterrupted, for it certainly need not be interrupted during the night, when we dream.

This, then, is the answer to Mr. Muir: violence interests us because we are violent. And the gentlest outwardly can be the most turbulent inwardly. This possibility has indeed been stressed to the point where by now we suspect every Milquetoast of being a repressed Torquemada—every Jekyll a mere mask for Hyde. But violence is not limited to persons of nonviolent demeanor. It is present in all except, on the one hand, the exceptionally enfeebled and, on the other, certain kinds of saints. And while feebleness may be congenital, nonviolent saintliness is not. The violence has been burned out of a saint by ceaseless moral labor. Now saints do not need the drama; and the feeble of mind and body cannot get to it. Everyone else welcomes the violence in it. And I have sometimes wondered if it wouldn't make better sense to teach budding playwrights, instead of the usual Dramatic Technique, two rules grounded in human nature: if you wish to attract the audience's attention, be violent; if you wish to hold it, be violent again. It is true that bad plays are founded on such principles, but it is not true that good plays are written by defying them.

THE IMITATION OF LIFE

What is the relation between the violent material and the finished plot?

Art mirrors life. Aristotle's word is *mimesis.* We are too sophisticated if we do not allow the word to carry its literal denotation: sheer reproduction. Would art exist at all if men did not desire to live twice? You have your life; and on the stage you have it again. This is simple, but not on that account less valid. Greek scholars are always explaining that, for Aristotle, imitation does not mean imitation. Nevertheless, it does.

The instinct of imitation is implanted in man from childhood [Aristotle writes], one difference between

9

him and other animals being that he is the most imitative of living creatures. . . . Objects which in themselves we view with pain we delight to contemplate when reproduced with minute fidelity. . . . Thus the reason why men enjoy seeing a likeness is . . . that they find themselves . . . saying . . . "Yes, that is he."

"Objects which in themselves we view with pain we delight to contemplate when reproduced with minute fidelity." In other words, a raw slice of life may be served up as art. It is not any deviation from life that we are enjoying. The fact of imitation is sufficient to turn pain to delight.

Any attempt at a psychology of dramatic art should start by acknowledging the impulse toward sheer imitation. What can be said against such faithful mimicry is not that it is unsound in principle but only that its possibilities are extremely limited in practice. We begin to glimpse what other possibilities there are at the moment when we permit deviations from strict fidelity. It remains a mistake to reject the raw material. The "vigorous events" and "violent actions" of which Mr. Muir spoke are not things to be relegated to lower classes of art. They may be low in themselves but only as the soil is low: from it spring the flowers. The flowers of dramatic art have their roots in crude action.

It was said once by a dramatic critic of *The New York Times* that a dramatist must be something of a charlatan. This is not true but a truth is involved. A dramatist is not an old maid. He seldom forgets the animal part of our nature. He will not refine upon human nature, much as he may also be interested in human refinement. The most civilized great tragedy ever written, perhaps, is *Phaedra,* but Phaedra was the half-sister of the Minotaur and step-daughter, as it were, to a bull. Although to some Anglo-Saxon readers, Racine's kind of drama seems narrow and specialized, it actually ranges from the peaks of the human spirit to the depths of animalism. If it is ultracivilized, it is also ultrabarbaric.

Then there is Shakespeare. There are things in Shakespeare that stare us in the face but which we either cannot or will not see. Modern respectability resembles neo-Classic good taste: it is a form of blindness. Unless one shares Shakespeare's "irresponsible delight in vigorous events" one is too genteel to appreciate what he did with such events. Shakespeare's comedy is much earthier than modern producers admit, his tragedy much less uniformly sublime. Certain recent European productions allegedly influenced by Communism have been far better than the American and British productions we see, mainly because they are influenced, first, by crude life around us and, second, by crude art around us (gangster films, pulp fiction, and the like).

No dramatist is afraid of crude action as Mr. Muir was. Maeterlinck himself uses crude action almost to the point of pornography in *Monna Vanna*. Shaw talked against plot but used plenty of action in most of his plays and, for some of the best of his plays, constructed an intricate plot. Chekhov placed his camera in an unusual relation to the violent action, but that action was still there and was still crucial. Only his skilled legerdemain prevents an audience from realizing that Professor Serebriakov, Natasha, and Madame Ranevsky are predatory animals—they are the villains of the plays and give them an action of horrifying and traditional destructiveness.

Drama is cruder than lyric poetry and the novel in this respect: that it does not even conceal its connection with those raw elements which interest us "irresponsibly." This is the explanation of the well-recognized fact that a good play can be enjoyed on distinct planes by audiences of differing degrees of refinement. It is important to recall which plane is most necessary: the soil can exist without the flower, but the flower cannot exist without the soil.

ASTONISHMENT AND SUSPENSE

THE ART of the drama is firmly grounded in human nature, and to be human is to revel in mishaps and disasters. Aristotle adds that pleasure may be taken in the mere mimicking of such mishaps or disasters. But simple imitation—imitation so simply undertaken—will never yield a plot. Indeed the gap between life in the raw and life in the narratives of the dramatic masters is so wide that we may wonder how it ever gets bridged. It is hardly surprising that some people suppose that raw life can be completely disregarded.

There is a halfway house between life and plot, and that is story. If one has a supply of incidents, all one needs to make a story of them is the word *and*. The psychology of stories is primitive. It is all a matter of that interest in violent actions which Mr. Muir takes a low view of. For if you have this interest in gossip, in scandal, in casualties and catastrophes, all I have to do is tell you incident A, and you wish to know incident B. Then, as I work my way through the alphabet, your appetite grows with eating, and you won't let me leave off. It's like an appetite for certain foods. You may not especially like them, but you can't put them down. Such was the secret of Scheherazade in *The Arabian Nights*. She would get the king so interested in A and B that he would refrain from beheading her in order to hear C and D. This king resembles the "resistance" of every reader; and Scheherazade, every storyteller and dramatist.

What creates suspense? Not merely ignorance as to what will happen next, but an active desire to know it, a desire that has been aroused by a previous stimulus. The first of the passions, says Descartes, is astonishment (*admiratio*). Incident A has to astonish before we become eager to know incident B. The violent, raw material I was discussing is apropos from the start because our interest in it can be counted on. To get from the first incident to the second requires a minimum application of the narrator's art.

Such are the two ingredients of suspense in narrative. They suffice for the composition of the crudest fictions, such as soap operas and TV Westerns, and once again I refer to the crude phenomena, not to scorn them, but in a sense to embrace them. Like other symptoms of childhood or neurosis, they are not to be banned by adult and relatively healthy persons but to be included within the definition of maturity or health. As Nietzsche says, one should not throw rubbish away, one should be an ocean and be able to hold it.

The formula of soap opera and Westerns is a sound one. If we don't spend our days and nights watching them, that should only be because we have other things to do. Possibly they would prove monotonous after a while, but possibly, like peanuts and cigarettes, they would not. Even on a TV screen violence in action and suspense in narrative can seldom fail to hold interest. The psychology is sound and each man is a human being—a specimen of human psychology—before he is a scholar or a gentleman.

There is one argument for doing without soap opera that is especially relevant here. We can do without it in its petty and pure form because we can get it as part of a larger and complex form. Great narrative is not the opposite of cheap narrative: it is soap opera *plus*. A French critic once went to some pains to show that the stories of Corneille's plays were the same as the stories of the movies in the era of Rudolph Valentino. That you like Valentino is not presumptive evidence that you will like Corneille, but you will dislike Corneille if you read, so to speak, from the neck up, if you prevent the movie fan in you from finding and enjoying in Corneille what he has in common with Valentino. A certain gentility, still a tradition in academic life even in this age of extermination camps, tends to divide not only society but each individual into highbrow and lowbrow.

THE IMITATION OF THE ACTION

THERE IS life with its events, really large and seemingly large, life which is all drama yet in which the dramas are not written, staged, enacted. There is narrative, which I have exemplified in its most rudimentary form: the mainspring is suspense and the method is the arrangement of incidents in chronological order. Finally, there is plot, which is narrative with something "done to it," something added. The something done to it is a rearrangement of the incidents in the order most calculated to have the right effect. The something added is a principle in terms of which the incidents take on meaning: even the principle of causality will turn a story into a plot. As E. M. Forster says in his *Aspects of the Novel*, "the king died and then the queen died" is story, but it becomes a plot if we write: "the king died and then the queen died *of grief*."

Plot, then, is nothing if not artificial. Plot results from the intervention of the artist's brain, which makes a cosmos out of events that nature has left in chaos. In Richard Moulton's words, it is "the purely intellectual side of action," "the extension of design to the sphere of human life." Plot being a high and intricate example of Art, as Art stands in contrast to Life, how can plot also be considered an imitation of life? It cannot. It can incorporate some of those exact imitations which Aristotle mentioned but it is itself an alteration of life and an improvement on it.

Aristotle does not say that plot is an imitation of life. He says: "the plot is the imitation of the Action." What is the Action? Aristotle forgot to tell. A French critic, Pierre-Aimé Touchard, suggests that it is "the general movement that brings it about that something is born, develops, and dies between the beginning and the end." The remark is helpful in not being too helpful. It would be vain to expect to locate Action except where Touchard very obviously locates it—in our minds. We would never affirm the existence of such a general movement unless we claimed to have already felt it. But this is what we do claim, when under the influence of a plot. For the dramatist, correspondingly, to imitate an Action is to find objective equivalents of a subjective experience. An Action is a definition in terms of incidents and events of something undefined that lurks inside the dramatist. This is not to say that this is *all* an Action is, and that therefore the drama deals only with the writer's internal world, but only that, whatever a play covers, in outer or inner worlds, its author is indeed the author of its being: its life is his life. There have been good playwrights whose comprehension of the great world was slight indeed, but a playwright whose sense of the "general movement" of an Action is slight could only be a slight playwright.

Another French critic, Henri Gouhier, has suggested that the idea of an Action will become clearer if we trace it back to the creative process. Psychologists have long been aware that the creative imagination, whether of scientists or artists, does not always work away at details and leave the discovery of all-embracing unity till the end. It often starts out from a unity vaguely apprehended and discovers details as it proceeds. Kepler worked that way. And the dramatist could be regarded as working that way.

In a profound chapter of his book *Mind-Energy,* Bergson calls such a unity a "dynamic schema." Applying Bergsonian views to the drama, we would postulate a process in four stages: first, the author's creative emotion; second, his hazy yet at the same time tenacious general idea or "dynamic schema"; third, his Action, which is an "imitation," objectification, and elaboration of the dynamic schema; and fourth, the completed play, or Action fitted out with characters, dialogue, and spectacle.

Another thinker who has contributed to the understanding of dramatic psychology is Lord Raglan. He took it as his job in his book *The Hero* to stress the extent to which plots are *not* a direct imitation of life. In effect, he rewrites even the dictum that plot is the imitation of the Action. For Raglan, plot is the imitation of myth. Remarking that "plots are like nothing that really happens,"

Raglan has this to say of the plot of Shakespeare's *Henry IV:*

> The Prince Henry of history, who spent his time trying to suppress the Welsh and the Lollards, and the Prince Henry of the stories, who spends his time roistering with Falstaff, may meet on the field of Shrewsbury, but they are creatures of quite different worlds, and the world of the latter is the world of myth. In this world of myth the principal characters are two, a hero and a buffoon. . . .

Taken as the imitation, not of history, but of legend, the Falstaff story makes better sense, and the rejection of Falstaff comes to seem, not improbable, but necessary. What Raglan is "on to" is a theory of narrative archetypes, such as Miss Maud Bodkin was later to put forward in her well-known book, *Archetypal Patterns in Poetry.* Incidentally, Miss Bodkin did not really need to base her conclusions on the special theories of Jung. Her main point, surely, is that in art, recognition is preferable to cognition: a good story is one we have heard before; that is, a good storyteller aims at the effect of re-telling, a good dramatist at re-enactment. This is where ritual comes in— ritual *is* re-enactment. Gilbert Murray had said the following (as Miss Bodkin acknowledges) of the appeal of primitive stories to modern men:

> in part, I suspect, it depends on mere repetition . . . these stories and situations . . . are . . . deeply implanted in the memory of the race . . . there is that within us which leaps at the sight of them, a cry of the blood which tells us we have known them always.

* * *

And if the old stories are ever new, new stories must always be old if they are to take hold of us. It is a question of our only being able to learn what we feel we already know, of the uselessness of knowing without realization, of all learning being a conscious or unconscious Recognition (*anagnorisis*).

Plot, says Santayana, in *The Sense of Beauty,* elaborating on Aristotle, is "the most difficult portion of dramatic art." That is why it has been the least explored and remains the least understood. Why has it in modern times come to be also the least respected?

THE PREJUDICE AGAINST PLOT

SOME RESENT life; others, art. Both resentments show themselves in the prejudice against plot. The raw material of plot is resented for its rawness. The finished plot is resented for its lack of rawness, its artificiality. Both resentments may be felt by the same person. The late John van Druten said: "A play that was all atmosphere with no plot at all would be my preference." The preference for *no plot* corresponds to the modern distaste for artifice, and the phrase "all atmosphere" expressed the modern distaste for violent action.

If Edwin Muir is an example of a critic who looks down his nose at the literature of violent events and vigorous actions, an equally distinguished critic who is embarrassed by the finished story and the finished plot is E. M. Forster. "Yes," he says wearily, "oh dear yes, the novel tells a story." And he finds that the price Henry James pays for virtuosity in the weaving of narrative patterns is that "most of human life has to disappear before he can do us a novel."

Mr. Forster also says that the drama is properly dominated by plot.

In the drama all human happiness and misery does
and must take the form of action. Otherwise its existence remains unknown, and this is the great difference
between the drama and the novel.

But he adds:

The drama may look towards the pictorial arts, it may
allow Aristotle to discipline it, for it is not so deeply
committed to the claims of human beings. Human beings have their great chance in the novel.

As a result of their skilled patterning of incidents, the
dramatists and Henry James achieve beauty—but at the
cost of truth. And in a rash moment Mr. Forster applies
this theory to Racine.

In plays—the plays of Racine, for instance—[Beauty]
may be justified because [she] can be a great empress
on the stage and reconcile us to the loss of the men
we knew.

Could anyone not momentarily carried away by an idea
represent Racine of all dramatists as sacrificing "the men
we knew" to an effect of beauty?

Mr. Forster has left many things unsorted out. For
example, though plot is important in all good drama, it is
not always plot in the popular sense of an intricate network
of incidents. Racine would have associated this popular
definition with the work of his rival, Corneille, and
himself aimed at an Action reduced to the smallest possible number of incidents, and these related to each other
in the most direct and simple way. It would be very hard
to make of this kind of plot an obstacle to the portrayal of

men, which Mr. Forster apparently considers all plot to be. It is equally hard to speak of Racine and Henry James together, since the latter did use an intricate patterning of incidents. And with James, even more sorting out is needed. Mr. Forster may be right that he sometimes let his ingenuity desiccate his stories. The question would be if that happened often enough to be characteristic of its author. Mr. Forster would seem to have been seduced by a possibility: it is possible, by overstressing the plot, "the purely intellectual side of action," to lose touch with the nonintellectual, emotional side—it is possible, that is, for plot to lose touch with its own raw material. But this is no more *to be expected* than for the flower to lose touch with the root, and the collected works of James are there as evidence that the Master very seldom lost touch with his own *daimon*. A better thesis than Mr. Forster's is Jacques Barzun's: that James was at heart a melodramatist.

THE PROVOCATION TO THE PREJUDICE

THE PEOPLE who originally brought plot into disrepute were the champions of plot. The great champions of plot have been the French. Not of course all the French, but most of their theorists and most of the playwrights during a great and formative two hundred years of theatre— approximately 1650 to 1850. And what the French said and did in drama laid down the rules for the rest of the world. Never perhaps in the whole history of theatre has a given way of writing plays been so insisted upon and other ways so scorned. In stark contrast is the Elizabethan Drama or the Spanish Drama. No one tried to impose the method of Shakespeare and Lope de Vega upon the world. It was not only not imposed, it was forgotten. What we have to reckon with here is the French passion for cultural propaganda and legislation.

There would have been less to deplore had the propaganda been on behalf of Corneille, Racine, or Molière, but all three members of that great trinity, though much influenced by current theories, failed so signally to conform to them as to be fiercely attacked for incorrectness. What I am calling the French idea of drama was the work of critics, theorists, and minor practitioners, and it did not reach its final and most influential form till the eighteenth century—in the commentaries of Voltaire.

The neo-Classic or Voltairean theory of drama is a reduction of Aristotle. If Aristotle's argument is pushed further, it is pushed only along one thin line. Aristotle had said that plot was the soul of tragedy. Voltaire says the soul of tragedy is the prolonging of an uncertainty as much as possible, which sounds like Aristotle adjusted to our modern courses in playwriting.

A tragedy [says Voltaire], should be all action. . . .
Every scene should serve to tie and untie the intrigue, every speech should be preparation or obstacle.

The Abbé d'Aubignac had declared flatly that the law of the theatre was suspense. Yet another neo-Classic theorist—Marmontel—gave thought to the ways and means: speed, he thought, like any Broadway critic, is the *sine qua non* and, as for suspense, he advises the playwright to keep the interest always rising by letting the situations unfold in careful gradation.

A corollary of this approach to theatre is the contempt for Shakespeare for which the French of the eighteenth century are famous. That French doctrine spread beyond

French boundaries is clear enough from the utterances of Frederick the Great of Prussia, Voltaire's pupil, who described Shakespeare's plays as "farces worthy of the savages of Canada." Voltaire himself has often been quoted to much the same effect, and he took just as low a view of the Greeks, whose plays, with their dances and choral poems, hardly seemed to that age to be drama at all. Even the masterpieces of French Classicism were not classical enough: Voltaire says that they are all too long, and gives chapter and verse by declaring that the whole last act of Corneille's *Horatius* is superfluous.

In the early nineteenth century the face of the drama changed. Prose more and more replaced the alexandrine, and the modern setting, the ancient. The idea of drama changed less. "The action of a [dramatic] poem," Marmontel had written, "can be considered a kind of problem of which the dénouement forms the answer." The remark bears witness not only to a theory but to a state of mind. Suspense. Tempo. Rising interest. Graded situations. The prolongation of uncertainty. The tying and untying of an intrigue. Action, action, action! We of today cotton to this vocabulary rather quickly. It is used on the marquees of movie theatres and in newspaper reviews of plays. Only "the tying and untying of an intrigue" sound old-fashioned. It was still modish, however, a hundred years after it was written. The nineteenth-century theatre was the theatre of the Well Made Play, and the Well Made Play is a form of the classical tragedy—a form of it that can be called degenerate or ultimate, according to the point of view.

This kind of drama is "all plot," and even if one knew no Well Made Plays one might guess why the genre eventually made enemies among thinking people. Because it is all plot, there is nothing for plot to mesh with or impinge upon. There is plenty of bustle, but no movement in a particular direction. We can get from it no "sense of something being born and growing and then declining." Applying Bergson's four-fold formula, we find no fullness of drama because there is no integrating Action, no Action because there is no dynamic schema to inform it, and no dynamic schema because there is no creative emotion behind the whole effort.

This least intellectual form of drama—this drama for nonintellectuals as such—fails from a lack, not of brains, but of emotion. True, it is a device for the creation of one emotion—the itch of suspense—but it cannot touch the other emotions. And it is put together by brains alone, if one can include in the concept "brains" the possession of a theatrical knack. We do use the word "knack," most often, of mechanical facility, and the Well Made Play was put together according to a *mechanical* scheme, not, like any really good work of art, according to an *organic* scheme.

The plot imitates an Action, says Aristotle. It imitates a myth, I have imagined Lord Raglan rejoining. In either case it is not the whole play but a part. And it is not detached from the meaning of the whole play but, on the contrary, contributes to that meaning and is, in turn, shaped by that meaning. This is yet another way in which plot differs from simple imitation of life.

The creative plot [says Ramon Fernandez], is not merely a faithful transcription of probability. It owes its roundedness, its impact, and its interest to its meaning.

It contributes to that vision of life which is provided by the play as a whole.

Since the Well Made Play monopolized for a while the stages of the nineteenth century, one can readily understand how plot came to be a dirty word.

> When the critics [wrote Bernard Shaw in his music column] were full of the "construction" of plays, I steadfastly maintained that a work of art is a growth, and not a construction. When the Scribes and Sardous turned out neat and showy cradles, the critics said: "How exquisitely constructed!" I said: "Where's the baby?"

Now Shaw was not really against construction, much less incapable of it. The Scribean devices are overlooked in his plays because he put them to work, made them serve a purpose. Since what was wrong with the Well Made pattern was the isolation of plot from the rest of the drama, Shaw was setting matters to rights. That he proceeded to talk as if his plays had no plot at all could, of course, prove misleading.

Shaw found the meaning of plot in its artificiality. He used plots parodistically in a running contrast of what-happens-in-Scribe with what-happens-in-real-life. Ibsen was able to take the Scribe plots straight. They happened to be just what he needed. If he is the first of the moderns, he is the last of the French classicists.

Ibsen and Shaw were both of them exceptions. The main movement in the theatre was Naturalistic, and Naturalism stood for the rejection of plot. It substituted the documentary conception. The subsequent revolt against Naturalism in the theatre was called Expressionism, but in one important respect—and the one that concerns us here—Expressionism was continuous with

Naturalism. It sought a drama without plot. The same had been true of a movement that existed alongside Naturalism in the nineties: Symbolism. The Symbolist Maeterlinck advertised a drama not only plotless but eventless, a drama which has "lost the name of action."

The man who rescued the idea of plot for the twentieth-century drama was Bertolt Brecht. He did not propose a return to the Well Made Play. One of the appalling things about the Well Made Play is that it limited everyone's image of plot to that particular kind of plot. Brecht did not want a drama that was "all plot," nor did he want Scribe's closed and claustrophobic structure. His conception of action is derived directly from Büchner and hence indirectly from Shakespeare. What better model could there be? The playwright whom the French champions of plot despised as a barbarian was himself the supreme master of the art of the plot. But it was a different mastery from theirs and a different sort of plotting.

SHAKESPEARE

FOR THE PAST CENTURY and a half Shakespeare has been a popular author, but on what account? Chiefly, it would seem, for the Poetry and the Great Characters. The Poetry can be exhibited in extracts. The Characters could be celebrated in books which abstracted them from the play and invented for them what the poet had forgotten to mention. This way of thinking has latterly been criticized; but it has by no means disappeared. And the tendency to detach the poetry from the play has only been reinforced by the twentieth-century interest in imagery.

Throughout the whole modern epoch it has been assumed, if not asserted, that Shakespeare's way with a story was far from noteworthy. Little jokes against his plots have become a staple of semisophisticated journalism. Disrespect for his storytelling has expressed itself in the cutting of the plays by stage directors and movie directors. Could anyone have followed the Olivier film of *Hamlet* if he had not known the play already? And one must ask of much lengthier stage *Hamlets:* is most of the Fortinbras story omitted only because the play is too long, or because we are insensitive to the relation of one piece of narrative to another? If the latter, then we are hostile to Shakespeare's narrative method.

Even among professional scholars and critics, only a few seem to have thought Shakespeare showed much talent in the making of plots. We hear about all other departments of his work, and, as to plot, are fobbed off with the statement that he took his plots from other writers. He often did take the *stories* from other writers, but he usually changed them, and he always had his own *plot* to make. Even if plot-making were only the blending of two stories it would be a subtle enough craft. Shakespeare made of the interaction of two stories a high art, and a vehicle of profound meaning.

It seems to me useful, perhaps even necessary, to become a little child again and read Shakespeare as if one did not know him already—which means, above all, *following what goes on.* It sounds easy, but there are at least two obstacles. First, we have been spoiled and do not readily surrender ourselves to pure narrative. Second, far from being in themselves simple, Shakespeare's plots are complicated, sometimes to the point of being baffling. How much information we are supposed to pick up in the first act of *Hamlet!* In taking no notice we are following the line of least resistance. No wonder we don't wish to hear about Fortinbras later on!

Here is a play about which hundreds, if not thousands, of books have been written, and in which one might expect every detail to have been gone over *ad nauseam*. Yet I wonder if what is gone over is not always the same four or five points, illustrated from the same couple of dozen speeches or scenes. I have read a sampling of this *Hamlet* literature and can think of many primary experiences one has of the play which, though they are not simple, are very seldom mentioned. To me, one of the most puzzling parts of *Hamlet* has always been what follows Hamlet's return from England. How does Hamlet now stand related to Claudius? What is the reason for his greatly lightened mood? By any familiar logic, the final killing of Claudius is accidental. What would have happened but for this accidental circumstance? . . . One can read thousands of pages of what is reputed to be the best *Hamlet* criticism and not find the primary questions dealt with if these be questions of plot.

It may well be that Shakespeare's plots are unappreciated precisely because they are so good—because they are invisible, because at every point they touch the theme and the characterizations, and we cannot discuss one without the others.

Richard III has often seemed to modern persons a crude affair—such crude things happen in it! It reveals itself as a superb piece of "play-making" when we see on what lines the play *is* made, when we see, in Richard Moulton's words, "the intricate design of which the recurrent pattern is Nemesis." Moulton was able to show, I believe definitively, that this play often held to be loose and meandering, is exact and close-knit. Shakespeare's calculations are mathematically accurate, and pay off in marvelous feats of plot, such as a turning point that carries immense excitement because it is prepared and placed so unerringly.

Or take the scene which modern persons have often rejected for its improbability, the courting of Lady Anne. The play presents civil war. The Yorkist wreaks vengeance on the Lancastrian, in one case after another, and then the Lancastrian on the Yorkist. Lady Anne is the greatest sufferer of all the Lancastrians at the hands of the Yorkists and Richard has inflicted most of the suffering. Just for this reason, Lady Anne sees marriage with him as a possible path to peace and reconciliation. But through the channel in which she seeks an end to the curse she falls victim to the curse. What we have here is a most skillful arrangement of scenes, a very bold imagining of events and confrontations, and all in terms of the main idea, which had been brought into high relief by the initial encounter. Such is dramatic narrative in the hands of a master.

Again speaking of *Richard III,* Moulton says:

> Plot presents trains of events in human life taking form and shape as a crime and its nemesis, an oracle and its fulfillment, the rise and fall of an individual, or even as simply a story.

In the plots of the masters, no detail is too small for study, and much can be learned from watching how Shakespeare or Lope de Vega ties one incident to the next. Yet that is, in every sense, the least that they did. Great plots are not arrived at by adding one and one and one, but by the application of certain integrating principles.

An oracle and its fulfillment constitute such a principle. In plays, prophecies are not made for nothing. Anything prophesied in Act One is going to come true later, and the audience knows this. Logically there is something childish about such a proposition. But that is just it: it is the child in us that responds to stories, and the modern antagonism to narrative is much too exclusively adult an attitude for an artist. In any healthy public (as against a group of doctrinaires) you can rely on the proper childlike attitude to such a thing as a prophecy. Once the prophecy is made, the childlike mind is interested in seeing it fulfilled.

Then what happens to suspense? Surely, to know the conclusion is the direct opposite of being kept suspended. Logically, yes. Psychologically, no. It is a matter, not of the forestalling of suspense, but of its complication. Although we have no reason to be in doubt as to the issue, we still do feel in doubt, and we wish to see if the prophecy will really, really, come true. What we want is not so much information for the head as reassurance for the heart. Which is analogous to the many situations in life where we have been apprised of what will happen but, even as it happens, we find ourselves saying: "I still don't believe it." One should bear in mind this psychology when one reads that the Greeks always knew the story of the play. They knew it, and their knowing it made a difference. Yet this difference was not a reversal of the psychological situation, it was a complication of it. An unstable equilibrium is established in the mind between certainty and uncertainty. (I think the phenomenon has only filtered through into criticism and scholarship via philosophy. In discussing the meaning of Greek tragedy, critics have often intimated that a delicate balance is achieved between freedom and necessity, free will and determinism. In other words, the outcome is a foregone conclusion, *and at the same time it is not*.)

The rise and fall of an individual might at first seem to have little in common with an oracle and its fulfillment. Psychologically, the pattern can do the playwright a similar service. The end is prefigured in the beginning. Even though the fall is unannounced, it is one of those things that an audience senses, and the playwright relies heavily on such things as an audience senses. They save explanations and time. More important: they have that tremulous effect that goes with a sense of inevitability and doom. And they have this, as I have said, without removing the suspense.

If I make it sound as though a pattern can do an artist's work for him, that illusion can be dispelled by comparing one artist's work with another's, as, for example, some of the early Elizabethan rises and falls with a supreme example of the genre such as *Macbeth*. The less-great artist perforce does rely too heavily on the patterns (that is, on the work of others). For example, he tends simply to increase the speed of the fall. That way he may prove persuasive to the many who agree with Voltaire that the dramatist should always take the quickest way to his goals. One thinks of popular formulas like Hurtling To His Doom and indeed of all the phrases used in advertising movies and other cheap fiction. The superiority of Shakespeare is seen in his using, not the accelerator, but the brake. The fall of a Macbeth has great momentum. Such a fall will become more horribly impressive if that momentum is somehow counteracted. Then we get the effect of a man, not falling off a wall, but sliding inch by inch down a rock slope. And this is the effect Shakespeare gets.

A PLOT IS NOT A PLAY

THE RAW MATERIAL of plot is life, but not the mean average of daily living in its external banality: rather, the extreme situations of life's rare climaxes or of daily living in its secret, not wholly conscious forms. The outlook that rejects these extreme situations is antidramatic.

Plotting is the ordering of this material. It entails the application of a rational principle to the chaos of the irrational. Hence any plot has a dual character: it is made up of violently irrational matter, but the "making up" is itself rational, intellectual. Interest in a plot—even the most rudimentary one—is interest in both these factors, and, even more perhaps, in their interaction. We are reluctant to grant an intellectual element in soap opera and other melodrama. It is the obverse of our reluctance to grant a crudely emotional element in higher art. However, the intellectual element in lower art is very restricted. It is only on the scale of the intellectual element in children's games. Yet games demand real ingenuity for the solution of the little problems they set. A plot is like a checkerboard: its challenge and appeal are in considerable part due to the love of ingenuity.

"All men by nature," says Aristotle, "wish to know." In a detective story we wish to discover "the unknown murderer," and in so wishing we are philosophers. The emotion concerned is the itch to find out—we call it the thirst for knowledge when we approve, inquisitiveness when we disapprove, and curiosity when we are neutral.

I become curious if you surprise me and leave the surprise unaccounted for. I am on hot coals till you have enlightened me. On such hot coals, simple drama is cooked. The word is suspense. The term "clever plotter" signifies an ingenious manipulator of surprise and suspense.

Yet not all drama is marked by "clever plotting" in this sense, and most of the drama that is so marked is second-rate. If the end in view is first-rate drama, the end in view is not surprise and suspense, is not plot. The theory that it is has been "derived" from Aristotle, but in defiance of his own expressed intention. Even when he speaks of plot devices such as Reversal and Recognition as "the most powerful elements of emotional interest," it is clear that Aristotle has more than curiosity in mind. He envisages an audience that "thrills with horror and melts to pity." Horror (or fear) and pity are of course the emotions cited in Aristotle's most famous, if not most lucid, pronouncement—that tragedy effects through pity and fear "the proper catharsis of these emotions." Suffice it here that, for all the varying interpretations of this sentence, no one has ever tried to reduce it to a defense of the drama of mere "interest" (or curiosity).

What is a good plot? The question is a hard one because a plot is not good in itself but as part of a pattern. In calling plot the "soul" of tragedy, Aristotle is saying, perhaps, that in his view it is the playwright's principal instrument among several. If drama is an art of extreme situations, plot is the means by which the playwright gets us into those situations and (if he wishes) out of them again. Plot is the way in which he creates the necessary collisions —like a perverse traffic policeman, steering the cars, not past, but into each other. The collisions arouse curiosity, and can be arranged to create suspense. Thus far we have a sound, second-rate theatre. Some of the things plot can do to create a first-rate theatre I have suggested in this chapter. It remains to suggest what can be contributed to such a theatre by character, dialogue, thought, and enactment.

2

CHARACTER

THE RAW MATERIAL OF CHARACTER

PERCEPTION IS RIVETED to need. Our real needs being relatively few, our perceptions are relatively few. They are also relatively faint and incomplete and inaccurate. This is one reason why it is not easy for us to reproduce any section of life in the theatre. The man in the street sees that life is on the doorstep, and concludes that it shouldn't be too hard to shovel up some chunks of it and throw them on the stage. But what do we *see* on the doorstep? Do we see what a camera sees? What kind of a camera? With how powerful a lens? We loosely call photographic any kind of detailed rendering. What a camera really does is variable and selective. It would be hard indeed to say when the camera's "vision" was the same as that of the human eye, or even as one particular human eye. There is an image on the retina; but one does not see with the retina.

All too often we do not see; we do not look; we have preconceptions. Casting a hasty, nervous glance in front, to make sure that we don't actually collide with anything, we fit together what we half-see with what we assume we know. What is half-seen in this manner is quite often a specimen of the species *homo sapiens,* and from such half-glances may derive that "knowledge of human nature" for which human beings are famous in song and story. In songs and stories, that is, of human authorship.

All too often we look at a stranger for two minutes and decide this isn't someone else but Uncle George all over again. Would that we knew even Uncle George to the depths of his soul! But Uncle George is the label we have stuck on some nightmare of childhood. And if a million nervous sidelong glances do not make one good look, we have never looked even at Uncle George.

Or take our knowledge of our parents or, conversely, of our children. Are there any such complete strangers, Shaw has asked, as a parent and his child? They enjoy propinquity. They engage in conflict, perhaps unceasingly. Very likely they feel mutual affection; that is natural. They may even attain to what could fairly be called love; that is sublime. But none of this provides a shred of evidence that they have ever seen each other or that they will ever know each other. Traditionally, only God is credited with the gift of knowing men, of penetrating their inmost thoughts, their inmost feelings; for any being who could do this would *have* to be a god. In another existence, we can conceive of ourselves as seeing face to face: in this existence, it is through a glass darkly; or through a glass falsely; or not at all.

If the raw material of plot is events, particularly violent events, the raw material of character is people, especially what are regarded as their cruder impulses. It is said that babies, being attached to the mother first by the umbilical cord and then by the breast, believe the human world to be all one piece. If so, one concludes, this is paradise, and the dismissal from Eden comes when we decide, as it seems we do in later babyhood, that the world is divided into two parts: oneself and other people. Later still, with our intellects, we make more elaborate divisions: as patriots, we insist on nations, as Marxists on classes, and so on. Even so, the distinction we live with each day remains simply that between oneself and other people. And the primordial group of other people—our family —makes up the original cast of characters in the drama of life, a drama that we keep on reviving later with more and more people cast for the same few parts. As for oneself, one is the invisible man. One cannot see oneself, one can only see those with whom one has chosen to be identified.

The raw material of character, then, is not very raw after all. It has already been worked over. It has already been turned into a kind of art: the art of fantasy. Life is a double fiction. We do not see others so much as certain substitutions for others. We do not see ourselves so much as others with whom we are identified. When Plato said we see, not life, but shadows of life flickering in the firelight on the wall of a cave, he was an optimist. Or perhaps he made allowances for the extraordinary distortions and suppressions of shadow play.

FROM FACT TO FICTION

IF A WRITER does not see all of life and reproduce it, does he see part of life and reproduce that? The public is very confused on the point. On the one hand, it lends an ear to the notion that the artist does not imitate at all but writes from sheer inspiration to the end of sheer invention. On the other, it is slow to accept the many deviations that art must make from life and quick to complain that an historical romance is "full of inaccuracies."

Now even the story or play that strikes the naïve spectator as "lifelike" reveals itself under analysis to be unlike life. An Aldous Huxley character complains that in fiction there is no menstruation. That is a taboo subject. There are others. And there are many subjects that *can* enter in but which must not enter in as often as they do in real life or we shall be bored. Washing one's hands, for example. Or take the most decisive human experiences of all. As Apeneck Sweeney says, they are birth and copulation and death. Of the three, only the last can readily be enacted on stage. And that is a problem, for if dying is an experience, it is one that none of the audience has had: the possibility of recognition or understanding is nil.

Very much, then, both in trivial and in vital experience, is necessarily missing from literature, and what is present in literature is there in different proportions from those of life. I have given examples of what is missing. What is there more of? Most obviously: emotion—and emotion, not just placed there in giant containers labeled Hatred, Love, Envy, and the like, but dynamic, moving up and down the poem, the story, or the play. Such emotion is the element we live in as we read or watch or listen.

E. M. Forster writes:

> If you think of a novel in the vague you think of a love interest—of a man and woman who want to be united and perhaps succeed. If you think of your own life in the vague, . . . you are left with a very differ-

ent and a more complex impression. . . . The constant sensitiveness of characters for each other . . . is remarkable, and has no parallel in life. . . . Passion, intensity at moments—yes, but not this constant awareness, this endless readjusting, this ceaseless hunger.

If the novelist is reproducing a part of life, he also puts it together in a quite new configuration. "Art is art," Goethe said, "because it is not life." The housemaid would not have needed the penny novelette if such goings-on had been prevalent on the backstairs, nor must one fool oneself that *kitsch* is a special case. None of us would listen to a Beethoven quartet if we had such serenity and such ecstasy at our beck and call. Beethoven is Beethoven because he is not oneself. Or, one might put it, there were two Beethovens. The second was a musician who created the emotional freedom which the first, a neurotic bachelor, failed to create in his relations with his nephew and the world at large. And *we* go to Beethoven's music for (ultimately) much the same kind of reason that *he* went to it for. The genius of the writer—in novel or play—will be found in the skill with which he projects and controls that constant sensitivity, that endless readjustment, that ceaseless hunger. He has to find the buried river of the emotions and then work as an engineer, damming it here, deflecting it there, but always making the fullest use of its natural power.

To return to the question: does the artist reproduce at least the bit of life that he can see? Sheer reproduction does happen, but the process is not simply a duplication of the skimpy motion picture on our retinas. Fiction is a good word to describe it, and perhaps one should use the word to include plays as well as novels. Both are made up. Fantasy makes possible a continuity and wholeness in both which actuality would preclude. Truth *is* stranger than fiction, for fiction makes sense in a way that truth does not.

> In daily life [as Mr. Forster puts it] we never understand each other: neither complete clairvoyance nor complete confessional exists. We know each other approximately, by external signs. . . . But people in a novel can be understood completely by the reader, if the novelist wishes . . .

And Mr. Forster pushes the point home with a contrast between novels and history books. The history book is limited to what actually came out into the open. The novelist tells the truths that stayed inside people's heads. But he knows them only through fantasy; his truth is an invention. It is not just his story, either, that is "false." The method produces a world which operates on partly different principles from the world we know. For everything in it is purposive, and the purpose is one we in some degree understand. Though the physical universe, as we envisage it today, is so far from anthropocentric, man remains the center of the universe of art. Of dramatic art he tends to be both center and circumference.

Though Mr. Forster himself does not think the playwright can do as much with people as the novelist can, the principle he states does apply to the drama. The play too is a clairvoyant and confessional form. The drama too has laws which are not of this world. And a main reason for going to a play, as for reading a novel, will always be the need for emotions that are coherent and continuous as well as strong.

There is an interesting comment on the difference between drama and life in Edward Bullough's much-quoted essay on "Psychical Distance":

> The exceptional element in tragic figures—that which makes them so utterly different from characters we meet with in ordinary experience—is a consistency of direction, a fervor of ideality, a persistence and driving force which is far above the capacities of average men.

Released from the compulsion to wash his hands, as it were, a stage character may concentrate on his main purpose in life. In real life such "main purposes," when they exist at all, hide in closets and dark corridors. Our rooms are full of towels, toothbrushes, business letters, telephones, and TV sets.

A modernist author may find precisely this duality of creative interest. It is the pleasure of Chekhov, for example, to display the trivial furniture, and clothing, and conversation, while suggesting precisely that the closets and dark corridors are haunted. Behind the whiskers and waistcoats are primordial yearnings. But Chekhov's has not been the traditional method. The traditional method has been to isolate and thus emphasize the larger driving forces. Hence, as Bullough implies, the marked difference in kind between our impression of Hamlet and our impression of Jones, our impression of Macbeth and our impression of Smith. Now if Smith and Jones are individuals, what are Hamlet and Macbeth?

IN PRAISE OF TYPES

PLOT HAS NOT for a long time now been something the reviewers praise a playwright for. They praise him for the characters he has created, and they praise them because they are Real Human Beings. An alternative expression is Believable Human Beings, and the opposite of this is a Type. A type is a Bad Thing.

Now, though this doctrine is most influential among the semi-literate, the semi-literate had to get it originally where they do get such things: from the literate. And the literate continue to give the semi-literate too much comfort. Mr. Forster, for example, calls individuals "round" characters and types "flat" characters and in doing so indicates an unmistakable preference for the former, since they respond to new situations, and truly live, and speak truly. . . . The people of Racine or Emily Brontë are "round."

The nub of Mr. Forster's definition is that "round" characters are free and therefore unpredictable and surprising, whereas "flat" characters can only do what they do, and one knows what this is in advance: they are fixed quantities. That is assuredly to be as unflattering as possible to the flat characters. And yet—even within the bounds of a narrow definition and an unflattering metaphor—is there not a place for the flat character? A person whose future is predictable because he has set a fixed definition on himself is a creature of habit. But appallingly enough, most of us are creatures of habit; and it is legitimate for any writer to picture us as such. A creature of habit, not responding to new situations, but repeating his responses to old ones, speaks mostly falsehood. If he knows it, he is a hypocrite. If he does not, he is a self-deceiver. In either case, he is very apt material for one large genre of drama: comedy (including farce) . Mr. Forster recalls that a master of the novel—Charles Dickens—uses flat characters, and comments:

Those who dislike Dickens have an excellent case. He ought to be bad.

Then Mr. Forster's sense of humor gets the better of his logic and he adds:

[Dickens'] immense success with types suggests that there may be more in flatness than the severer critics admit.

The close connection between types and comedy has been urged by none so strongly as by Henri Bergson in his essay on laughter.

Every comic character is a type. Conversely, every resemblance to a type has something comic in it . . .

It is unfortunate that, having once seen that types could have a place in the world, Bergson proceeds to delimit that place with Gallic overprecision.

Not only are we entitled to say that comedy gives us general types, but we might add that it is the only art that aims at the general . . .

From here the argument runs downhill into a belittlement of comedy as hardly an art at all but a sort of cross between art and life. It presents types because it is superficial:

Settling on the surface, it will not be more than skin-deep, dealing with persons at the point at which they come into contact and become capable of resembling one another.

To make light of the "point at which [persons] come into contact" is surely to make light of all human relations. Here is what Bergson holds out as the alternative:

What interests us in the work of the poet is the glimpse we get of certain profound moods or inner struggles.

If the emphasis here is placed on mood, then Bergson had too lyric and romantic an idea of dramatic poetry. If the stress is on struggle, then it was a mistake to find profound struggle in tragedy alone, especially since the leading French master of comedy, Molière, wrote out his inner struggles in comedy quite as fully as Racine did his in tragedy.

Bergson makes the searching observation that when the writer of comedy groups secondary characters around his protagonist these characters tend to be the protagonist over again in a reduced or partial form. But then he too absolutely denies that the tragic poet can do this and declares that while comedy presents the type, tragedy presents the individual. Surely the minor characters in a tragedy are types in the simplest definition—they are "flat"? What is Horatio but the loyal friend? What is young Malcolm but any other fine young prince? And so on?

"All art," says Bergson, "aims at what is individual." Dr. Johnson had said: "Nothing can please many and please long but just representations of general nature." Those are two philosophies of art, and on the face of it irreconcilable. They become reconcilable, however, once we realize that an artist's "just representations of general nature" are, in each case, thoroughly individual. Bergson seems to go wrong by a play on words: Art is individual, therefore it should present individuals. Which is a *non sequitur*. In fact, as I have just said, even tragedies contain many characters of the kind traditionally known as types.

Since Bergson concedes that comedies certainly do, one is tempted to ask: is the tragic hero the only character in drama who is not a type? We ask of an individual in real life, what is he like? and our friends supply a thumbnail sketch. Can we do the same for the most celebrated tragic protagonists? What was Oedipus like? The only suggestion I have heard is that he was a rash man. But it is none too clear in the *Oedipus Rex* that he is unusually rash for a king; and if rash is all that he is, then he is a type in the simplest sense.

What of Hamlet—the classic instance of an individual in world drama? It has been said that Coleridge saw Hamlet in his own image. It has been said that Goethe saw Hamlet in his own image. Now Goethe and Coleridge didn't resemble each other any too closely. And, for that matter, later critics of different kinds *also* saw Hamlet, either in their own image or in the image of their dream self. The great Russian rebel Belinsky saw him as a great Russian rebel. Salvador de Madariaga sees him as a Machiavellian Prince. This would seem to be proof that Hamlet is not limited by his author to one highly individualized physiognomy. The world's imagination seems tacitly to admit as much, for while the text says Hamlet is fat, the world has often thought of him as thin. Then is not Hamlet a type?

The pedagogue's standard observation on types—that the human race is not divided into jealous men, choleric men, and the like—is quite valid, and there is no reason to think the classic dramatists did not know it. On the contrary, instead of trying to reduce you and me to a desiccated formula, they put much of the affective life of you and me into their types. If on one definition a type is a part of the human species (nation, class, race), on another a type cuts through boundaries of nations, classes, races, and the like and is a part of each human being. Through his Peer Gynt, Ibsen reaches the self-deceiving, romancing liar in each of us. Through Don Quixote, Cervantes reaches the soul-sick, questing romantic in each of us.

(I oversimplify. Actually, Definition One would fit Don Quixote better at the beginning of the book, where we meet, not ourselves, but an eccentric of the *hidalgo* class, very much of the Spanish nation and the Latin race. Then this definition gradually ceases to have point, and the other one is called for. The same thing happens in Dickens' *Pickwick Papers*—English *Don Quixote* as it is— where a nitwit bachelor of the gentleman class, very much the Englishman and the Anglo-Saxon, gradually becomes a mythic figure, sufferer for lost causes, representative of a lost innocence. In a terminology I am about to define, the Don and Pickwick change from *minor* to *major* characters, and from *type* to *archetype*. To refer forward to a yet later part of this book, there is a transition from *wit* to *humor*—almost from *comedy* to *tragedy*.)

Furthermore, before he is an individual in the sense in which a person seems an individual when painted or well photographed, a fictitious character is *a force in a story.* We are accustomed to admit this, but querulously, in the case of minor characters whom we can belittle as only cogs in the wheel of plot. But it has always been legitimate for some characters in a play to be cogs of that kind. The messengers in Greek drama are never any more. The minor characters in Shakespeare do no more to meet the requirements of twentieth-century directors who wish them to have a "biography" or "case history" than project a single quality (tone, color) . They exist less as themselves than as part of a group, gang, or partnership. Such characters resemble members of a *corps de ballet* more than the people in a novel.

Even the major Shakespeare characters are not what the modern novel reader might wish. They do not have a life story behind them. Their motives belong to a less familiar world, and/or are not as fully gone into as is expected. If the world of the novel is "real"—and novelists have gone all out to make this word their own—it may well follow that many of Shakespeare's personae are "unreal." Iago's motives, or lack of them, have become the subject of a standing controversy. What is significant is that the matter ever became a problem. And it did so, only because even if Iago has motives they do not make him a character in a nineteenth-century novel. First and foremost he is a force in the story. When Wilson Knight describes him as an acid corroding all higher values, the metaphor is apt because it suggests a doing, and not a being. True, Iago is not a type in the commonest modern sense: no one is going to cry, "There are lots of Iagos in our town." But he is a type in the sense that there is an Iago in each of us.

TYPE AND ARCHETYPE

I HAVE BEEN speaking of both major and minor characters, but it may already have become apparent that the major characters are not types in the same sense as the minor ones. Osric, a minor character, is a type much in Mr. Forster's sense: a "flat" character. One would hardly wish to apply that word to Hamlet. Or take a major character of Shakespeare's of whom some would make a type of the simplest sort. Othello, to these, is "a jealous man." Now aside from the fact that the phrase "not easily jealous" is in the play—the phrase is Othello's own, and not necessarily true—one can hardly describe Othello as *merely* jealous or the characterization as an attempt to deal with jealousy alone or even primarily. On this point, Coleridge's words seem definitive:

> Jealousy does not strike me as the point in [Othello's] passion; I take it to be rather an agony that the creature whom he had believed angelic . . . should be proved impure and worthless. It was the struggle *not* to love her. It was a moral indignation and regret that virtue should so fall.

Now it could be argued that some or all of the experiences here mentioned—the agony, the struggle, the indignation and regret—are very commonly connected with jealousy. Yet they are not jealousy itself, and in any event Coleridge is not pretending that jealousy is *absent* from the play. One's thoughts about it start out from jealousy, and Shakespeare presumably planned that they should. His art is shown in the way he then displaces the accent, carrying us from the static idea: "a jealous man" to an experience of jealousy. Being an experience, it does not consist of abstract qualities, nor can it be defined by them. It is defined by dialogue (poetry), and action (including the inner action, or struggle, as mentioned by Coleridge). The impression given is less that of a typical character being tagged than that of a man having a typical experience. The experience is not wholly implicit in his character, and so does not merely illustrate his character. And it is not merely a "being jealous," as with Master Page, in *The Merry Wives of Windsor* (a "flat" character). It is the devastating loss of the noble image of a beloved person. If we had to say Othello is there to illustrate something,

47

we could say that he illustrates the nature of such devastation and such loss.

Another instance of this "displacement of accent" is provided by *The Misanthrope*. Molière calls Alceste "the misanthrope," a character type by definition. And in the seventeenth century it was common to write descriptions of such general types in the form of a short set piece of prose. But Molière's character does not correspond to such a *caractère* of a misanthrope. He is an idealist. His hopes for the human race are, originally, all too high. He is not only capable of feeling for another, he is head over heels in love with Célimène. Nor is he solitary by nature. He has a chronic need of someone to grumble to, even of a group to be at once the audience and the butt of his railery. The nearest he gets to misanthropy, even at the end, is that he would *like* to be a misanthrope. As the curtain falls, he can rely on being pursued by his friend, just as he could when the curtain rose on Act One.

If Othello is "the jealous man" who proves better or worse than jealous, Alceste is "the misanthrope" who proves better or worse than misanthropic: and one of *his* real troubles is jealousy. Does this mean that Molière does describe jealousy, does present such a state of being, does write, essentially, about qualities? No more than Shakespeare. He makes more use of the *"caractères"*—at least one such set piece is inserted into the text—for that was his tradition and the tradition of his audience. But his method of presenting a protagonist is the classic one of the drama: by action. Passions, in his plays, make events, and are seen *in* the events, among which are included inner events—though they become outer ones by means of dialogue. Jealousy in drama, like any other passion, cannot just be: it must surge up in word or deed. It proceeds from

Alceste in a torrent of articulateness. It also has both a starting point and a destination, for scenes must not only move, they must move from one point to another in a certain direction. One "scheme" which we may imagine to have been in Molière's head is the idea of starting from Misanthropy (it is in the title), proceeding to Rage (it is in the opening lines, and then almost *passim*), and only after that showing that the man is Jealous.

That the major characters who are types should be more complex than the minor ones is in itself neither surprising nor revealing, but it is a pointer toward a much larger phenomenon: they tend, in the hands of the masters, to become archetypes. If the traditional fixed characters typify smaller things—groups and their foibles and eccentricities—the archetypal character typifies larger things and characteristics that are more than idiosyncrasies. Don Quixote and Peer Gynt have been mentioned. Then there is the plastic archetype, such as Faust, who had a development through the centuries.

What is the difference between "the men we know" in life and such archetypes? Suppose that, for a moment, we hold in our mind's eye an actual person who has reminded us of an archetype or of whom an archetype has reminded us. I shall think of my friend X who has the reputation of a Don Juan. Which of the Don Juans in dramatic literature resembles X? Bernard Shaw's, now the most famous, we might agree to set aside as a paradox or a parody. Zorrilla's, well-known to Hispanic audiences, is also "unusual," since he proves in the end as susceptible to theological as to sexual seduction. Mozart's? Here is a Don Juan which could receive a hundred-page analysis from a great theological psychologist—Kierkegaard. Listen to the statue music—or even merely to the so-called champagne aria.

49

Either passage will give you the Mozartian character. But no statue has ever come for Mr. X, nor has the latter's promiscuity ever presented itself as a demonic circularity such as the whirling aria defines. As we retreat to the seventeenth century, the mystery, far from clearing up, only deepens. Directly opposite interpretations have been offered of Molière's *Don Juan*. Some have it that Molière takes the part of atheism in this play; others that he is attacking it. Atheism now! My friend X is a devout church-goer: aren't the churches full of young ladies? Nor is it true that, in Molière's play, atheistic theory takes pre-cedence over character. That Don Juan is not merely the mouthpiece of a philosophy. He embodies an attitude. He is the outsider and rebel in a social as well as a theological way. A slight shift, and we would feel sorry for him, he is so isolated. His seductions are not displays of sensuality but of technique. He likes to feel his power and even to show it. Sganarelle is a welcome audience. The theatre audience identifies itself with him, and is the voyeur to the Don's exhibitionism. In the end, the Don is punished with hell fire: but can we take this seriously, let alone literally? Perhaps we *can;* but it is by no means certain that we *should.* As Ramon Fernandez has noted, Molière made a great dramatic theme out of impunity: he was inclined to see bad men as getting away with murder. The ultimate punishment of Don Juan is given so much less emphasis than the impunity that precedes it that the comedy as a whole prompts the thought: would the ending be like this in real life? Molière's is a Don Juan who walks in the shadows. And the same could be said of the first of all Don Juans, the "trickster" of Tirso de Molina. It is all very well to observe that Tirso's *Trickster of Seville* is theo-logical rather than psychosexual provided one adds that the theology is worked out in dramatic terms—which is also to say in emotional terms. No more than in Molière is the theology pure and abstract. It is given social forms. The Don defies God by violating godly customs, the law of hospitality, the sacrament of marriage, respect for age, paternity, kingship. Though this Don is no atheist, and lacks the grandeur of Molière's, he too is a great rebel and concentrates in his single person the rebelliousness of thousands. . . . And so on. And so forth. The more we see the size of the legend the more the actuality is dwarfed by it. Though X is a human being, and his claims to individuality would be pressed not only by himself but by his contemporaries *en masse,* individualists all, he fades into insignificance beside the Don Juans of the great dramatists, who are only types.

TYPOLOGY AND MYTHOLOGY

IN SHORT, what Mr. Forster calls the flat character and Bergson the comic type does not by any means exhaust the element in dramatic characterization which can fairly be called typical. It does not, finally, even do justice to the traditional fixed types themselves, if it is these types whom we find in the comedies of the classical masters. Ben Jonson's characters, for example. They are "flat" enough, if the reduction of traits to one, or few, be the criterion. They are close, in many instances, to the formulas of Roman and Italian comedy. But neither the "flatness" as described by Forster nor the "mechanical" quality stressed by Bergson goes far toward indicating the kind of life they possess. No mean theorist himself, Jonson gets closer to the bone in his celebrated description of what he calls "a humour"—that is, a character in Jonsonian comedy:

51

As when some one peculiar quality
Doth so possess a man, that it doth draw
All his affects, his spirits, and his powers,
In their confluctions, all to run one way,
This may be truly said to be a humour.

How feeble and effeminate the customary descriptions of comic character are beside this one! The image is not of a mere oddity, something silly or cute, mincing or feebly foolish, but of a creation at once more vital and less humane, further gone, utterly unhealthy but living at the pace of a whirling dervish, a monomaniac. What the theorists—be it Forster or Bergson or, for that matter, Meredith—fail to suggest is that the center of interest is, not character traits, but human and inhuman energy.

Now among all those who know that the *commedia dell' arte* was for some centuries the main carrier of the tradition of fixed characters, how many realize that it was also the carrier of the tradition of comic brio, verve, and *diablerie?* The second fact is not necessarily more important than the first, but the first is a lame and vulnerable fact without the second, for it permits the view of types we have found wanting, the view that they are regular characters with something missing, rather than valid and positive creations.

If, as is widely agreed, the *commedia dell'arte* is theatrical art in a pure state, then it can be cited to show what a dramatic theatre can do without and what it cannot do without. It can do without perpetually fresh and original studies of individual character. It cannot do without ready-to-hand characterizations and, if the audience wants nuance and novelty, it will have to find them, not in new people, but in new performances and their rendering of ever-new, living contact between people.

A book could be written to establish more firmly that the fixed characters are a positive achievement. It would have to go thoroughly into the subject of typology. Is it profound to use words like Extravert and Introvert, and shallow to use words like Pulcinella and Scaramouche? To realize that it is not is to embark on the study of what is perhaps the classical typology in Western tradition: the typology of traditional theatre in general, and the *commedia dell'arte* in particular.

From typology, such a book would have to proceed to mythology. That the archetypes plunge us deep into myth is obvious: they *are* myth, and their creators are among the great myth-makers. At this point, if not before, we realize that our two kinds of type characters are not fundamentally separate. Even the nonarchetypes, the more modest fixed characters of Latin tradition, constitute a mythology, as Fernandez has ably argued. We are slow to see it, only because mythology in drama means to us the stories that underlie tragedy. In the tragic tradition, the characters can be different every time, because the story remains the same. In comedy, it was the characters who remained constant, while the changes were rung on plots. If tragedy makes use of narrative myth, comedy makes use of character myth.

The point of any myth is to provide a known element as a starting point and preserve us from the vacuum of absolute novelty. Art is a matter of satisfying certain expectations, and myth sets up expectations with a minimum of fuss. Art is also, as I was saying in the previous chapter, a matter, not of cognition, but of re-cognition: it does not tell you anything you didn't know (the telephone directory can do that), it tells you something you "know" and makes you realize. Now it is generally admitted that the Greek myths offer perfect material for the enforcement of such realizations: hence, to take one example among a thousand, all the Electras from Aeschylus to O'Neill and Sartre. Less justice has been done to those character myths of New Greek Comedy which have proved their vitality by living over two thousand years. Bernard Shaw, for one, was happy to acknowledge the support he received from the tradition of Punch, and of Harlequin and Columbine. But many people are far too busy chattering about individuals to notice what can be done with types.

MODERN PSYCHOLOGICAL DRAMA

THE VIEW that the drama deals with "individuals, not types" derives to a considerable extent from modern psychological drama. If the case for this view were at all strong, it would have to apply at least to drama of this school. But in fact even this drama has much about it that is "typical."

Among the "psychological" dramatists of any great merit, the most psychological are Ibsen and Chekhov. Chekhov was from the first drawn to the standard type characters, and he put the farcical types to dazzling use in his one-act plays. Also from the first he worked at the creation of archetypal protagonists. His first full-length play was intended to present a Russian Don Juan; his second, a Russian Hamlet. Of the latter, *Ivanov,* he wrote: "No matter how bad the play is, I created a type that has literary value." As for his masterpieces, those who take them to be all mood and nuance have missed some of the more solid features, such as that each play contains a traditional Villain who serves the traditional purpose of villains in dramatic plots, namely, to drive the Action toward catastrophe. The Professor in *Uncle Vanya*, Natasha in *The Three Sisters*, and Madame Ranevsky in *The Cherry Orchard* do just that. In *The Seagull* the villainy is divided between Arkadina and Trigorin.

Ibsen also may be said to have started out with attempts to create huge archetypal protagonists: Julian the Apostate, Brand, and Peer Gynt. Then, as the whole world knows, came a change, but, even after it, Ibsen's chief figures would be justly celebrated for their representative character. Bernard Shaw observed that the action of *A Doll's House* was located in every suburb in Europe. Rilke noted the vast, cosmic resonance of *The Wild Duck* —a play in which, as many have noticed, Hjalmar stands as the archetype of lower-middle-class idealist. Most startling illustration of all: when Sigmund Freud was looking for the most typical case of a certain neurosis, he confessed himself unable to find any among actual patients who was as thoroughly typical as one of Ibsen's heroines. And it is Rebecca West's life-story that he included in his essay on "Character Types."

Those who champion individuals against types often pursue the thought further, and come out in favor of a drama in which character takes precedence over theme, plot, and dialogue. The challenge here is especially to the traditional, Aristotelian view that character must be subordinated to plot. John Galsworthy countered with:

> A human being is the best plot there is. . . . The dramatist who hangs his characters to his plot, instead of hanging his plot to his characters, is guilty of cardinal sin.

* * *

55

Since such views undoubtedly grew out of the modern movement, it is fair, even imperative, to ask if the modern masters consciously or unconsciously, in theory or in practice, subscribed to them.

In explaining that he wrote three drafts of his plays, Ibsen added that these drafts differed "very much from each other in characterization, not in action." In other words, the action was not subject to revision, while the motivation was. Ibsen supplies further particulars:

> [In the first draft] I feel as though I had the degree of acquaintance with my characters that one acquires on a train: one has met and chatted about this or that. With the next . . . I know characters just about as one would know them after a few weeks' stay in a spa: I have learned the fundamental traits of their characters as well as their little idiosyncrasies, yet it remains possible that I may be quite wrong in some essential respect. In the last draft, I finally stand at the limit of knowledge: I know my people from close and long association—they are my intimate friends, they will not disappoint me, I shall always see them as I now do.

Traits, then, even fundamental ones can be quite misleading "in some essential respect." The modern psychological dramatist is less interested, ultimately, in the traits and idiosyncrasies he makes use of than in "some essential" factor to which these traits and idiosyncrasies do not necessarily point. What is finally effective about Ibsen's characterization of Mrs. Alving is not any of the traits so ably presented in the first two acts, but rather, the agonizing revelation in the last act, to herself and Oswald and us, that she shares the guilt which she had previously projected onto her husband. In other words, Ibsen is not on John Galsworthy's side. In his work, action does not play second fiddle to character. Like the older playwrights, he is less concerned to accumulate information about a person than to reveal some great truth about them in a flash of dramaturgic lightning. In this, of course, character is not playing second fiddle to action, either. Character and action are so well coordinated that the question of priority loses all relevance.

If modern drama is "all psychology," "all character," then Ibsen is not a modernist. He is a social dramatist— but in a sense much deeper than was intended when he was praised or attacked long ago for the supposed message in *A Doll's House* or *Ghosts*. If his protagonists are unheroic in moral caliber, they nonetheless have the representative quality of the heroes of old. (We tend to forget that the Greek hero was not necessarily either a gladiator or a Boy Scout, but did necessarily represent his community: when he died, they died, and *vice versa*.) What struck Rilke about *The Wild Duck* was the sense of doom that rings out in it. Ibsen once said he did not let a character go "until his fate is accomplished," and it is essential to see that Ibsen people have a fate, not just a character. As for the old tag: Character *is* fate, if it means what it seems to mean, it was never true until the rather bad and excessively psychological drama of the nineteen twenties. Character was never fate *all on its own*. Fate was always the word for whatever was outside men but which bore down on them—"a force not ourselves that makes for righteousness" or for the reverse. The idea that fate is wholly *inside* men will yield at best, not plays such as Ibsen's, but plays such as Eugene O'Neill's in which psychology commits incest with psychology. Fate in Ibsen, as before him, is a name for what we say is "in the air," and what for a dramatist *is* in the air, as thunder is in the air on a sultry day. An essential feature of the characters of Ibsen and Chekhov is that each carries and gives off a sense of a doom that is more than his own doom. Because what was doomed was a whole culture, they are both in the widest sense social dramatists. Their people typify a civilization and an epoch.

BEYOND TYPES AND INDIVIDUALS

BUT it would be disingenuous to drop the matter there, leaving an impression that Ibsen and Chekhov not only stood *for* a drama of types but resolutely *against* a drama of individuals. Ibsen also said, and his words would hold for Chekhov too:

> Before I write down one word I have to have the character in mind through and through. I must penetrate to the last wrinkle of his soul. I always proceed from the individual. The stage setting, the dramatic ensemble, all *that* comes naturally and does not cause me any worry, as soon as I am certain of the individual in every aspect of his humanity. I have to have his exterior in mind also, down to the last button, how he stands and walks, his behavior, what his voice sounds like.

Words like these bear witness to a kind of drama that was as new in its day as, say, the Elizabethan drama in the age of Elizabeth. If we see it negatively, it is because we know it chiefly in the products of its subsequent decline during the twentieth century. Ibsen and Chekhov were among the finest spokesmen in art for the modern sense of the individual's significance. I would emphasize the words *in art,* for no advocacy of any *ism* is involved. Individual*ism,* especially, was something both had seen through. The celebrated individualism of the freely competing economy was proving hostile to the life of individual. It tended indeed to stifle him. Ibsen and Chekhov were enemies of this individualism because they were friends of individuality. In different ways, their work is imbued with the love of individual being, and they seem to have invented a new method of character presentation which for lack of a better word we may call biographical. A character now has *a life story behind him,* and if the dramatist cannot unfold it in a single passage, he will let out the information in bits and pieces which the reader or spectator can later fit together. This, along with a notation of realistic detail inspired by the novel, would seem to be the most original feature in the "new drama," so far as its characters are concerned.

It is not clear, however, that the result should be described as "individuals, not types," first, because of the typical features mentioned above and, second, because the definition of "individual" remains vague. The word *type,* useful for a while, as I hope I have shown, also reaches a point of diminishing returns. When *types* have to be subdivided into two kinds, and when one of these kinds is complex, and includes Hamlet, it will pardonably be asked if he might not be called an *individual* after all. This would be to define an *individual* as a complex *type!*

The distinction must, willy-nilly, be left behind at a certain stage, for the great dramatists' interest in Character, whether typical or individual, had limits, even if some people's interest in it has none. Aristotle observed this but made his observation seem to depend on another point: that Plot is more important. Plot by itself may not be more important. I shall argue in a later chapter that it is the play as a whole, not the plot, that is more important. In regard to character, the point is the same. Character is subordinated to something else, and the subordination is a very strict and confining one. There is much about human beings that the playwright is prevented from saying by the exigencies of plot, dialogue, and theme, not to mention performance. This is to say that strict limits are placed upon the dramatist's opportunities to create either "types" or "individuals."

When I say the dramatist's interest in Character is limited I mean also that he does not see human beings as merely Characters, either individual or typical. What other way is there of seeing them? What *is* character? Suffice it here that it is something that, in life, can rationally be regarded as a bad thing. In Wilhelm Reich's *Character Analysis,* it is portrayed as a kind of armor which the child puts on as protection against the world—a psychic carapace. Sandor Ferenczi put much the same thought this way: "Character is . . . a sort of abnormality, a kind of mechanization of a particular way of reacting." Literature has not taken its "characters" to be only this, but such interpretations do help us remember to what a degree character even in literature is only an idea—a man's idea of himself, an author's idea of a man. Such ideas follow set patterns, conform to conventions. When we speak of "a very well-drawn character" we are bestowing an accolade for a new performance of an old routine. Even the slang sense of the word, as in "He's quite a character!" contains the implication of artifice: it is as if such a man were not alive but came out of a play.

"Well, what's wrong with the characters in plays?" Even the greatest writers have to use them and accept the attendant simplification. But we have seen in *Othello* how a playwright can move on from the protagonist's character to his humanity. Shakespeare often shows less interest in attributing qualities to people than in providing a demonstration that they are alive, that they are in the world. We identify ourselves with a Shakespeare character less in the sense of: "I am this man, I have these traits of character" than in the sense of: "Becoming this man, I know what it is to be alive." What the drama lacks in character-drawing, it makes up for in a concrete rendition of the dynamics of living.

There is a kind of simplicity about this, reminding us of the sense in which, as Goethe observed, all art is superficial: art works with the surfaces of life. What is so evidently true of painting is in some respects equally true of the drama. The surface of life, for a dramatist, is human beings walking and standing and sitting and talking and shouting and singing. To show this activity on a stage is theatre.

Very suggestive is a phrase of Benjamin Constant's: "that undulating mobility which pertains to human nature and forms actual beings." Before he presents characters, the playwright presents this undulation, this mobility which forms us, which *is* us. And perhaps one should prescribe for playwrights that they give life, rather than create character. Such is their *imitatio Dei*—and of Him we learn that on the sixth day He made man, though we do not learn if the man had a character.

"The whole of theatre is existential," says Etienne Souriau, "to make imaginary characters exist is its triumph and heroic act." This dictum makes the best sense, in my view, if the stress falls on the word *exist* rather than on the word *characters*. The playwright's first intention, as to his people, is to create existences. A particular mode of existence is implied: action. Aristotle took note of this, and George Santayana in *The Sense of Beauty,* has added that the dramatist is, in this, a sound philosopher of life:

> Plot is the synthesis of actions, and is a reproduction of those experiences from which our notion of men and things is originally derived; for character can never be observed in the world except as manifested in action. . . . The acts are the data, and the character the inferred principle.

Now I may seem to have been speaking as if actions happened in a vacuum and characters were out on their own somewhere. A portrait painter, after all, may present a single person's likeness. Why should not a playwright do likewise, or even present several people each in his singleness? Were character not, for him, a matter of actions, he might try. But "no man is an island," and no man's actions are insulated from other men. On the contrary, they are mainly and essentially things done *to* other men. We should not have been surprised to learn from modern psychology that even the ultimate action against oneself—suicide—is at the same time an aggression against the survivors. Or even against nonsurvivors: for a suicide may be a working off of hatred against someone long dead, in which case self-murder is an aggression in fantasy (like some plays): "how so-and-so would have been hurt by this." We speak of a man's relation with himself but how shall we get at it, how shall we even find words for it, except through his relations with other men, alive or dead?

In principle, the drama presents human relationships—

the things men do to each other—and nothing else. Other things are not presented on stage but, if "there" at all, are merely implied. In *King Lear,* much is *implied* about Nature and the gods, but *presented* on stage are a king and his subjects, a father and his children. Dramatic criticism emphasizes the implications at its peril. Had those been the writer's chief interest he would not have chosen the dramatic form. Milton was right not to choose it for a poem whose intention was to "justify the ways of God to men." And, *per contra,* the Spanish religious drama, when it is great, is great because it presents theology existentially: that is, in terms of existent, mutually interacting human beings. While theologically these beings are God's subjects, dramatically even He is subject to them. Such drama adds to the tension between art and life that between art and theology. Hence its fiery, tremulous character. The Catholic theologian Gilson has asked whether every great work of art does not involve to some degree a renunciation of God, and the Catholic dramatist might be said to be looking for trouble. I shall later be affirming that the great Spaniards delighted to do just that.

Ours has been an age, not of theology, but of individualism, and what has upset people about the dramatist is that he is, in a profound sense, less concerned with the individual than with society. Karl Marx said that a man was the ensemble of his relations with other men, and, in this respect, the soul of the playwright is by nature Marxist, though he may define society in terms of family rather than class. For instead of attempting static portraits on the analogy of painting, the playwright presents the dynamics of relationship. This explains why the naïve modern reader can go to the dramatic classics and find such a notable absence of "real human beings." He finds plot and theme. For the naïve modern reader is an individualist and does not consider it possible that the essence of humanity is to be found in the quicksilver of relationship rather than in the dead weight of isolated being.

What of the monologue? Can at least that stand as an individual portrait in dramatic form? It would seem not. Whether one thinks of Eugene O'Neill's *Before Breakfast,* Jean Cocteau's *The Human Voice,* or even of a poem not meant as a play such as Browning's *My Last Duchess,* the trick of the monologuist—a good trick—is to make an off-stage character as real as the one on stage, and otherwise to proceed on orthodox dramatic lines, making drama out of the relationship between people. As for the soliloquy in a regular play, it is fenced in on both sides by dialogue, and could be defined as but a long "aside," in which the drama of human relationships is momentarily continued by other means (direct address to the audience).

When we see a play, what is it we see? Possibly against a pictorial background, we watch people encountering each other. This, and, in principle, nothing else: if, say, acrobatics are added, it is strictly as an extra—or as a more demonstrative mode of encounter. The statement that the drama was born when a soloist stepped out of the chorus and uttered a monologue should perhaps be emended to: the drama was born when two soloists stepped out of the chorus and spoke dialogue. Or perhaps the first soloist took the chorus itself for his partner, and dialogue was invented that way. In either case, the encounter is what makes the acted drama as we know it.

In making the personal encounter the focal point of living, and so of therapy (the correction of living), J. L. Moreno, the founder of "psychodrama," is truly psychodramatic. In a personal encounter, made without inhibitions, we function fully and openly in the most direct relation we are capable of: that with a single other being. Such an encounter is "a scene from a play": it is fully enacted. Conversely, plays contain an enormous number of scenes of two people meeting. Even scenes with many characters on stage are often, in essence, scenes of two people meeting. "Ill met by moonlight, proud Titania!" The presence of bands of fairies, in the famous scene in *A Midsummer Night's Dream*, does not prevent that scene's being mainly the encounter of king and queen. Ludicrous, from a Naturalistic viewpoint, how many pairs, in the drama, just "happen to meet"! An encounter is a rendezvous with destiny. Paths cross that swords may cross.

This is the paradox of "drama and life": life is dramatic but its drama cannot be defined and presented without departures from life's usual procedures. In our usual "life as it is lived," inhibitions reign. Meetings do not often become encounters. Nor could they: it would be too inconvenient, too exhausting. Rather than encounter and face people all day, one needs devices for keeping them at arms' length. Courtesy, etiquette, mores, conventions are names for such devices. We say, "I'm glad to see you" to avoid giving offense when we are *not* glad to see someone. In this way the "scene" of offense given and taken—ending perhaps in a duel and a death—is not enacted. On stage it would have been *the* scene, the *scène à faire*. Life on stage is not inhibited, it is acted out; which is one reason we can only stand a couple of hours of stage life at a time. As for the devices for putting life at arms' length, they are not needed on stage to fill this natural function, but will be found there, willy-nilly, sometimes as documentation proving that human beings do use these devices, sometimes (and this in comedy) to characterize behavior as indirect, as existing on two planes at once. Comedy of manners, by definition, deals specifically with these devices, offers just these to the audience's eyes and ears, and yet, to achieve a work of art, has to make them fail in their objective of concealing human feeling and avoiding real encounters. There is comedy in the very fact that such ceremonious creatures try to avoid encounters and do not succeed. This is perhaps most amusing when a couple use manners to imply a lack of love when in fact they are courting at that very moment. Congreve's Mirabell and Millamant spring to mind.

On stage, meetings *are* encounters. Even to dramatize a nonencounter—the meeting, say, of two persons who talk past each other—the writer has either to accompany it with real encounters of other people, or make the non-encounter turn out to be an encounter after all. An example of the latter paradox is to be found in Alceste's meeting with Oronte in the first act of *The Misanthrope*. These two cannot meet in mutual respect or even mutual understanding. Hence the elaborate politeness with which they weave a screen between each other. But if there is no respect nor, on one side, understanding, there is on both sides anger. And from this mutuality ensues, finally, an encounter, an accomplished scene.

The essentially dual life of comedy tends to complicate encounters. They are seen more simply in tragedy and *drame*. And one might push the idea of Moreno a little further with the help of a thinker who belonged to the same group of young Viennese intellectuals in about 1910: Martin Buber. Life in a true encounter is life as we would wish it in something more than the good health of its psychology, the hygiene and efficiency, so to speak, of the little communications system that is set up. Buber would put it that in meetings which fail to be encounters we are reducing persons to things, and making of our fellow man an *It*. In an encounter, the other man is inescapably a *You,* and one could add that in languages that have the intimate form he is a *Thou,* a *Du,* a *Tu.* Now, outside of "real life," most of the great encounters of *I* and *Thou* are to be found in the dialogue of the master playwrights, not to repeat that any good scene in a play is likely to consist of, or contain, such an encounter. Where is the "I love you" of fourteen-year-olds more fully expressed than in *Romeo and Juliet,* or that of adulterous infatuation than in *Antony and Cleopatra?*

While we have been brought up to believe that what interests us in the life shown on stage is the character of separate individuals, a factor that probably does more to hold us fascinated is the spectacle of a more adequate kind of communication with others, hence of relationship with others, than we can find in life. Such is the relationship of real encounters in which (with exceptions that are significant as such) every *I* finds its *Thou.*

(Works by good playwrights who question whether such relationships can exist are no exception. In order to say that human beings cannot reach each other, Brecht, in *In the Swamp,* has to write scenes in which they do reach each other—albeit sado-masochistically. And in order to have his Father agonize at his apparent isolation from all, in *Six Characters in Search of an Author,* Pirandello uses the endlessly repeated traumatic encounter of Father and Stepdaughter. It may be said that the isolation comes after the trauma; the point is that Pirandello must then, *a fortiori,* return to the trauma to define it.)

THE STUFF OF DREAMS

LET ME append here, since it has a certain bearing, an observation on greatness in dramatic characterization. The "great" characters—Hamlet, Phaedra, Faust, Don Juan—have something enigmatic about them. In this they stand in stark and solemn contrast to—for example—the people of the present-day psychological play who are fully *explained*. The effect of such a modern play is of a naïve rationalism: reason has either explained everything, or is in process of doing so, and a cast of characters is at best a row of extinct volcanoes. The enigmatic nature of great characters also carries a cosmic implication: that life is but a small light in the midst of a vast darkness.

>   We are such stuff
> As dreams are made on, and our little life
> Is rounded with a sleep.

The lines are so familiar, we forget that they may, or even must, be taken as the final conclusion of the greatest of playwrights on his principal subject: human beings. How true, in any event, these words are of human beings in the plays of William Shakespeare! How faithfully they represent the life of the plays—so luminous at the center yet shading off toward the edges into a metaphysical mystery!

A sense of that mystery is strong and majestic throughout Greek tragedy, nor is it absent from Greek comedy. Roman drama is second-rate in lacking it. Racine has it always, and Corneille whenever he fails to suppress his sense of the painful and contradictory truth of things. It clings to the great Fausts and Don Juans through the changing interpretations of their characters. The opening

68

speeches of Dr. Faustus tell us that Marlowe has got it, and we infallibly recognize it on the first page of Tirso's *Trickster of Seville:*

> *¡Ah, cielo! ¿Quièn eres, hombre?*
> *¿Quièn soy? Un hombre sin nombre.*

> Great Heaven, what man are you, for shame?
> I am a man without a name.

Kleist and Büchner imparted it at the beginning of the nineteenth century; Ibsen and Strindberg and Chekhov at the end. Pirandello gives it a distinctly twentieth-century form—as an emanation of characters in plays still in the making. Even Shaw has it at moments: as in the presentation of Joan in her epilogue. It was something that Bertolt Brecht would never have wished upon himself and yet, *malgré lui,* he gave it to his archetypes of self-division, Galileo and Mother Courage.

If the final effect of greatness in dramatic characterization is one of mystery, we see, once again, how bad it is for us, the audience, to demand or expect that all characters should be either predefined abstract types or newly defined concrete individuals. A mysterious character is one with an open definition—not completely open, or there will be no character at all, and the mystery will dwindle to a muddle, but open as, say, a circle is open when most of the circumference has been drawn. Hamlet might be called an accepted instance of such a character, for, if not, what have all those critics been doing, with their perpetual redefining of him? They have been closing the circle which Shakespeare left open. Which is not foolish, but very likely what Shakespeare intended. Foolish are only those critics who assume that the great geometrician would leave a circle open by accident.

3

DIALOGUE

"TALKING!"

ALL LITERATURE is made up of words, but plays are made up of spoken words. While any literature may be read aloud, plays are written to be read aloud. It is because the drama presents men speaking that the theatre hires speaking men to communicate it. This is expensive. And nothing testifies more surely to people's interest in hearing words spoken than their willingness to pay for it.

A grown-up person will sometimes claim to have learned a foreign language without learning to speak it or to understand it when spoken. Anyone who has tried this knows how very small an experience he can expect from it. Words learned in that way ("Turn Right," "Beware of the Dog") may have a certain utility but can never be what words are in the languages we do speak and hear. Language at bottom is so little a matter of strict utility. A certain kind of textbook will have it that children learn words in order to ask for things. Actually, the strongest way of asking for the kind of thing infants ask for is to scream for it wordlessly—which children do both before and after they learn to talk. Anyone who has listened to two-year-olds knows that they do not talk to get things as much as they talk for pleasure. At two years old, my son Philip said: "Mama, don't talk! Philip talk!" He liked to hear the sound of his own voice, and he differed from an adult only in being unashamed of this.

And on the sixth day, God made man, and man said: Man talk! and man talked, and has never stopped talking since. Ontogeny repeats phylogeny. Each of us can truthfully state: I should like to talk incessantly. Why? In the first instance, because Narcissus is Narcissus, and used a mirror only because the tape recorder had not yet been invented. Talking is surely, among all the forms of life we know, the prime mode of self-assertion, from the cradle to the pulpit, and from the log cabin to the White House. Nor is it guileless. Often likened to the lovecalls of birds, it might equally be compared to the growls of hungry beasts. In their indefatigable efforts to hurt one another, men use a million words to every bullet. For, even more than bullets, words enable them to combine the maximum of hostility with the maximum of cowardice.

It is interesting that psychoanalysis is an exclusively verbal therapy. Therapist and patient do nothing but talk or leave pauses between talking. That, even more than the couple of dozen volumes of his collected works, is Freud's tribute to the Word. For, from a man's way with speech, everything else about him can be deduced. Quite aside from what he says, it can be deduced from his not knowing when to stop, or his not knowing when to begin, from his stammering, from his refusal to leave pauses for people to reply in. Lack of style is the man.

Freud saw men as self-betrayers. Others, Judaslike, they may betray with a kiss; themselves they most often betray with words. With his eye for the humanly significant, Freud early hit on what seemed the odd subject of slips of the tongue and verbal errors generally. Reading what he has to say, we realize that it is characteristic of the tongue to slip, and that words are what men usually have to err with before their error can become action. Before the murders of Julius Caesar or King Duncan comes the decision to murder them, a decision reached in words. Right there is the dramatist's opportunity.

Great orators, we say, weave a spell, and magic, in a more literal sense, is from the beginning the end in view. By talk we hope to control things. To believe in magic is to believe in the maximum power of words: for, if spells are valid, then words can move mountains. Faith in words has always been stronger and more widespread than faith in faith. Men with no belief in God will mutter the verbal formulas of such belief when they are in a fix. They are not thereby regaining their faith in God, they are maintaining their faith in words. For more civilized folk, the phrase "the magic of words" is figurative. It covers phenomena both good and bad: Hitler too was a magician with words. On the positive side, "the magic of words" connotes the magic of literature and, especially, of dramatic literature.

It also connotes that I should like to talk, not only incessantly, but incomparably. At the age of two I am convinced that I can; perhaps also at the ages of three and four; but somewhere along the line this illusion is lost along with others, which is fortunate, since, in a world of so many million people, it is hardly practical for each person to talk all the time. Disillusioned, one falls silent; and for the first time, is free to listen. Luckily one's make-up includes a mechanism that prevents one from succumbing to mere envy if what one hears is incomparable talk. This is the act of identification. If you can't lick 'em, join 'em. If you cannot be a great talker, identify yourself with the great talkers. Singing "O Sole Mio" in the bathtub, one sounds (to oneself) remarkably like Caruso. Rivaling Caruso, one can rival Winston Churchill, Demosthenes, Laurence Olivier, David Garrick, Oscar Wilde, Bernard Shaw. And, provided such rivalry is not taken seriously, the situation is a healthy one, and indeed a necessary one if living contact is ever to be made between great words and oneself. "In the end," says Nietzsche, "one experiences only oneself," and whether or not this remark embraces the whole truth, it calls attention to certain unalterable limitations upon one's powers and possibilities. If one is not eloquent, one latches on to the eloquence of others. No one, it seems, can just do without eloquence: it is as indispensable as it is irresistible. We may regret this when thinking of the eloquence of some rabble-rouser or evangelist, but to it we owe also the perennial human interest in great drama, which, as Ronald Peacock says, "is based on the poet's voice."

THE PLAYWRIGHT AS TALKER

WHY are we not eloquent? Why are we not only not orators but fail to converse as we might wish to? Talking involves the whole man, and talk between persons involves the whole society. Superlative talk would exist only among supermen in a utopia of supermen. Among men as we know them, in societies as we know them, talk is bad—either positively or negatively—either, that is, because of what people say or because of what they fail to say. Everyone talks too much or too little. Some people talk alternately too much and too little. Some cannot stop talking; others cannot begin. We have had a President of the United States who quite regularly got lost in his own sentences. Conversation does not exist any more except as an idea; in practice there are only people talking past each other. Introduced to the "greatest conversationalist of our time," one encounters only the composer of the world's longest monologues. Introduced to some of the wisest men of our time, one finds them too shy to speak.

A talking animal, man is not a success as a talking animal. And in each of us, except the glib, a sense of inarticulateness, of verbal ineffectiveness, is a potent, if negative, force—the linguistic component of our human portion of suffering. A sense of inarticulateness argues a respect for articulateness. The more inarticulate we are, the more reason we have to covet articulateness. After all, we only learn to talk in the first place because, all around us, are grownups talking in a fashion so fast and furious it would be beyond our wildest hopes to match it. From a sense of inadequacy within, and a sense that somewhere, without, there is adequacy, comes our respect for eloquence. Of course we don't understand what the grownups are saying: its wisdom, even its dependability, are taken on trust. But such trust comes easy to children. If words are magic, magic needs words for its spells. To name the demon, to find a word for him, is to exorcise him. As children revere and accept the imagined eloquence of grownups, the grownups revere and accept the messages of any whose power over words arouses a similar feeling or is similarly superior to their own. An orator is impressive in the degree of one's own lack of eloquence.

Such is life. The arts are compensatory. For the bad writing of everyday, literature provides good writing to astonish and delight. For the bad talk of everyday, the drama provides good talk to astonish and delight. The drama is the talker's dream and the taciturn man's revenge. For it is "all talk." A play is written by someone who wishes to do nothing but talk for an audience that is resigned to do nothing but listen to talk.

Of course the wish to do "nothing but talk" includes the wish to play all the parts. "The boss comes up to me and he says . . ." The narrative formulas of talk introduce those one-man dialogues which are the *pièces de resistance* of every talking soloist. The nonstop talker puts words into many mouths, and the really fluent nonstop talker will often be found to have done his homework— which is to listen to talk and remember it. All of us do a little listening and remembering, otherwise we would not know *what* the boss comes up to us and says, and in that case we could not invent later the brilliant retort we forgot to make at the time. Much dialogue being invented in daydreams, everyman his own playwright, he who hopes to be the playwright for everyman starts perforce with everyman's daydreams.

We like to tell ourselves that the drama does not idealize, and in one sense that is true: the drama does not gloss over the grimness in life. Yet there is one sort of grimness it can and should and often happily does gloss over: the grimness of our bad talking and of our taciturnity. Bad talk and silence can in a play be used only as exceptional effects. For example, the point can be made that bad talk is bad. This may be done by surrounding the bad talk with good. Or by exaggerating the badness to the point of the ludicrous; i.e., of the comic. But to make a whole play out of silence would be to write the scenario of a pantomime, and to make a whole play out of bad talk would be to make a bad play. I see no real exceptions to this rule. The apparent exceptions are plays in which the talk is not wholly bad or plays in which the author is depicting people who talk badly but manages to do so without writing bad dialogue. The latter task sounds impossible yet it has often been performed. Eloquent and expressive pages of dialogue can be made out of the stammerings of semiarticulate people: Büchner's *Woyzeck* was perhaps the first proof of this. I shall return in a minute to the anti-eloquent drama. It *is* exceptional. The rule is that the talk of life is idealized on stage. A dramatist takes an Eisenhower speech and makes it sound like Churchill. Hence the primary pleasure of dramatic dialogue: the pleasure of perfect articulateness. Nothing pertinent is left unexpressed. Each speaker says all he should say, and says it perfectly—according to the kind of perfection that is appropriate to the context, be it witty and concise or poetic and elaborate. Which may seem a straightforward enough thing for it to do but, in the face of the confusion of things in this world, and the inadequacy of most people to most occasions, a piece of good dialogue is always of itself a source of delight and comes with the shock of surprise.

Büchner is articulate in presenting the inarticulateness of Woyzeck, but to write a whole play around such a man was an unprecedented procedure. Shakespeare had made fun of the inarticulate Dogberry, and got rid of him in a scene or two. For generally speaking, the drama has room only for proficient talkers. True, it would not be sound criticism to conclude that Racine's people are meant to be taken as garrulous because Racine's plays are written in long speeches, but it is equally true that an understood part of each Racine character is verbal adequacy to the most taxing of human situations. In life, none of us is verbally adequate to these situations. One could no more find words that do them justice than one could find music to do them justice and burst into song when something terrible happens like some hero from Verdi or Wagner. What is involved here is not so much the characterization of particular roles as the assumption that human nature is able to give an account of itself in words. For the dramatist human beings are articulate. Words are the sign and insignia of their humanity. One thinks of the young Helen Keller, whose humanity could only become manifest if and when she found out about words.

ELOQUENCE IN DIALOGUE

IN GENERAL, a dramatist has to write eloquently, which is to say that he has to achieve a level of speech, not for a character but for whole plays, that is far higher than our talk in life. This is in itself a task of such size that it can, at a given time in history, prove impossible. At another time, it may take a whole generation of dramatists to achieve it. The eloquence of Shakespeare's early plays, as has often been recognized, was the achievement, not of Shakespeare only, but of those predecessors of his who invented blank verse and gradually made it an eloquent medium. In the history of the drama the forging of such weapons rightly occupies a pre-eminent place. The French eloquence of the seventeenth century would be inconceivable without the alexandrine which, when Racine came along, had been, as if deliberately, made ready for him. Traditionally, the playwrights have not worked with the language of the street, but with language as rendered more expressive by predecessors and colleagues in a specially eloquent medium that belongs, not to life, but to literature.

"Le théâtre," says Robert Brasillach, *"c'est le style."* And traditionally, the style has been set by the poet, not the stage designer, nor the director, nor even the actor, all of whom have to adapt themselves to the style of the writing. I once had the opportunity to ask Jean Vilar what it was in Paul Claudel's plays that made it possible for him to put them across to uneducated miners. He replied, *"L'éloquence,"* and went on to maintain that *"l'éloquence"* was the one thing necessary in any difficult play if it is to get across to an audience.

But the diagnostic of dramatic dialogue cannot be found either in "style" or "eloquence," for these it has in common with all other literature. What sets dialogue off from the rest of literature is precisely dialogue, as opposed to monologue, verbal intercourse as opposed to verbal discourse. Dialogue, it is true, occurs in the novel, but if a novel were wholly in dialogue, it would be that much less a novel, that much more a play. The Spanish masterpiece, *Celestina,* to cite the most celebrated case in point, has alternately been called a play and a novel in dialogue. An opposite tendency is found in the play with excessive stage directions which may well indicate that the author is a novelist who has not found himself. Conversely, a born playwright is a man who does not need stage directions: reality as he sees it—that part of reality which he sees— can be *com*pressed into dialogue and *ex*pressed by it.

If eloquence and style are qualities of single speeches, the special problem of the playwright is the relation between speeches. Take the duration of a speech. In life, each speech in a conversation is either too long or too short. In drama, each speech is exactly the right length. Not only does each person know how to communicate fully, he knows when to leave off, he knows when the next man's turn has come, he knows how to take as well as to give. The famous discussion scenes in Shaw plays are dream discussions, the only perfect discussions, probably, that one has ever known. That is one reason why they are so delightful. However, there are few scenes of discussion even in Shaw, while the principle of perfected talk holds for all dialogue, and exact rightness of length characterizes the speeches of all the first-rate playwrights. This rightness has a significance that goes beyond good manners and morals. The drama's "element" is time; and drama is a brief form. These two facts bring it about that each unit of time—second, minute, or whatever—is at a premium. George Cohan said he measured criticism by the inch, and any dramatist measures dialogue by the split second. How long a person speaks can be as important as what he says. A dramatist's first draft of a group scene might well contain such an entry as "here A speaks for five seconds." For the writer may have sensed the size and rhythm of a scene before having arrived at all its content. To break this rhythm would be more fatal than to omit such and such a statement. Stark Young has pointed out how fatal it can be for translators of a master dramatist to render a short phrase in a long sentence "to get in all the meaning." Dialogue is under no compulsion to cover any particular territory: it is no essay or treatise. It is bound by the exigencies of the drama alone.

79

Hence a character in a play does not talk merely to show what he is like, nor is he allowed to talk himself out. He is limited in his utterances to what bears on the play as a whole, keeps it moving, advances it just as much as it needs to be advanced, and at the proper rate of speed.

And this constitutes a supreme idealization of life, for it signifies a life which has a clear and unitary meaning, a direction, an utterly purposive movement toward an end. In this respect, dramatic art is one of the great wish-fulfilling dreams, for there is nothing human beings more ardently crave than to be persons in such a drama. In the Middle Ages, it was official doctrine that humanity did belong in such a drama; and so the art of the drama represented a metaphysical fact. But this art has as great a poignancy—or greater—in an age like our own when the universe is generally felt to be unintelligible, amorphous, undramatic. For today art offers the only integrated drama, and we can be persons in a perfectly constructed Action only, it would seem, when we read or see a play.

NATURALISM

IF DRAMATIC DIALOGUE is ideal talking subordinated to the play as a whole, a very wide field of possibilities is open to it. But excluded in principle is talking, even ideal talking, that is not subordinated to a drama, and to this excluded category belongs, of course, all the actual talking we do in life. We have witnessed in the past several generations various misguided attempts to make dialogue out of just this, for we live in an age that is ever ready to make a cult of life, particularly raw life of any kind, an age which is inclined to ignore or deny all differences between life and art.

It is the age of the tape recorder. And it will be convenient to describe different kinds of dramatic dialogue in the degree that they diverge from tape recordings of actual conversations. I insert the word "actual" to exclude conversations which the speakers know are being tape recorded, for such knowledge would constitute the first departure from spontaneity, and so the first approach to art, good or bad. If people know they are being tape recorded, they make adjustments both of form and content, they begin to talk for posterity, they begin to be artists. The next departure from raw life comes when a tape is edited. Editing brings in a degree of selectivity, and this of itself gives us art, albeit of a primitive kind. In other words, art can be life minus something, rather than life plus something, if the subtracted element is the dead wood of stuttering, pausing, repeating, going on too long, and so forth. (Art can be life minus something, if we speak in terms of pure durational quantity. It is still life plus something if we introduce qualitative terms such as purity, intensity, saliency, austerity. . . .)

The word for dialogue which is as close as this to actual talking is Naturalistic, and obviously Naturalistic writers will often run the risk of failing to edit enough, thus tumbling out of art into life—of which the result is not an impression of the vividness of living but the dullness of art that is not art. If this is the besetting sin of Naturalistic writers, their merit is their sense that content matters, that life is what art is about. Since drama is spoken words, it must always retain a discernible relation to the language as spoken. This relationship may be hard to discern in the most highly wrought styles, such as that of French classical drama, particularly if we try to discern it in languages other than our own, but if anyone takes the most highly wrought language of great drama in his own tongue, he will find, I believe, that this language makes use of colloquial rhythm, and even vocabulary, more than, say, the language of epic and lyric poetry does in the same culture. (An English-speaking person could compare the style of *Antony and Cleopatra* with that of *Paradise Lost* or Chapman's Homer.)

Also in favor of the Naturalistic approach is the fact that language is not raw material, except relatively speaking. It is not completely amorphous, but, on the contrary, has to be shaped and formed before talk can be even talk. The dramatist can think of the community that shapes and forms a language as his collaborator. John Synge, famously, thought of the Irish, and especially the Aran, community in this way, but the example should also serve to remind us that some languages or dialects are much richer—esthetically speaking—than others. Given speech as rich in wit and imagination as that of the Irish, it is true that, given also an Action, dramatic dialogue might be created more by editing than by writing. The existence of such a rich dialect offers possibilities, as does the dialect, for that matter, of some of the big cities, such as New York. A large part of the life of Clifford Odets' plays comes from his good remembering of what people do say in the Bronx. One hears that he sat in bars taking notes, and, for *The Flowering Peach*, resorted to the tape recorder itself. Sean O'Casey's dialogue, at its best, seems to me a little more "creative"—i.e., created. He seems not just to remember and edit but also to develop the material, working it up to giddier heights of fantasy on his own. John Synge, despite his own remarks, seems to have invented an Irish dialect which no Irishman ever spoke. If he is a Naturalistic playwright, then Naturalism contains a delightful element of blarney.

The appeal of Naturalistic dialogue, when this is not unusually witty or imaginative, is to our human concern with the actual—our wish to give the nod of approval to a claim to accuracy. This is something that interests three-year-old children a good deal, and what one might call the three-year-old element in art is never lightly to be discounted. The three-year-old child will indignantly reject a wrong name for a thing or a wrong account of an incident. There is evidently much pleasure for *Homo sapiens* in the mere assertion that things *are thus* and not otherwise. The historian, says Leopold Ranke, must show the object as it actually was—*wie es eigentlich gewesen*—and each human being, even each little person of three, likes to appoint himself a judge of historians and other truthtellers.

The pleasure seems to reside in the act of recognition. "I remember things to have been as you say, and now you bring the memory back to me, and I enjoy this." One person will tell another the story of a movie, which both have seen, and the two will chuckle together over having the various incidents recalled to the mind's eye. The Naturalistic play, as we have known it on Broadway in our time, specializes in reminders of hearth and home. "*We* have a rocking chair on our porch; and this man's play features a rocking chair on *his* porch." Dialogue, in such a theatre, becomes a series of reminders that homey people speak a homey idiom. Character is rendered by phrase-ology that reminds one of Aunt Lucy and Uncle George. In the lower-middle-class mentality of the drama which presents the lower middle class will again be noted the drift of Naturalism toward mere life, toward nonart. The dialogue tends to be unimproved and all but unedited talk, and, interestingly enough, it seems proportionately harder for the playwright to create a play to which the dialogue can be subordinated; hence the tendency of Naturalism toward the episodic—which is nothing more than a tendency to meander, a tendency to lose track, a tendency, in short, to formlessness.

Probably the better type of Naturalistic play—the kind in which the talk is well edited, and even a little developed by brains and imagination—seems to most modern persons to be the very type of drama as a whole. Anything else would be classed as "unusual." Which is a fairly reasonable response to the theatre as we have known it in the past couple of generations. To the theatre of the past two thousand years it would be an unreasonable response, no such closeness to everyday talk ever having been envisaged. Literary theory offers some oft-repeated phrases to the effect that the real language of men is heard on the comic stage ("language such as men do use"), but we have only to remember that comedy was written in verse until the Renaissance, and even sometimes after that, to be reminded that such phrases are elastic, and that one man's formality is another's colloquialism. Former ages were much less prone than ours to let art bog down in the mess of living. Their temptation was ordinarily the opposite one—to let art, at times, dry up by excessive abstraction from life. If the great fault of modern dialogue is characterless vernacular, the great fault of dialogue at earlier periods is empty rhetoric—in his day Shakespeare was perhaps the only dramatist who consistently escaped it.

84

RHETORICAL PROSE

ALL stage dialogue except the modern is highly rhetorical; that is to say, it is raised far above the colloquial by deliberate artifice. Minimally, it is "rhetorical" in the popular sense—highflown, florid, oratorical. For example, the prose plays of the nineteenth century before Ibsen are couched in a conventional oratorical mode which, as a result of Ibsenite modernity, has come in for a lot of ridicule since. The rhetoric of Victorian melodrama is but the rhetoric of all the prose drama of the period, and was accepted by the whole culture. Dickens is not above using it in his novels. Nor did the first generation of Naturalists eschew it. Zola's *Thérèse Raquin*, the very manifesto of stage Naturalism, is "rhetorical" from beginning to end. Present-day reviewers would call it "corny."

The rhetorical prose of drama in the nineteenth century can be traced back to the eighteenth. One is told that the eighteenth century invented the drama of drab middle-class life and so turned from verse to colloquial prose. But how colloquial is colloquial—in the eighteenth century? Actually, it would seem that the dramatists of middle-class life looked for a rhetoric which would provide a kind of bourgeois equivalent of poetry. George Lillo, for example, is so unmodern that he finds it hard not to write blank verse.

The most interesting school of prose drama in the eighteenth century is that of the German *Sturm und Drang*. The name of the movement applies par excellence to the dialogue of the plays. Certainly, the subject of Schiller's *Love and Intrigue* is middle-class, but the dialogue, far from being antirhetorical and subdued as befits middle-class drabness, is, to an almost intolerable degree, bizarre, florid, extravagant. But if everything in the *Sturm und Drang* is overdone, more or less on principle, the intention was an honorable one, and the intention was, while admitting the famously undramatic bourgeois milieu, to surrender no degree of the histrionic in style. And the histrionic is compatible with bad taste, but not with monotony. The theatre prefers garish colors to none at all.

Now there is this much evidence for the proposition that the natural medium of drama is verse: prose dramatists seem desperately to need rhetorical substitutes for meter. Meter brings an element of the expected, whatever may be its surprises in rhythm and content, and this makes for solidity. While the man in the street will think of prose as gloriously free, the prose artist will know that this freedom constitutes precisely the difficulty in making prose effective, especially in making it effective as dialogue, and he will seek features that set limits to the freedom. For example, the form of a catechism, rudimentary as it is—the merest questioning and answering—is better than nothing—"nothing" in this case being to talk "freely" on. The catechism also introduces an element of ceremony, of ritual; and that, too, helps. The dialogue "routines" of *commedia dell'arte*—such as Molière is still using in great plays like *The Miser*—are often no more complex than a catechism and are sometimes precisely a catechism.

Prose rhetoric could be called more Naturalistic than the rhetoric of verse, not just because people speak prose, but because it relies more heavily on patterns from life, not art, or, more exactly, on patterns from *other* arts, and more practical ones, than literature. The theatre, in this department of prose rhetoric, has drawn very heavily indeed upon two other "artistic" institutions: the church and the law court. Usually, when people call a prose play "preachy," they are referring to content, but there is an organic connection between preaching and the style of dialogue of a great deal of prose drama. It is unfortunate that the word "preaching" carries a slur. The modern world seems to have forgotten that the sermon can be one of the most sublimely thrilling of all performances. That, and not dull moralizing, was certainly what Lessing had in mind when he put forward his idea of the stage as a pulpit. Prose drama seems to have suffered somewhat in prestige along with that homiletic art upon which it has been so dependent. Yet if we realize that the theatre's chief preacher within living memory is Bernard Shaw we shall perhaps be prepared to grant that preaching is not all it has been cracked down to be.

It is true that the influence of the church is hard to isolate. When is prose homiletic and when not? It would be hard to draw a line. One can be a good deal more specific about the influence of the law courts, for the drama abounds in trial scenes, good and bad. The reason is not that playwrights tamely follow in each other's footsteps. It is that the stage and the law court are two versions of the same thing—our human refusal to obey the precept, Judge not that ye be not judged. Plays are, in a symbolic sense, "trial scenes"; and it is inevitable that they run to thousands of trial scenes in a literal sense. This being so, it is also inevitable that the language of the law court should creep in too. Judge, prosecutor, advocate, plaintiff, defendant—what play could not be written with these five characters and a witness or two? Courtroom language is a dramatic language in that it finds itself under the dual compulsion of the theatre: to keep things moving and to be at each moment esthetically impressive. It is subordinated to a larger whole but it needs to have every artistic merit—eloquence, grace, dignity, wit, and so on.

RHETORICAL VERSE

IT IS NOT just the prose drama that makes abundant use of homiletic and forensic oratory. Taking another step away from everyday talk, we come to drama in verse which is not poetry in the fullest sense but, meter aside, operates much on the lines of the drama of prose rhetoric. *Nathan the Wise* is an example; its author came of a line of clergymen. Schiller's work falls in this category; which explains why any comparison with Shakespeare is bound to be so damaging to him. His use of language could not be less Shakespearean. Instead, it is homiletic and, even more, forensic, a language of splendid preachments, formal accusations, majestic defenses. Such dialogue cannot give anything like so full an account of man as Shakespeare's. But what style can? Schiller matches, not Shakespeare, but the Cicero and the Burke of the great statesmanlike orations. His kind of dialogue is fully adequate to his purpose, which is the presentation of dialectics in a key of sublimity.

Sublimity has long been out of fashion—out of something more than fashion, indeed, since one must impute its disappearance to something more than snobbery and caprice. Sublimity no longer fits. Schiller was perhaps not only the last dramatist who did write sublimely but the last who could have. Already, in his younger contemporary Kleist, sublimity is coming to seem only a face that is put upon things—a form of hypocrisy. A quarter-century later, in Büchner's *Danton's Death,* we hear the sublime note only as an echo in the distance. Today very few realize what has been lost. To speak only of sublimity in rhetoric, how unfortunate that it is thought of as necessarily meretricious! Far more, of course, is involved than a mode of speech. It is the whole mode of culture that has changed. To appreciate Schiller's tone of voice, one would have to appreciate Sir Joshua Reynolds' portraits and Handel's operas—and Washington's Inaugural Address.

There is something the Germans call by the term *Pathos* which was a legitimate feature of the old style in theatre and which is now counted a fault. Pathos implies a heightened form of language and of delivery. We say "declamatory." The word Pathos conveys not only this but also the feeling of elation that goes with it. In short, the term implies that when the "declamatory" style is properly achieved, a certain elation does go with it. To describe this particular form of elation one would have to draw on adjectives like noble, dignified, grand, splendid. And an acknowledgment of sadness is there too. It was not by chance that Beethoven chose words by Schiller for his symphony, since Beethoven is pre-eminently the *pathétique* composer, as Schiller is the *pathétique* dramatist. And Schiller's plays would be of high interest even if this Pathos was all they had to offer. It yields a splendid mode of theatrical utterance; one may wonder if any subsequent mode can be said to match it.

POETRY

ON THE OTHER HAND, it is inferior to the Shakespearean mode, and the difference might loosely be defined as that between rhetoric and poetry. The rhetorician takes the language as it is, and marshals his words with all the professional skills of pulpit and law court. A case is stated, and if it is stated with more than clarity and concision, then what is added might be considered flourishes—of humor, wit, cleverness, or what not. But the poet does not regard words in this way, as tools already made. They are tools he makes and remakes while using them. The rhetorician is rightly said to clothe thoughts in suitable words, and that is to imply that the thoughts already existed fully enough for us to judge that they are now *suitably* clothed. Now if they existed, they existed in words—presumably other words, and less suitable ones. Hence the rhetorician is an improver of phraseology, a professional "rewrite man." His aim is to put down "what oft was thought but ne'er so well expressed." The poet, on the other hand, likes—if I may paraphrase D. W. Harding—to get at a thought before it is fully a thought, before it has been pinned down with words. With him, the word-finding and the thought-thinking proceed together, and the result is, not necessarily new vocabulary, but new language, new phrasing, new combinations of vocabulary, new rhythms, new meaning. We do not congratulate a poet on "putting it well," but rather on producing a new "it."

For English-speaking persons the great instance of fully poetic drama is inescapably Shakespeare. Ben Jonson's tragedies are comparatively "rhetorical," the tragedies of the Restoration crudely so. Even John Webster's claim to have created a fully poetic drama, in this sense, is dubious. He is, rather, the creator of "poetic drama"—in the modern sense of drama in highly colored language.

I have spoken of the poet as making up his language as he goes along. Today such a statement suggests the devices of *Finnegans Wake*, but the Shakespearean experimentality was diametrically opposite. Joyce will have his joke—on the basis of erudition and memory. His book is an experiment to end experiments, and wholly retrospective in method. Shakespeare faced forward, and could get away with it because he had the luck to live at a time when the language was young and unsettled. He helped to mold, not only an English of his own, but the English of English culture. One hardly needs the Oxford Dictionary to confirm that so many expressions are first found in Shakespeare, one has while reading him so lively and spontaneous a sense of being present at the birth of meanings. Philosophically, there are in Shakespeare's works reiterations of older views; but the *experiencing* of these philosophies is ever new. This is one reason why Shakespeare means more to us than those who would teach us more. He takes us back to a point before that at which "teachings" are formulated. He does not (primarily) contend or confute, he enables us to melt down our own contentions and confutations—after which we can, if we are capable of it, remold them for ourselves. His spiritual strength is unique, for he is the teacher behind the teachers.

The most obvious characteristic of the Shakespearean style and method is rich and original imagery. All writing contains images, but the images of rhetoric are only those of conversation worked up with a fuller vocabulary and better rhythm. That is to say: they are old images, which the rhetorician uses again, with more or less acknowledgment of the fact. Even his "new" images are old. Either it will be found that they have been used before, or they represent so slight a departure from the old as to enforce no new way of seeing the object or the point. Orators no doubt "think of" metaphors and similes, but *what* metaphors and similes they think of is a matter of habit, helped out by logic. Their kind of imagery is merely illustrative, and we can all "think of" such images insofar as we are not dim-witted.

The difference between Shakespeare and Schiller is in nothing so marked as in their use of images. Schiller does in this line all that a good orator can do. Shakespeare thinks in images. It is by means of the image, more than by any other single means one can readily name, that he comes by his uniquely fresh vision of things. Our difficulty is keeping pace with him. The images say so much, and shift so rapidly, one could not possibly "take it all in" at first hearing. Even to see the main pattern, let alone notice the details, one has to go more slowly than actors ever could. Is this because some of the words are archaic now? Is it because we are less quick in apprehension than our ancestors were? Whatever the reason for the failure, one characteristic result is that producers of his plays feel compelled to simplify him. And rather than slow the dialogue down to the point where it might be clear but would probably be tiresome, they maintain a proper tempo, sacrificing all detail. Now, from a speech delivered too fast to follow in detail, one retains just certain general impressions, broad ideas. From the Shakespearean point of view, it is not enough. No wonder a comparison with a rhetorician like Schiller becomes possible, for under these conditions Shakespeare may well *be* a Schiller, his poetry having been reduced to rhetoric.

And there are those who seem to say: so much the better. When a Shakespeare play is read thus loosely, not only are its specific significances missed, but the way is open to any loose interpretation that takes anyone's fancy. In the edition of *Twelfth Night* that commemorates Orson Welles' production, we learn that the play has a thesis, and that it is this: "Dost thou think because thou art virtuous, there shall be no more cakes and ale?" Which is as though the play had been written by Sir Toby Belch. And it seems that when Welles staged *Julius Caesar* he made Fascists and anti-Fascists out of Caesar's party and their enemies, respectively. This kind of interpretation would seem to yield political drama of a type positively inferior to Schiller's because, since Fascists are bad, and anti-Fascists good *ex officio,* it cannot be so very interesting to get to know either party: all we have is a crude melodrama made pretentious by forced allusions to current events.

In describing four kinds of dialogue, I have not sought to provide a scheme that will cover all drama. The dramatic poetry of Racine, for example, does not really fit into any of these categories. All I am doing is taking examples of dialogue that depart in different degrees from ordinary talk, and making the point that they appeal to different human beings or to the same human beings in different ways. Naturalistic dialogue is homey, and says: "Please note how close our playwright has stayed to the ordinary conversation of ordinary people." The rationale could be called democratic: "This is *your* theatre." Rhetorical dialogue, in prose or verse, is aristocratic. It is an ideal speech, and will tend to consort with plots and characters above the ordinary. I chose Schiller for my main example. A simpler choice would have been Corneille, the archetypal "undemocratic" writer, who asks us, not to recognize the ordinary, but to be awe-struck by the superior. Now my fourth category, poetic dialogue, can include the other three (Naturalism, Prose Rhetoric, Verse Rhetoric). In Shakespeare there are Naturalistic bits, and there are "Cornelian" bits, but the poetic dramatist does not limit himself to these kinds of appeal. Even Corneille and Schiller seem narrow when compared with Shakespeare. The rhetorical drama tends to limit them to the public and professional side of life. Using a homiletic and forensic type of dialogue, they present a cast of characters who, if they are not all preachers and lawyers, live in the world of preachers and lawyers, the world of public issues. Shakespeare does not belittle the public issues, but his universality consists not least in this: that he presents the inner life of man, not instead of, but as well as, the outer life. Nor does his presentation of the inner life consist of "psychologizing," as I hope my chapter on Character has shown. What it does consist of is only in part relevant here. Not to wander from the topic of Dialogue, let me simply remark that Shakespeare's image of man requires, among other things, lyric verse to define it. How inconceivable that anyone should sing a little love song in a play by Corneille! It would be breaking with more than the Unities, it would be breaking with his world. Influenced by Shakespeare and the Greeks, Schiller very much wished to introduce lyrical elements into his plays, but his kind of lyric is itself "rhetorical," and when Mary Stuart bursts into stanzaic verses after two acts of iambic pentameter the sense of change is minimal. In Shakespeare, on the other hand, the presence of little songs here and there is a token of an omnipresent lyricism that goes to the making of the Shakespearean verse texture, the Shakespearean dramaturgy, and even the Shakespearean *Weltanschauung*.

The division Dramatic, Epic, Lyric is misleading if it suggests that any one of the three normally excludes the others. The dramatic is made up of epic and lyric elements. The plot is the epic element. The lyric element will be found in the dialogue or nowhere. That in so much modern drama it is found nowhere is hardly a recommendation of modern drama; and, as I have been pointing out, much of the drama of the seventeenth and eighteenth centuries was antilyrical too. The whole modern period—since the Middle Ages—tends to specializations. Opera is our lyric drama, if one is to speak of achievements. Among the failures is the occasional outcropping of a kind of drama that is too exclusively lyrical. In our day, *The Lady's Not For Burning* struck me as being drama of this sort. I would certainly place in this category the plays of Gabriele D'Annunzio. Many of the products of the various revivals of poetic drama inevitably turn out to be over-lyrical, though it seems to me that T. S. Eliot went the other way, left the poetry out of most of his poetic plays, and developed a verse rhetoric of considerable expressive and dramatic power.

It is tempting to see the history of drama since the seventeenth century as a steady decline. Yeats has written:

Shakespearean fish swam the sea, far away from land;
Romantic fish swam in nets coming to the hand;
What are all those fish that lie gasping on the strand?

The French classicists, followed by the playwrights of the other countries, exclude lyricism. The Naturalists later exclude even eloquence. What is left?

ANTI-POETRY

ONE WOULD HAVE to say "very little" if all we had witnessed in the past century was ordinary Naturalistic drama written in the manner of edited tape recordings.

Actually, though some of the great modern playwrights have been classed as Naturalists, they have one and all been hostile to Naturalism. They have all rejected banality, and have demanded a larger dramatic world. What confuses us is that they were often quasi-Naturalistic. A person may open a volume of Ibsen and conclude: "Well, this *is* just ordinary conversation." There is nothing in the individual sentence, or sometimes on the individual page, to give him the lie. The dialogue of Ibsen, Strindberg, Chekhov, and Pirandello does start both from ordinary conversation and from the kind of dialogue most closely related to it. The unit remains the actual uttered remark, but the units are then related to each other with extreme sophistication. Actors who till then had noticed only the banality of each sentence in a Chekhov scene are suddenly amazed to find that the scene as a whole is a poem. Ibsen should be credited with the invention of an anti-poetry. He made a fine art of the understatement, the evasion, the unfinished sentence. In a sense his writing undercuts poetry—and reduces it to triviality. This happens with Hedda Gabler's poetic phrase "vine leaves in his hair," and with Hilda Wangel's "harps in the air." How little the literati of Ibsen's day were wise to this rhetoric of his is shown in Arthur Symons's dismissal of just these phrases on the grounds of their inadequacy as poetry.

Nietzsche speaks of the really deep calm being one like that of the sea, under which turbulence and power can be sensed, and the work of Ibsen suggests that the really effective prose in drama is that under which poetry can be sensed. The ordinary Naturalist achieves mere in-eloquence and therefore *non*art. Ibsen contrives anti-eloquence and makes *another kind of art* from it. It is not facile wisdom after the event to say one can feel the presence of the early Ibsen in the work of the late Ibsen. After all, he was the last playwright in the world who could have come to the theatre with a tape recorder or the mental equivalent thereof. He had prepared himself in just the opposite way. Arguably *Peer Gynt* and *Brand* are his greatest work and he made a mistake to turn from that path. Mistake or not, he did—and this is history—make other great plays by a complete reversal of method. In *Peer Gynt* and *Brand* he was the eloquent poet par excellence writing a magnificent verse rhetoric that had its roots in the literature of the previous hundred years. Reading a lecture by Georg Brandes in 1872, he decided that modern drama had to be far more modern in its form, starting with the dialogue. We find him telling a correspondent some years later that the verse drama was obsolete. The text of his plays, from *Pillars of Society* on, tells us that prose rhetoric had been dismissed along with verse. Well and good, but behind the assiduously subdued and unrhetorical prose of these plays is the hectic poetic temperament of the author of *Peer Gynt*. The pressure of this temperament is indeed felt with a peculiar intensity under the new restraints. Granted, the *problème du style* is posed in a new way. In a sense there is now no "writing" at all. The Aristotelian idea of the primacy of the Action takes on a new meaning. The Ibsenite Action is so all-embracing that people can hardly get a word in edgewise. Words are spoken only when they are pried loose by the situation, and the situation is one that will not let many words be pried loose. The greater the pressure, the less people can say. Still, a hundred pages of words—much the usual amount for a play—do finally get down on Ibsen's writing paper, and it is fair to ask:

97

how have they been chosen? I think Pirandello found the best phrase to answer this question with, and since he regarded Ibsen as second only to Shakespeare, it is fitting that he should have. His phrase is: *l'azione parlata*—the Action spoken, the Action in words.* This distinctly Aristotelian formula is that of the great modern dramatists as a group. If the resultant writing must by its nature lack all the luxuriant richness of direct poetry, and even all the Pathos of declamatory rhetoric, it has the opposite virtues of leanness, economy, accuracy, and consistently ironical understatement.

ANTI-PLAYS

THE better drama of the Ibsenite era was anti-lyric and anti-eloquent but it was not anti-dramatic. The idea of anti-dramatic dramas, anti-plays—belongs to quite another school, and one which to date has much less to show. Is the anti-play, as its name suggests, the point at which drama liquidates itself? Or is it simply another step in the drama's development? Terminology is polemical, and so one cannot blithely assume that what is called an anti-play will in fact not be a play. Eugène Ionesco's anti-plays are far more conventional than the talk about them suggests.

* The context reads as follows: "But, to the end that the characters should leap, living and self-propelled, from the written pages, it is necessary for the dramatist to find the word that shall be the action itself spoken, the living word that can move, the immediate expression, conatural with the act, the unique expression which can only be what it is, that is, appropriate to this given character in this given situation; words, expressions which are not invented but which are born when the author is truly identified with his creature to the point of feeling it as he feels himself, desiring it as it desires itself." This passage appears first in the essay "*L'azione parlata*" (1899), and is used again in the essay "*Illustratori, Attori, e Traduttori*" (1908).

Samuel Beckett's *Waiting for Godot* has established itself as the most original contribution to dramatic literature since 1950. The distinction of the writing is undeniable. All kinds of good things may be said about the dialogue, "but is it dramatic?" Let us set aside the fact that very little happens in the play, for this is true of so many good plays. And many good plays have wrongly been found undramatic ("not a play") by their first critics. The first critic to make the point, and repeatedly, that Beckett's dialogue is not dramatic is Beckett himself—in that dialogue. For this "criticism" is inherent in the recurrent joke of letting the conversation simply dry up and having one character tell the other to say something. In this, Beckett has put into a play what "cannot be put into a play." For in a play, the dialogue cannot conceivably dry up. A play is, so to speak, a much longer piece of dialogue, reduced to the number of lines one sees in the final text by the craftsmanship of compression. Pauses can only occur when they are equivalent to dialogue, when their silence is more eloquent and packed with meaning than words would be. The dramatist fights against time. He cannot "get it all in." His craft is the filling out of every nook and cranny that each second as it passes may offer him, just as the painter's craft is the filling in of each square inch of canvas. That any part of the dramatist's precious couple of hours should stand empty, and that there should be any difficulty about filling it, is absurd. But *Waiting for Godot* is "drama of the absurd."

Not to settle the matter with a pun, let me add that on the face of it, Beckett's work is too Naturalistic for drama. It is in life, not in drama, that there may be a problem about filling in the time. It is in life that we "kill time"; in drama, time kills us. A dramatist will show the sands

99

running out on Dr. Faustus and hell approaching. He will not show time stretching endlessly, inorganically out, and Godot not coming. And, as far as dialogue is concerned, a dramatist cannot use garrulousness (talk, talk, talk) except incidentally and framed by nongarrulousness. (If a Mr. Jingle breezes in, he must soon breeze out again.) *Waiting for Godot* seems anti-dramatic in that garrulity is the all-but-declared principle of its dialogue. These men talk to kill time, talk for talking's sake. It is the opposite of *azione parlata,* which implies "a minimum of words, because something more important is going on." Here we seem to have a maximum of words because nothing at all is going on—except waiting.

But this is a big exception, and it saves Beckett's play. It makes no difference that the waiting may be for nothing. Here is a play with a very slight Action, with only the slightest movement from beginning to middle to end, and yet there *is* an Action, and it enables us to see the totality, not as *un*dramatic, but as a parody of the dramatic. After all, Beckett is not himself finding it hard to fill two hours with words. His play is actually jampacked and like any other good play could easily be thought of as a compression of some five-hundred-page version. He is *presenting* people who have trouble filling up *their* time. In the theatre, the moments where Vladimir and Estragon dry up are not gaps *for the audience:* Beckett has made comic points of them. And so *Waiting for Godot* is not, after all, "the end of the line," it is only one of many modern works *about* the end of the line. Now an art is never threatened with extinction by good works of art *about* extinction. It is threatened only by bad works of art, though they cry nothing but: Eternal life!

Waiting for Godot is not, I suspect, a tombstone but a

landmark. If the form of the dialogue is derivative (from the music hall and so, one might say, from the *commedia dell'arte* tradition), there is freshness and originality in the application of that dialogue to these purposes. Behind the mordant flippancy of the clowns we are made to hear —if in the distance—another voice: Beckett's own perhaps, or that of the Lamentations of Jeremiah, desolate and dolorous, a voice of cosmic doom not untouched by human dignity.

4

THOUGHT

THOUGHT AND FEELING

No SUBJECT is more beclouded with prejudice than the subject of thought (intellect, ideas) in drama. The trouble arises from the modern tendency to separate thought and feeling, and to want one without the other. After all, in science it is often imperative to exclude personal feeling and attitude: what is sought is truth in areas outside these. And to live in an age of science is to live in an age when the criteria of science invade areas where they do not belong.

Even within the area of scientific work, it seems necessary to point out not only where emotion need not and should not enter but also where it should and always does. Popular fallacy has it that scientific work is as "cool" and "detached" as its conclusions. In reality, all interest is emotional, all great interest positively passionate. The pursuit of "cold" facts would never happen were it not actually the pursuit of "warm" pleasure, and the pursuit of cold facts *is* a warm pleasure, or human beings would not take it up. It is perhaps mainly because most of us do not take such pleasure in the sciences that we omit to notice that scientists do. We make the Philistine assumption that, in Bernard Shaw's phrase, a Casanova gets a lot more fun out of life than an Isaac Newton. But it is foolish to think that the "objectivity" of a science rubs off on the scientist himself, and it is arbitrary to think that facts *are* cold, hard, inexorable, and so forth. A phrase like "the brute fact of the matter is . . ." too readily leads to the assumption that anything not brutal is not a fact—which indeed often *is* assumed by the school of literary thought that considers itself closest to science, Naturalism.

An age which can consider the scientist unfeeling, just because some of his findings have a validity independent of feeling, can obviously consider the artist unthinking. When the popular mind wishes to be friendly to the artist it makes of him an ethereal genius who does not descend to "mere" reason. When it wishes to be unfriendly it makes of him a madman who could never rise to reason's sublime heights. Friendliness and unfriendliness can also be mingled to yield the mixed image, now the most usual one, of the mad genius, half angel, half devil, or half superman, half idiot. The great artists whom this formula comes closest to fitting, or to seeming to fit, are carefully picked out from the rest to support the thesis. It is obvious, for example, that, by forcing, one could make a Hollywoodian film about Beethoven; it would be harder to make one about Bach. And even on a plane higher than the Hollywoodian, there are many teachers who would cite the phrase "spontaneous overflow of powerful feeling" as a definition of poetry without adding that Wordsworth, its author, was one of the great *minds* of literature whose magnum opus was specifically about the poet's *mind*. In the twentieth century the average schoolboy undoubtedly thinks of art as a product of pure feeling without the mediation of knowledge or thinking. And the child, as our intellectual poet put it, is father of the man.

The mistake, surely, is to make of thought and feeling a sort of funicular railway on which one car must go up when the other comes down. That reason can be driven out by passion—hence thought by feeling—is well known. Whether it is the normal function of feeling to get rid of thought is quite another matter. A tragedy about the defeat of reason by passion in its protagonist does not itself exemplify the same process or it would be a bad tragedy. It is Phaedra who loses her reason, not Racine. He writes a play which judges her from the standpoint of reason. Whether or not *Phaedra* came to Racine in a spontaneous overflow of powerful feeling (and we do not know that it did), the created work not merely is written from the viewpoint of reason but is itself a rational structure. Writers who have lost their reason, as Phaedra did, fail, as she did, to attain their ends.

Not all artists are prodigies of intellect, or of feeling either for that matter, but all art draws on both the intellect and the feelings, and presupposes that the two work, not at loggerheads, but in harness. Any other situation is an unhealthy one for the artists—and their public. In art it may often be legitimate to demand more of either intellect or feeling, but it can seldom be legitimate to demand less. If ever there were a general demand for art of less feeling and more intellect, it would be the critic's job to object to that. In the twentieth century, since there is a fairly wide and frequent demand for less intellect and more feeling, the critic's job is to object to this.

THE PATHOS OF THOUGHT

NOT LEAST the critic of the drama. For since the theatre keeps closer company with philistinism than the other arts, it is more susceptible than they to popular fallacy in general and to anti-intellectualism in particular. Reviewers of plays in the English and American theatre may be expected to be anti-intellectual from the very nature of their position in society, but they are only an extreme case, and academic criticism, though more stately in tone, can be equally tainted with the anti-intellectual prejudice. Like antisemitism, this prejudice knows every shading from the mildest aversion to the most frenzied hostility. What in one dramatic critic may produce an elaborate rationalization, in which the prejudice against mind parades as love of the people or even as honest love of pleasure, will drive another to "come right out with it" in a declaration (and this one was made by a man of brilliant intellect) that drama, like all fine art, "deliberately spits in the eye of intelligence."

The deeper error of the anti-intellectual position is that it is unfair, not to thought alone, but to feeling too. The dramas that attain the highest intensity of feeling will be found, one and all, to be, like *Phaedra,* elaborate structures, into the making of which went a remarkable mind. For one thing, intensity of feeling is not just a large quantity of feeling. In a play, intensity has to be there but it cannot get there by a mere piling up of "more of the same." Greater intensity can result from an admixture of feelings which are less intense. The most intense plays, even those in the concentrated form of the Greek and the French classicists, present feelings of varying degrees of intensity. One could scarcely exaggerate the range and subtlety of this variation. But actors appreciate both when they endeavor, against heavy odds, to make their voices express the modulations of feeling in any great speech.

In literature, feeling *needs* thought. In life it often doesn't: you can have your twinge of pain and let it go. In a play no twinge can be inflicted on an audience which is not part of an intelligent, intelligible pattern and has a meaning as such.

Thinking, on the other hand, is impossible, even in life, without feeling. It is impossible to do any thinking without also feeling, and the content of the thinking will also be mixed with feeling, except where thought is divorced from language itself, as in mathematics. The proposition 2 times 2 is 4 may have emotional associations but they are no part of the statement itself. And the proposition does not *necessarily* have such associations. The proposition "God exists," on the other hand, is far less clear but is weighted with a pathos of some kind for everyone who is thoroughly familiar with both words. Hence philosophy, though it has thought as its principal ingredient, and feeling as a lesser one, cannot altogether dispense with feeling and, in its great masters, has not tried to. The German of Hegel, for example, though it is not elegant, and can even be condemned as a style, contributes to the pathos of Hegel, whose world-shaking pronouncements would have shaken the world a good deal less without it. Many other philosophers, from Plato to Bergson, have been stylists: like poets, they seduce with beautiful words—words, that is, in which feeling runs both delicately and strongly. The tonality of a philosopher can be, in a sense, his crowning achievement. The splendid Beethovenesque melancholy of Schopenhauer continues to gleam after the Kantian metaphysics of his great book has begun to look tarnished. That Schopenhauer holds pessimistic views may well have less effect on his readers than the fact that he is sad—intelligently, sensitively sad, like Jeremiah and like his beloved Baltasar Gracián.

Or Blaise Pascal. Pascal is a great thinker but his great thoughts convey, like Schopenhauer's, an immense melancholy and, unlike Schopenhauer's, a profound sense of the mystery of being and the magnitude of this mystery. Is there less feeling in this thinker than in a dramatist? One would have to pick one's dramatist carefully indeed to answer the question in the affirmative.

Philosophic thought—thought about the great issues, "matters of life and death"—has its own peculiar pathos, and the dramatic poet is free to exploit the fact. Shakespeare's plays are studded with philosophic comments on these matters of life and death. Sometimes critics observe, with malice or otherwise, that Shakespeare filched them from Seneca or Plutarch or such another. If he did, we should be glad, for they add another color to his rich canvas. "The readiness is all." "The quality of mercy is not strained." "As flies to wanton boys are we to the gods . . ." "We are such stuff as dreams are made on . . ." The champions of "pure poetry" would be hard put to explain the tremor that runs through us when we come to such dicta in the plays of Shakespeare.

In her richly suggestive book *Feeling and Form,* Susanne Langer has issued a salutary warning against valuing art on nonartistic grounds, and especially against valuing literature as ethics. It is true enough that we need an aesthetic that will enable us to avoid rating *Uncle Tom's Cabin* higher than *Othello*—as better men than ourselves have done—but surely we would not become devotees of literature at all if we did not in some sense attach importance—very great importance—to the thought therein. Perhaps the question is: what kind of thought? Certainly we do not demand from literature the whole argument, say, whereby Bishop Berkeley proves that the world does not exist except in the mind of God. What we want is not philosophy but (to use a traditional if not scientific distinction) wisdom. The German term *Lebensweisheit* says a little more: what we want is a wisdom that bears upon our being alive (and about to be dead) as men, a thought that relates itself to our pleasure, suffering, and mortality. A Berkeleyan metaphysic does become literature when related, as in a sense it is by a Pirandello, to the torment of experience. Just as philosophy cannot, without mathematical symbols, divest itself of its literary and experiential element, so literature cannot help having a philosophic and moral interest. Reading the Bible "as literature" is a ridiculous proposition, unless it amounts to the same thing as reading the Bible as nonliterature: unless, that is, the term "literature" is permitted to include morality and metaphysics. People who discover that the Bible is literature are only discovering that thought has its own pathos. (The discovery is announced in the popular press with a phrase like "as exciting as a novel," which is all too flattering to novels.) The "literature of philosophy and theology" *is* literature, and, conversely, literature has no separateness but partakes of philosophy and theology. Santayana is not less a philosopher for being a stylist; Dante is not less a poet for being a student of theology. Something nearer the opposite is the case:

Santayana's philosophy becomes what it is in considerable part through the prose, Dante's poetry becomes what it is in considerable part through the thought. The pathos of the thought adds to the total pathos of Dante's poem. Instead of constricting the life of the feelings, thought, in art, can serve to intensify it.

BAD IDEAS

So MUCH in justification of thought, which happens to stand in need of it. The relevance of thought once established, one may turn around to observe that mere thought, thought per se, is nothing to congratulate ourselves upon. I have been discussing thought of some distinction. Most thought, like most feeling, is undistinguished, and should not be respected. It is only in forgetfulness that we ever speak about ideas as uniformly lofty and unemotional. Most ideas are neither, as the history of religion and ideology will attest. Nothing is stranger in the mentality of dramatic critics than their way of assuming that only cold intellectual fish are concerned with ideas. One could almost say: Would that it were so! In actuality ideas have provided the most inflammatory of fuel for all the most inflammable mobs of history. Violence has seldom been done on a large scale *except* on the score of ideas, and even today there is nothing that can so quickly upset a man's mental balance as a theory.

Perhaps, after all, one should approach the whole subject of thought in the arts from below instead of above. If one did, one would find oneself stating that ideas, before they could enter into art, had to lose a little of their natural frenzy, and be brought to terms with civilized feeling. Seen in this perspective, feelings would seem the milder phenomenon, ideas the wilder one. And this is no arbitrary way of putting things. A fanatic is tamed, if at all, not by a rival idea, which only excites him, but by sobering contact with gentle feelings.

It is the worst men who give themselves to ideas most unreservedly. Hitler is a blatant instance. *Mein Kampf* may not contain any good ideas, it does not even contain many clear ones, but it contains *nothing but ideas,* and expresses the mentality of one for whom *ideas were all.* If we are to speak of all literature, and not just of good literature, then we are speaking of a literature of bad ideas as well as good, and bad ideas, too, have their pathos: what book has aroused as much emotion as *Mein Kampf?* But just as it is an error to look for an art in which there is nothing but emotion, so it is an error to accept emotional excitement irrespective of its source. If all one wanted was to raise one's emotional temperature, one could do it at any time by performing some abominable action. Is this too obvious to need saying? Let him who thinks so take a look at popular dramatic criticism, in which excitement—mere amoral palpitation—figures as the *unum necessarium.*

PROPAGANDA

In turning from good to bad ideas in literature, I have turned also from one way of using ideas to another: I have turned from philosophy to propaganda. And it is usually only propaganda that people have in mind when they speak of ideas in literature, especially when they speak of them disparagingly. The topic here is properly *didac-*

ticism, of which propaganda is an instance. Though all art (in the old left-wing slogan) may be propaganda, in the sense that all writers wish to be persuasive, there remains an immense difference between a merely persuasive presentation and an all-out attempt to push somebody from one view to another and thence into immediate and possibly violent action. Many who say they object to a "literature of ideas" only object to the propagandist use of ideas.

Propaganda is the *extreme* instance of didacticism, but admittedly the borderline between the extreme and the nonextreme would be impossible to draw, as, for that matter, would the borderline between the didactic and the nondidactic. Art in general may be held to teach *something.* When is it positively "didactic"? One cannot avoid a somewhat imprecise formulation like: "when the teaching tendency is overt," and as to deciding when the teaching tendency *is* overt, competent judges will differ; and indeed the truth about a single work may well be different, in this respect, at different times. One can only say that if some moderns give themselves overeagerly to the didactic idea ("art is a weapon" or "art for the Faith") , others, in revulsion from this tendency, tend to become far more anti-didactic than most of the great critics and artists of the past. It was not Karl Marx but Samuel Johnson who said: "It is always a writer's duty to make the world better." If a man's eagerness to propagandize, or to defend propaganda, can be excessive, so can his hostility either to propaganda or to didactic purpose in general.

The modern separation of thought and feeling enters in here to create further misunderstanding. Those who oppose didacticism in art often do so on the assumption that we don't go to art "to be taught things" and that the reason we don't is that art is emotional, while learning is intellectual. The implied psychology of learning is that of a dull educational routine in which very little could actually be learned. When much is learned, there is always much attendant emotion. It is the painful emotion which comes first to mind: the expression "to learn from painful experience" is often called for in this life. But pain and pleasure go together; it is only anesthesia that stands apart; and learning is in the first instance a pleasure. It is through delight at discovering something that we hold on to the discovery and see its implications: it is indeed through the delight of discovery that we discover. No child becomes "good at arithmetic" who is not enjoying figures and his mastery thereof: nor can finding out what twelve times twelve is be rated a lesser pleasure than the acknowledged pleasures of sheer recreation. . . . All of which was said in the classic textbook on dramatic art, Aristotle's *Poetics:*

> To be learning something is the greatest of pleasures not only to the philosopher but also to the rest of mankind, however small their capacity for it; the reason of the delight in seeing the picture is that one is at the same time learning—gathering the meaning of things. . . .

A PLAY IS AN INTELLECTUAL THING

Now if intellect (from which come thought and ideas) plays an important part in literature generally, it presumably plays one also in dramatic literature. I say "presumably" because in the twentieth century there have been both critics and dramatists to make of mindlessness the unique attraction of the drama. The burden of proof is on them, and they will need to point to other mindlessness than their own if they are to make a convincing case. Of literature it can be said that the grandest thoughts and the grandest feelings are to be found in the same works, and of drama it can be said that it is not only more emotional than the current notion of it but also more intellectual. Great drama has occurred only sporadically in history, and historians have often shown that a new wave of drama rolls in on a new wave of vitality. The vitality is intellectual as much as it is anything else. Great drama generally rolls in on an idea, that idea being the informing thought of a new movement in history, a new image of man. At such points in time, ideas don't just happen to be selected by playwrights in search of interesting material: drama is a sort of river bed into which mighty ideas flow. In a sense, then, the playwright of such a moment is thoroughly unoriginal. He does not canvas his own special opinions; he may therefore not need the protection of a bill of rights or even a "climate of freedom" such as publicists nowadays represent to be a *sine qua non* of great art; he gravitates toward the center of historical significance. The lesser playwrights of such a moment are those who fail to find it or who, not finding it for themselves, become epigones, reciters by rote.

Modern anti-intellectualism has devised the doctrine that the drama is nonintellectual in its origin. Did it not begin in Dionysian rites? Watching the theories of Nietzsche, Gilbert Murray, Jane Harrison, and F. M. Cornford percolate through the American educational system, I have had occasion to notice what an impression is made when the drama is said to stem, as it often is, from fertility worship. The image of an Orgy rises before the mind's eye to stop all thought in its tracks. But how close to an orgy are we in even the earliest known plays, which are those of Aeschylus? We are not at one but at several removes. For assuming that "the orgy theory" is true, one has to postulate a moment at which the frenzied horde of orgiasts split in two and one group became voyeurs (later known as spectators) instead. One has to postulate a later moment at which there was no orgy, even on stage, but only talk about orgies. For, at the earliest moment we actually know anything about, the audience is not actively participating in anything, but only looking on, and the performers are only talking, and not about orgies.

There is talk. In the beginning was the word. When the horde breaks into two and the orgiasts or communicants become voyeurs or spectators, when, too, as Aristotle reminds us, the single speaker steps out from the undifferentiated chorus, a new event is created of which the essence is men speaking to men. This is the archetypal dramatic event. The drama finds itself as it finds its voice.

And so the drama, at its birth, is an intellectual thing. Western intellect is a Greek invention, and the Greeks put it to use not in philosophy only but in drama. The two were not then so far apart. Even for Socrates philosophy was not only dialectics, it was also spoken dialogue: it would seem that he never wrote down a word. In teaching the West to speak, Greece invited the West to believe that the spoken word is the proper vehicle of mind and spirit.

The voice of the drama speaks poetry, and has done so from the very outset. It is equally remarkable that the poetry even then was the vehicle of majestic ideas. There have been those who would like to make a "primitive" out of Aeschylus because the technique of the drama developed a lot after his death, but if to be primitive is to stammer instead of speaking, or to think childishly instead of profoundly, then the drama of today is mostly more primitive than Aeschylus. No, development is not progress. Emotionally and intellectually our very first playwright achieved supremely great drama. *And intellectually:* this is the point here. *Great drama has been a "drama of ideas" from the very first.* And Aeschylus it must have been who first taught Western man that the great dramatist provides an image of his age as a whole, picturing its principal conflicts and triumphs (and failures, as we can feelingly add). The task calls for intellectual powers such as the average modern person would tend only to attribute to the statesman, the historian, or the scientist; and indeed there is something in Aeschylus's nature of each of these.

"No army can withstand the strength of an idea whose time has come." Victor Hugo's dictum suggests not only the power of ideas, and the relation of this power to history, but the reason why the drama has been a *locus classicus* for such ideas: ideas like these have antagonists in the shape of other ideas, or of battalions, or of both. The dictum also implies a point at which things come to a head. Drama, it is well known, tends to deal not only with antagonism but with culmination, not only with collisions but with final, decisive collisions. Naturally, then, it tends also, not toward ideas in general, but toward ideas belonging to the extreme situations, the "first and last things," the "matters of life and death." It seeks, as Strindberg once put it, the points at which the great battles take place.

A corollary of this is that there is no room in the drama for the elaborations which would be required either in the novel or in a historical or philosophic treatise. A philosopher would be entitled to put down a dramatist's treatment of ideas as insufficient. On the other hand, what the drama may lose in one area of reality it gains in the correlations it makes between different areas. A play may not fully analyze, for example, a world-historical encounter but, in proportion as it is a good play, it renders the interaction of idea and event in its existential concreteness. It can in this way provide a unique concentration of reality—as indeed is attested by the fact that, say, Freudian and Marxist critics can both find what they seek in it and both be right.

If what I am saying is correct, it follows that the vitality of any drama that *is* vital would be in part intellectual, and that we would find the ideas of the age contributing to the life of any significant drama whatsoever. This has in fact been shown many times over by scholarly critics of the Greeks, of Shakespeare, and of Corneille, Racine, and Molière. If there have also been dissenting voices, arguing that one or other of these had a bad philosophy, or even a second-rate mind, what I can say to refute them has already been said in this chapter. It remains to consider certain schools of drama that have often been deemed excessively intellectual ("abstract," "ideological," "doctrinaire"). There can of course be an excess of anything, but it seems to me that these schools would not have come under attack but for a prejudice against ideas in drama. Once intellect is seen as a potentially vitalizing thing, this body of work can also be seen as vital. I am thinking of medieval drama; the drama of the Golden Century in Spain; the German classics of the eighteenth century; and the modern "drama since Ibsen."

There was a time when scholars used to defend medieval drama on the grounds of the touches of modern realism that seemed here and there perceptible in it or the touches of an equally modern democratic sentiment. They were shamefaced about the bulk of the material as it stood because it was doctrinal in content and didactic in intention. Yet medieval drama will reveal its true merit only through this content and this intention, and when it has done so, the rather thin humor of the Second Shepherd's Play falls appropriately into the background, and what we become aware of is the grandeur and the sweep of the Cycles, which reflect the grandeur and sweep of a splendid vision of life. History is shown in terms of a guiding idea—the guiding ideal of civilized life in that age—and it is seen as a drama in many acts but with a definite beginning (the Creation), middle (the Fall and the Atonement), and end (the Last Judgment).

Incidentally, the Middle Ages provided the drama with what seems its definitive Villain, the Devil. All the villains since have had a little of Satan about them, whenever they have had any real energy at all. Popular melodrama as we know it is a decadent and usually feeble rendering of the Christian drama of life, man placed, Faustuslike, between good and evil angel.

THE SPANISH DRAMA

IT HAS often been said that Spain never emerged from the Middle Ages, and the Spanish drama of the Golden Century is in many ways in the medieval tradition. One finds readers of the later centuries tending, as they do with medieval plays, to accept only certain touches of what they regard as general humanity and rejecting the particular idea of humanity embodied in the work, because they dismiss the possibility that an idea may be, not a limiting factor, but a source of energy. Although the Spaniards were medieval in their total reliance upon Catholic theology, their work is more fully dramatic than the medieval Cycles because, not content to tell the Christian story and praise God, they insist on rendering the conflict between Christian idea and natural impulse. For them the idea is incarnate in fallible flesh, and, working out the dialectics of such conflict, they are not afraid to test the idea itself. So they have proved shocking writers. But the drama is an art of shock, and it is the great merit of ideas that, far from leading dramatic art toward the pallid and the dryly discursive, they generate their characteristic shocks. As for theology, though some people still think it is chiefly devoted to the discussion of the number of angels that can dance on a pinpoint, its *sine qua non* is the same as the *sine qua non* of the drama: the human sense of guilt. Theology being, among other things, a dramatization of right and wrong, a theological drama is a very legitimate branch of the "drama of ideas."

A famous pair of plays, both probably by Tirso de Molina, *The Trickster of Seville* and *Damned for Lack of Trust,* coalesce to provide a single illustration. They are about the same Christian belief, "grace abounding to the worst of sinners," the doctrine that God's mercy is so great it extends to all who repent, however late they do so and however much they may have sinned. Now it is as if the Spaniards asked whether this was just a bland piece of hyperbole not to be looked into too closely or whether it can actually be believed. If the latter, what does it mean, existentially speaking? One play shows that it is safe to accept the doctrine. A murderous robber chief, who repents in time, will go to heaven, says *Damned for Lack of Trust,* whereas a man of pious life who concludes that in this case he may as well become a murderous robber chief goes to hell—not for his bad deeds but for his "lack of trust" in God. In the other play, the Trickster is a man who plans his deathbed repentance long in advance, meanwhile deliberately devoting himself to a life of sin. The world has remembered—how well!—that Don Juan's sins included fornication and adultery, but Tirso's Don is less a philanderer than a blasphemer and iconoclast. He offends not only against the ladies but against father, uncle, and king. His sexual offenses against women are, even more, offenses against God, whose rules (e.g., the sacrament of marriage) are being broken right and left. Don Juan goes to hell, for repentance on one's deathbed must be spontaneous to be effectual: planned ahead of time, it fails to take place at all. Tirso is saying, too, I should think, that the kind of man who *can* plan ahead in this way has been incapable of repentance from the start. The hardness of heart is of a piece with the defiance which the Don also shows throughout. He is a philistine Faustus.

Over the years plays like *Damned for Lack of Trust* (Calderón's *Devotion to the Cross* is another) have scandalized some believers and brought comfort to some unbelievers. And it is too late for the sophisticated Catholic scholars of today to convince us that it was all a misunderstanding and that these are plays of unimpeachable respectability. Yes, Tirso and Calderón were priests, and priests without heretical tendencies. Even so their plays have more than a touch of that scandalousness with which Jean Cocteau has wittily characterized all original drama.

A dramatist is a man who may have his beliefs but who, if he dramatizes them, is likely to make a bad propagandist.

A propagandist behaves like a lawyer in court, passing over any good points the other side may have in order to make his own side seem the stronger. Propagandists and lawyers are concerned with what seems. But a dramatist is concerned with what is. Suppression of the other side's case would be against his interests, for he lives, not off victory, but off conflict. A man is not cut out to be a playwright if he is not unusually alive to "the other side" and the strength of its "case." A playwright is a dialectician. He is even an extremist, not in the sense that he espouses one extreme against another, but, rather, that he is inclined to push any contrast to both its limits. If he can sometimes be accused of "seeing things too much in black-and-white terms," he can never be accused of not noticing that black is black, white white. If, then, "Christianity" were not a theological term for respectability, amiability, and commonsense, but signified an invitation to a perilous adventure among the peaks and abysses of human joy and suffering, a dramatist might be a Christian. Living dangerously, he would be found wherever the dangers to the soul are greatest, which is to say that he would not veer away from what are humanly the sensitive spots of Christian teaching.

Does the parable of the prodigal son mean that it is better to be bad, so that later one can reap the harvest of repentance? Official apologetics on the point seem merely disingenuous. It takes a Dostoevsky properly to explore and present the human reality, and, when a Dostoevsky does so, it is to be noted that he comes much nearer to saying, "Yes, it *is* better to be bad," than any churchman is likely to. This is a result of an artist's extreme candor, and his commitment to the facts of experience. The same with Tirso and Calderón. There is something frightening, no doubt, about the way they enter so wholeheartedly into all the sinfulness. But there would be something very dull about their plays if they didn't. One cannot have it both ways. Either theological plays are dull because their authors stand outside the experiences they write of, or they become vivid because their authors present not only the idea but what it conflicts with—and all this in terms of human energy, especially sin. There is destructiveness of some kind in all plays, but destructiveness seen as sin has its own drama, as *Macbeth* and *Phaedra* so richly testify. For the Christian dramatist, sin represents a supreme opportunity.

If Christianity is not a sensible way of dealing with a sensible world, but a bold, rash, even wild way of attempting to deal with a freakish, opaque, and recalcitrant world, then it is with some justification that the Christian dramatist examines extravagant doctrines and extreme cases. Does the doctrine of grace only mean that good works are insufficient to save us? That is the conventional way of putting it—as blank as it is bland. What, humanly speaking, is the doctrine of grace all about? The disproportion between an infinite divine mercy and finite human deeds— a disproportion so staggering that only an extravagant legend can suggest it. Think of a man who commits all conceivable sins. Is the power of the cross sufficient to save *him?* No logic will convince us that it is. We would have to "see it to believe it." We would have to see the shadow of the cross fall upon him. . . . Something of this sort is what I would imagine to have been in Calderón's mind when he wrote *The Devotion to the Cross.* Even the free-thinking George Henry Lewes was scandalized at what he could only take as an invitation to murder and incest. But if this play is such an invitation, then so is the absolution of weekly confession. Is Christianity implausible then? This is the kind of question the Spaniards were not intimidated by. If the Spanish plays were not written by unbelievers, they could only have been written by men who thought their own most sacred beliefs must walk unprotected by pleasant plausibilities. In our age of "public relations," is that still intelligible? An effort must be made to imagine a state of soul in which one did not try to cover up difficulties, evade problems, suggest that adjustments are always possible, either/or decisions are never necessary, but in which, on the contrary, one delighted in the exposure of difficulties, the uncowed confrontation of the implacable, the choosing of the less impossible of two impossibilities. Making such an effort, one is imagining a state of soul close to great drama, and great drama in which great, if implausible, ideas play a large part.

THE GERMAN DRAMA

THE MEDIEVAL and the Spanish drama have not given offense on a large scale: they have been ignored. The "drama of ideas" that has awakened a resentment so burning that it is fanned back to flame any time a play with ideas in it is produced is the modern drama, beginning with Lessing and Schiller.

There are several reasons for this. One is that the ideas, from here on, enjoy no ecclesiastical privilege. They are "ideas," nakedly exposed as such, and no longer able to present themselves as sacrosanct righteousness. But this fact is part of a much larger one. Whereas the ideas of the drama in the sixteenth and seventeenth centuries favored the existing regime, the ideas of the great eighteenth-century writers, when not positively revolutionary, tend to be dissident, malcontent, reformist. Hostile to ruling interests, these writers cannot but arouse a corresponding hostility in the ruling classes, their parasites, friends, and admirers. Which is simple enough to understand, stated in these terms. It is only later when the "ruling interests" are more diffused, and less willing to be identified as such, that the modern theatrical situation is less easy to recognize.

It is a problematic situation since the dramatist is deprived in advance of what Shakespeare and Molière had: a national public. A drama that views with disfavor what the nation is doing is implicitly addressed only to the disaffiliated part of that nation. This is to state the case in political terms. Georg Lukacs stated it in social-aesthetic terms in a long essay he published in 1914 which said that up to the eighteenth century the drama proceeded naturally out of the theatre, whereas afterwards it offered itself to the theatre as the means whereby the theatre might be improved. The modern dramatic poets are one and all "above the theatre." They may descend into it and bore from within. Or they may wait for it to rise to their level. But they are not men *of* the theatre, à la Molière, whose theatrical work *turned out to be* great literature.

Lessing and Schiller are the first world dramatists of this new phase. Their work shows the wear and tear of the new situation, which, to be sure, is an unhealthy one. When they have to choose between literature and theatre, they choose the former. On the other hand, their work is "drama of ideas" in the grand tradition and not reduced to crude propaganda or mere monologue. *Nathan the Wise* becomes a bad, "preachy" play in English translation, because the quality of Lessing's language is lost. In the German, Nathan is not just a spokesman of sound notions, not just a nice non-Aryan uncle. His voice is that of a man who has suffered. His utterances come from the other side of tragedy. And what otherwise would be smug rightness becomes a hard-earned wisdom; which is dramatic.

Just as the Spanish Catholic "drama of ideas" is saved by a strong and positive sense of sin, so the German "drama of ideas" is saved by being considerably less goody-goody and unprejudiced than it sounds. Lessing may have vaguely had it in mind to say, as people say he said, that Christianity, Judaism, and Islam are all equally good, but in the end this rebel son of a family of ministers makes Christianity *less* good than the other two religions. Call *Nathan the Wise* prejudiced and impulsive, but do not call it doctrinaire and overabstract. Even the parable of the rings, which is the center of the play, does not state what one expects it to state. The inference is not that all three religions have an equally good pedigree, but that each pedigree may well be permanently uncertain. So it is better to go by results: "by their fruits ye shall know them." The play is addressed to Christians: it tells them they behave badly—worse than Moslems and Jews—and that they should mend their ways. Considering how grossly even modern playwrights have underestimated the dynamics of antisemitism,* it is astonishing with what unerring judgement Lessing chose the subject of the first modern—and German!—play of ideas. To write a play in 1764 that can logically be banned as subversive in 1933 is an achievement which later practitioners might look back on with envy.

Schiller, too, was sometimes in trouble with the Nazis, but, on the other hand, may in general be said to have been taken to the bosom of the bourgeoisie. German shop-

---

*E.g. Brecht in his *Resistible Rise of Arturo Ui,* Shaw in *Geneva.*

keepers' daughters imagine themselves Joan of Arc to the lines of Schiller's *Maid of Orleans.* The Marquis of Posa's line in *Don Carlos,* "Sire, give us freedom of speech," may have become subversive under Hitler, yet the Marquis was an "idealist" in so ethereal a vein that any carpet communist can "place" and refute him in a few sharp "realistic" phrases.

The case of Posa is crucial. On what one makes of him could justifiably depend what one makes of both Schiller and the modern "drama of ideas" generally. If *Don Carlos* was written, as has been assumed alike by Schiller's admirers and nonadmirers in great numbers, to celebrate the rightness of Posa's ideas, then the play forfeits its claim to greatness, not so much because these ideas are vulnerable, as because the play, so conceived, is but a melodrama, with Posa as its hero, and Philip II as its villain. Actually, *Don Carlos* can only be read this way by persons willing to be so carried away by the eloquence of individual speeches that they disregard all countervailing factors, particularly unspoken ones. For if it is the worst error in dramatic criticism to quote a character, taking for granted that he must be speaking for the author, the next worst error is to assume that a character is defined only by his own speeches and not by the speeches of others or, more important still, by his own actions. If the habit of quoting purple passages had not disabled criticism, it would have been seen all along that Posa's words are contradicted by his actions. He is an idealist who does not live up to his ideals, an altruist ruined by egotism. And in this, as in the fact that he is much better at getting off edifying sentiments about society than he is at understanding human beings, he constitutes a classic portrait of The Idealist. Within this framework, the circumstance that Posa speaks great thoughts which we sense are those of the author only gains in poignancy. But what, for that matter, could be more poignant than Philip's participation in the great encounter? The tact and restraint and human feeling in this "villain" are in marked contrast to the merely ideological enthusiasm of the "hero." "Enthusiasm" is indeed the word, with its eighteenth-century connotation of fanaticism. The German for it is *Schwärmerei,* and Philip has Posa's number when he calls him, gently: *"Wunderbarer Schwärmer!"*—"enthusiast extraordinary!"

Not that Philip is the hero, Posa the villain. That disposition of things would produce a paradoxical melodrama, but only a melodrama. What makes the encounter between Philip and Posa (Act III, Scene 10) one of the greatest "scenes of ideas" in the whole of dramatic literature is precisely that the author is on both sides. Both, not neither. To be on neither side is to achieve such an icy detachment as could only tend to detach one's audience from the whole subject. To be on both sides is to invest one's feelings on both sides, and then to be torn between the two sets of feelings. Posa's views are "right," and Schiller "believes in them," but were they practical in Philip's time? Philip based his stand on "necessity" and is he, too, not "right," in that it would *not* have been possible to proceed from sixteenth-century absolutism to eighteenth-century enlightenment by taking thought?

Some have spoken of Schiller's anachronisms. Perhaps he ought not, in the first place, to have attributed eighteenth-century ideas to a sixteenth-century nobleman? Historically, the proposition is absurd enough. And yet, paradoxically, the fiction allows Schiller to dramatize history and its perennial tension between freedom and necessity. All innovations are impracticable until they are practiced.

Philip II did not share the modern critic's absolute certitude that Posa's views would not be practical politics till much later: he could not, therefore, dismiss them as absurd with *that kind* of justification. But, on the other hand, Posa does not meet him halfway, pitting reason against reason. He makes as if to sweep him off his feet with magnificent rhetoric: which is to misjudge his man and evade the immediate issue. True to character, Posa is not really trying to persuade Philip at all: he is doing what idealists do—celebrating his own moral superiority. Had Posa succeeded in more than just making a personal impression, then either Schiller would have had to let Philip be won over, or he would have had to make him so villainous he is in no way accessible to reason. Either way, the scene would suffer. As Schiller wrote it, it is exactly what such a scene should be.

SHAW

THE TERM "drama of ideas" has been applied, loosely and often with sarcasm, to the work of all the great moderns from 1850 on. In the sense intended—that these men were principally propagandists for some ephemeral "cause"—it usually did not apply. *A Doll's House* was not a piece of propaganda for women's suffrage. *Ghosts* was not essentially concerned with syphilis. But of course modern ideas entered abundantly into Ibsen's plays, sometimes to be represented as noble, sometimes as false, always to be coordinated with plot, character, and theme, in the traditional fashion.

Just as Schiller has long been taken as the naïve representative of an Enlightenment of which he was in fact a critic, so Ibsen has been taken as the crude champion of the Victorian liberals, whom in fact he always combatted. Original with him is the subject of ideas affirmed by the intellect but not assimilated into the life of the affirmer. Mrs. Alving is the enlightened woman of her time, and what Ibsen shows is that the new ideas are only in her head, while the ghosts of the old ideas linger in her heart. People think they believe in new ideas, but they are actuated, particularly in crises, by old ideas. From this contradiction Ibsen is able to make a novel drama of ideas. He had found a state of affairs as rich in contradictions as the confrontation of Philip and Posa in *Don Carlos*.

Is the serious modern drama overintellectual? Since the generation of Ibsen, three names have been cited more than any others as evidence that it is: Shaw, Pirandello, and Brecht. For all three used thought unconventionally in an art form where it is not welcome to its critics even when used conventionally.

It is possible that the source of all the rancor about ideas in drama is Bernard Shaw. In his plays, the whole world has remarked, "people just talk." Which is in itself a popular definition of the drama of ideas. Elaborated slightly further, the popular view is that Shaw created a new genre, the drama-of-nothing-but-ideas. And, to be fair, he did approach such a "genre" in a few plays, such as *Misalliance* and *Getting Married*. These plays, as Shaw put it, are "disquisitory": they give their main topic an intellectual airing. Never before had any dramatist just proceeded to bring on a lot of people, sit them down, and let them sound off about life in general. And never again did any dramatist get away with it. The few attempts of others (such as J. B. Priestley) to write "Shavian drama" have failed. Why? Just to cite "lesser talent" is no explanation. Such lesser talent has been responsible for much more successful drama. Were Shaw's ideas better ideas? More urgent? Better handled? There may be something to each of these answers, yet surely the main answer is that Shaw's plays were never so wholly disquisitory as even he may have thought. That they were peppered with jokes, which no one could miss, was not just a matter of comic relief, it was the outward sign of an inner reality: the fact that Shaw, however intellectual he might get, or however sociological, never lost touch with the rhythm, the style, the ethos, the cosmos of comic drama.

This fact is the key to "Don Juan in Hell" (*Man and Superman,* Act Three) . The number of ideas in this scene, and the density of these ideas, may well leave the impression that we have here nothing *but* ideas. Yet if all he wanted was to set forth his ideas, Shaw would hardly need Ana and her father. He could just have written a debate between Don Juan and the Devil. Nor is the Commander *mere* relief. He and Ana fill out what finally we recognize to be a total view (better: a vision) of life that imperatively requires them.

And is the dialogue between Devil and Don a debate? Is it not, rather, a parody of a debate, in which Shaw is able to take off the elegances of parliamentary decorum with exquisite humor? Neither the word *debate* nor the word *discussion* will do justice to it, for it contains a dynamic element which neither word implies. Shaw has put the Devil on the defensive—a remarkable feat, and not the least brilliant of the many brilliant inversions in his plays. This is a Devil who almost pleads with his man. Don Juan, on his side, can afford to be boldly declaratory, even denunciatory. He talks *past* the Devil as much as Posa talks past Philip II, and here too the disrespect has a point, though a different one from Schiller's. In short, instead of debate or discussion, we have a drama: a conflict of opinion is compounded by a conflict of character which could not be deduced from the opinions themselves. The Devil is in fact one of Shaw's best character creations: the archetype of the "cultivated modern person." As for the Action, it hangs on a single hinge, the question whether Don Juan would stay in Hell. But it is enough for the purpose, and it *is* dramatic, if in the most rudimentary way—like, say, the Action of *Waiting for Godot*.

Brecht said of Shaw's characters that their most precious possession was a set of opinions. In defense of Shaw, it should be retorted, not that this is untrue, but that it is often the point Shaw himself is making. As with Ibsen, this "drama of ideas" is among other things an acknowledgment that we live in a society of ideas to a degree never known in history before, a society buzzing with theories and explanations, a society brought up to know all the theories and explanations—or, which may make for better satire, to half-know them. Ibsen was never more truly the social diagnostician than when he pointed a finger at Mrs. Alving's books, those books which wholly shocked Pastor Manders, and had enlightened Mrs. Alving—in part. The whole epoch of modern education is there, and all our libraries of "paperbacks," feeding us the brightest and best ideas in all fields. It is a point that Shaw could do more with than Ibsen, since half-knowledge and intellectual faddism, pedantry, and know-it-all-ism are natural subjects of comedy. When Shaw portrays the spokesmen of scientific medicine in *The Doctor's Dilemma* he is not so much inventing his own drama of ideas as making fun of *their* drama of ideas, the act *they* put on before the world. And if Ibsen had made savage fun of the fanatic Ibsenite, Gregers

Werle, Shaw will make impish fun of the "disciples of Bernard Shaw."

This category is much broader than the example of Louis Dubedat (in *The Doctor's Dilemma*) might suggest. For among the disciples of Bernard Shaw are all those suave and sharp-tongued ironists who walk or sit through his plays exposing the airy, garrulous impostors. On the face of it, Bernard Shaw may seem simply to be identified with the ironists, and by placing them at the center of his compositions to have reversed the traditional structure of comedy, which had a knave or fool at its center. But at least several of Shaw's comedies, and those among the best, turn out to be traditional in the end, as the ironist proves to be an impostor. Bluntschli, in *Arms and the Man,* is an example. For most of the evening, he is the ironist vis à vis two romantic impostors, Raina and Saranoff, and the laugh is on them. But in the end it turns out that the laugh is on him, and he too is shown to be a romantic and an impostor. So also Jack Tanner, in *Man and Superman,* makes everyone look false and foolish by his witty deflations of their errors and pretensions, but his victories are only verbal, and when it comes to living, he proves a fool—first in the matter of Violet's relation to marriage in Act One, and later in the matter of his own relation to it at the end of the play. What begins as a brilliance that carries all before it is finally exposed as a cleverness that is totally ineffectual. The many revolutionary ideas of Jack Tanner, commonly thought to be *the* ideas of one of the most celebrated dramas of ideas, are actually shown in a negative light.

One must also distinguish between the many ideas that come up *in* a Shaw play and the single idea that is the idea *of* the play. Even the latter is not what it at first seems to be. The idea of *Arms and the Man* at first seems to be that an antidote to romantic illusion can be found in men like Bluntschli who always see the prosaic reality beneath. But the play actually "builds" toward a more interesting idea—namely, that even those who see through some illusions are themselves fooled by others. Hence, life consists, not of two solid blocks, one labeled Reality, the other Illusion, but of realities and illusions intermingled or, if you choose, of "Chinese boxes" one inside the other —illusion within illusion. The idea of *Man and Superman* at first seems to be that the old-fashioned notions of a Ramsden or a Mrs. Whitefield are being punctured and destroyed by the radicalism of Tanner. This idea would yield the kind of left-wing, propaganda play which many have wished upon Shaw, but which he steadfastly refused to write. Beneath the social play is the biological one. Tanner's cleverness lies on the surface. Anne Whitefield's is that of life itself, with its deeper cunning and its fewer words. . . . If one speaks of the idea of a Shaw play, one must also speak of the idea behind the idea. The whole design will then reveal itself as dramatic.

PIRANDELLO

IF THE WORD we associate with Shaw is "ideas," the word we associate with Luigi Pirandello is "cerebral," for the Italian's reputation is not just for having one notion (that appearance *is* reality), but for harping on it, for being unable to let it alone. This, I presume, is what the word "cerebral" is intended to convey, and to deal with the point one must assume that appearance is *not* reality, since Pirandello appears cerebral and one would like to inquire whether he really is so.

If to be cerebral is to think without feeling, it is not possible for human beings to be wholly cerebral, and the question must be restated thus: Is Pirandello *unduly* cerebral? Is there *too little* feeling in his work? His being unable to let his idea alone suggests the contrary, since obsession is not a "coldly intellectual" factor but a hotly neurological one. Is it people who have got their Pirandello secondhand, through bad critics or bad translations, who think of him as "cerebral"? The first thing any sensitive reader would notice in his work is not an abstractness of thought but a tremor of the nerves. And if we pursue this clue we find that Pirandello, more of an Ibsenite than Shaw ever was, retained Ibsen's image of modern man as neurotic sufferer but in revising it deepened the shade of mental sickness. His starting point is not philosophy but emotional disturbance—and not the *theory* of emotional disturbance, as with so many post-Freudian playwrights, but the concrete fact—in short the emotion, the disturbance.

In all three of the Pirandello plays which have entered the world repertoire, *Six Characters, The Emperor,* (*Enrico IV*), and *Right You Are,* the principal characters are in turmoil to the depths of their being. If we do not in every case recognize this at once, it is because in our present-day plays such disturbances are labeled to orientate us, whereas in Pirandello we may never find out just what the trouble is, with or without labeling. In *Right You Are,* he makes it the point of the story that the psychic problems are unsolved—the psychic problems, not just the legal identities. Human nature is to be seen, he is telling us, not as a problem but as a mystery—he would have us look into the troubles of the Ponzas and Frolas with the reverent charity of religion rather than the inquisitive, inquisitorial microscope of medical science. Even so, in the two principal accounts of what has happened—one given by Signora Frola, one by Signor Ponza—case histories are provided of a mental distress that goes all the way to psychosis. One story is of a man who was so unable to bear being deprived of his wife's company that he had to conclude she was dead. The other is of a woman who was so unable to bear her daughter's death that she had to believe that another girl is her daughter, who had never really died. In both cases, the subject is delusion brought on by a trauma of deprivation. Traumas of this kind seem to be at the heart of things for Pirandello, and that is one reason why his work is dramatic. Theatre is shock because life is shock.

How did Pirandello proceed from these traumas to a type of drama the world would call cerebral? It is a question of the kind of significance he extracted from the material. Here Ibsen could not give him the answer. For Ibsen, man was neurotic. This was startling to his early audiences but it did not prevent him from writing a drama that was moral in the old way. For Pirandello, there is only a very special kind of ethics to be had—an ethics of compassion in the face of impossibility. The neurosis of man is seen as bordering upon psychosis and occasionally falling headlong into it. Though man may achieve compassion, he is first and foremost, not a moral being, but a pathological one. Yet pathology holds for Pirandello no clinical interest. Rather, it plunges him into despair about existence itself, a metaphysical anguish.

A schizophrenic is out of touch with us, and we with him. The reality of him is not only complex but somehow not there at all, "gone," lost. Such an unknowability and unreachability constitute for Pirandello the human condition generally. Which is a philosophical proposition; but before it is that, it is the "impression" life made on him, a shocking, agonizing impression. Biographical critics have spoken of Pirandello's psychotic wife, but nothing that might be discovered about the Signora could explain how the Maestro himself came to think her condition was, in a profound sense, that of the human race in general, much less how he could give to such an "unsound proposition" a vibrancy that would find a response in the world audience.

The existential situation is terrifying. How shall one probe its meaning? All that man has at his disposal for such a task is words and thoughts. So Pirandellian man, like other men, resorts to words and thoughts. They go round and round in his brain only to produce another terror, another vertigo. Man's intellect, to which alone he can look for explanations of anything whatever, and to which alone he can turn for an explanation of his own misery, fails him—and so becomes a further, more exasperating source of misery. Thought has assigned to itself the task of finding the reality beneath the appearance. It has failed. We have only the appearances, and must hail them, mockingly, despairingly, as reality. Pirandello's "little philosophy lesson" teaches little philosophy. What it teaches is both more than philosophy and less: terror, misery, despair. Pirandello's is the vision of Matthew Arnold's "Dover Beach"—a spectacle of ignorant armies clashing by night. Arnold speaks in that poem of the tide bringing in the eternal note of sadness:

> Sophocles long ago
> Heard it on the Aegean, and it brought
> Into his mind the turbid ebb and flow
> Of human misery . . .

* * *

Pirandello listened to this ebb and flow, and in a time called untragic recaptured the eternal note of sadness, restoring to it the turbulence of ancient tragedy.

BRECHT

THE QUESTION which the name of Bertolt Brecht brings up is more that of propaganda than of thought as such, but one can hardly discuss propaganda in isolation from the ideas propagated. For one thing, people who profess themselves to be opposed to propaganda in art nearly always turn out to be opposed only to the propaganda of "the other side," propaganda on "our side" not being propaganda at all but Truth issuing, disinterested and undistorted, from the mouth of God or one of his many accomodating vice-gerents. Because there is commonly such a lack of candor in the discussion of this topic it becomes necessary to state what ought to be obvious: that we all relish propaganda (given a minimum of eloquence) when we agree with it and conversely that we none of us relish propaganda (however eloquent) for a cause we hold in abhorrence.

The reason there is a problem has already been suggested: that the modern public is a divided one, and that writers belong to an "intelligentsia" which is a sectional and dissident entity. It is misleading for moderns to say "all art is propaganda," for most of the examples they will give—Aeschylus, Dante, medieval drama, Spanish drama, Shakespeare's histories—are "propaganda" on behalf of the whole social system they sprang from and to which they are addressed, whereas what the word "propaganda" suggests today is precisely the views of some of us and not of others of us—had "we" won over the "others," the need for propaganda of our sort would end. The demand for drama addressed to a hostile or divided audience is a modern phenomenon.

Theoretically, the writer of this sort of propagandist drama would have a choice. He could address one part of the divided public or the other: he could preach to the converted or seek to win over the heathen. Actually, very little propagandist drama is addressed directly to the "heathen," but quite a lot is addressed to those who are believed to be wondering which side they are on. In our time, the classic case is that of the middle-class liberal wondering if he can leave his conservative background and join the progressive left. A play on this theme (Stephen Spender's *Trial of a Judge* is an example) is directed in the first instance to similar middle-class liberals in the audience, but would also be welcome (it could be assumed) to the left-wing hordes whom the liberal is joining. That is, Spender could hope to address both the converted and the about-to-be converted. And though he could scarcely hope to keep the unconvertable in their seats, the noise they made leaving their seats might be counted on to create a scandal; and the scandal could be read as a sign of virtue, if not of victory.

I have used the word "conversion" advisedly because vis à vis a divided public, the conversion play is inevitably the principal kind of propagandist drama. In the thirties conversion plays were produced by the score: even Brecht wrote a couple. Generally speaking, Brecht was after bigger game. He did have his eye on the earlier "didacticism," that of Aeschylus, the Middle Ages, the Spaniards, Shakespeare's histories, and he *had* noted that none of these kinds of drama aimed at talking anyone out of one position and into another. Rather, they assumed that, for a community and an epoch, their main points had already been made, and they celebrated this achievement. Now supposing that what happened in Russia in 1917 was parallel to the achievement of democracy in ancient Athens, of Catholicism in the Middle Ages, of Tudor monarchy in Renaissance England? If Soviet Communism should be the "idea whose time has come" then no army could withstand it—or its drama. Brecht bet on this being so, as Pascal's hypothetical unbeliever bet on the existence of God. And how much he stood to gain! Should the claims of Marxism be valid, then not only is Marxism the philosophy of our time, it also offers a scientifically guaranteed understanding of all previous times. Through such knowledge, Brecht would be the first major dramatist in history who understood history, the first major dramatist who, to individual genius, could add a sure and certified knowledge of man and his society. I put this strongly, not to mock Brecht, but in order to concede that anyone who accepted Brecht at face value might well think he had more to offer than any other dramatist who ever wrote. When I lived among Brecht's intimates and followers, I was aware that this was exactly what they did think.

And Brecht liked to suppose that the converse was also true: he once said that, should Soviet Communism not conquer, his works would have no future. Perhaps this is a tautology, for it is part of the doctrine of Soviet Communism that Soviet Communism will *inevitably* conquer. If it didn't, then it would be false, and for true believers that would be the end of everything, and "everything" includes the works of Brecht.

Historically, Brecht differs from Aeschylus and the others in one obvious way. He is betting on the future where they were building on the past. And the speculative element introduces a hysterical note.

One is reminded that very bad writers can gain prominence by joining powerful political movements. The thirties produced dozens of Progressive Playwrights and Progressive Critics who could never have become just plain playwrights and critics. They rode what they hoped was the wave of the future and what was certainly the wave of that ephemeral present. If no army can withstand the idea, then no public can withstand the play (poem, novel, critical article) in which the idea is celebrated—that was the calculation. And Bertolt Brecht made a bid to be, not just a great writer, but The Writer of the Future.

That bid is only partially relevant to this chapter on thought because propagandist drama contains rather less thought than other drama does. The tendency of any drama celebrating the dramatist's eagerness to ride the wave of the future is toward mindless acceptance in the mood of a madly cheering mob. If it is "drama of ideas" to end a play with marching proletarians singing "All or Nothing!" to exciting music, then the drama of ideas is the drama of demagogy. And much that has been classed as drama of ideas—or even epic theatre—is just that.

But Brecht's famous theories of drama represented an attempt, not only to replace the commercial, capitalist theatre, but to supply a propagandist, anticapitalist theatre *of a more intellectual sort*. In his early formulations, it was defined as precisely a drama of thought, not emotion, of instruction, not pleasure. It was as if Brecht had taken over the motto of his senior colleague, Georg Kaiser: "The head is stronger than the heart."

The results are from no viewpoint insignificant. Written in the old way, *The Mother* would have been a quite different play. Given "the Brecht treatment," this "conversion plot" is carefully devulgarized. There is no crude assault upon the spectator's sympathy to make him feel that *he* is being converted too; nor is the wish to "teach" embarrassingly and hypocritically covered up. Brecht is able so far to admit the didacticism, and take it for granted, that he is free to use much fuller expressive means (more humor, more charm, more dignity). Keats said we hate a poet who has "a palpable design on us," and in *The Mother* we can salute, with relief, a propagandist who has no such design on us.

But why hasn't he? If Stephen Spender needed us, and all the left-wing dramatists of the thirties needed us, so that we might be converted and support the Popular Front, why didn't Brecht need us? Because he was much more deeply a Marxist, and truly saw the Revolution as inevitable and therefore not hard up for individual converts (undependable anyway). Rather, Brecht is able to get into *The Mother* a sense of the surging force of history and indeed of the "strength of an idea whose time has come." If the story is about the inevitability of the 1917 Revolution, well, that revolution *must* have been inevitable, since it had already happened when Brecht wrote the play. And if the playwright has no designs on us individually, we have also no doubt that he sees history as sweeping over our dead bodies if we do not consent to be swept along by it.

I once saw a "divided audience" with my own eyes: it was when *The Mother* was played in Paris by the Berlin Ensemble, and half the public rose to cheer, while the other half rose to boo. And this is a play that was designed to be cool and unemotional! Obviously, while certain feelings are cooled off by the Brechtian procedure, others are heated to boiling point. Indeed, the former are cooled off in order to leave more fuel available for the latter. The intellectual content of *The Mother* is slight. That much Marxism could be learned, I would estimate, in about twenty-five minutes. What the play has to offer in pleasures is more on the sensuous side. Had Brecht only written *The Mother* and the *Lehrstuecke* (Didactic Plays) , I would say his work was not overintellectual but the opposite, and that those who fear "drama of ideas" have nothing whatever to fear from him.

Brecht was an intellectual dramatist, but not because he took up with Marxist philosophy. Marxism brought him close at times to a Jesuitical "sacrifice of the intellect," an abasement before authority, a surrender to the "inevitable" and the "necessary." Just as one might say (to compare Brecht to a lesser writer) that Mr. Graham Greene's intellect is employed more in resisting Catholicism than in embracing it, so Brecht's intellect is characteristically employed in what doctrinaires on both sides might call subterfuge and evasion, rather than in celebration of the true faith. His awareness of the other side insured that he would remain more of a dramatist than a propagandist. Indeed "other sides" always proved a temptation and a lure to him, exactly as they had to Schiller and to Shaw. A less gifted playwright might have created Posa: it took Schiller to create such a Philip II. A less gifted playwright might have created the Shavian St. Joan: it took Shaw to create such an Inquisitor. A less gifted playwright might have created a Swiss Cheese or even a Kattrin: it took Brecht to create Mother Courage. Indeed, so shifting are the viewpoints, so manifold the ironies, that it is sometimes hard in Brecht to say which "the other side" is. *The Measures Taken* is spoken of as his most dogmatic play, and as such must be read as the defense of the realist against the idealist—Philip II coming into his own as Stalin's Party, the Marquis of Posa meeting his definitive defeat as the "purged" Comrade. But if Schiller had a lurking sympathy for Philip, the Brechtian text barely conceals one for the Young Comrade. The life of man finds expression, not in official sentiment, but in the sense of interplay, in the clash between one kind of sympathy and another. When this clash is dramatized—as in Brecht's conflicting sympathy for the cynical Mother Courage and for her heroic daughter Kattrin—the best Brechtian drama is written. And it is a superb best.

THE DIGNITY OF SIGNIFICANCE

THE DEFENSE of Brecht, Pirandello, and Shaw—and even Schiller and Lessing—against popular fallacy would be more than I should care to tax my "unpopular" reader's patience with except that it enables me to argue that none of them at his best wrote mere *pièces à thèse*. The *pièce à thèse*—the play that proves a thesis—would be the purest form of drama of ideas if it could fairly be called drama at all. For in it the idea is the spoiled child and gets all its own way. To "prove" a thesis in a play is no better than cheating: all the playwright has to do is stack the cards. And to concentrate on a purpose of this kind is to exclude all the traditional and mandatory substance of a play.

It is good that the thesis play exists, at least as a conception, since it can serve both as a reference point and as an awful example. It shows what happens to the drama when nothing is held to matter except to state an idea and to endorse it. Which is an heretical version of dramatic art, and a fatally narrow one. I have tried to show that the great playwrights, even those accused of such narrowness, even those sometimes guilty of it, did not in their best work isolate the ideas, in this fashion, from recalcitrant experience but, on the contrary, found "drama" precisely in the recalcitrance—in the interplay, that is, between idea and non-idea, abstraction and concretion, theory and practice.

Is the thought in a play the most important of its elements? Plot, character, dialogue, thought: each of these aspects of a play has its claims to primacy, and has had them championed by writers of note. Generally the motive seems to be to damage the claims of one of the others. Aristotle's famous promulgation of the primacy of plot is aimed at those who put character first. In modern times, those who wished to damage the claims of ideas (thought, theme) have often championed dialogue (style, words), taking as their cue Mallarmé's statement, "poetry is not written with ideas, it is written with words." Pragmatically, one can report that these polemics have often proved healthy. Modern scholars have, for instance, been able to rehabilitate the Spanish classical drama largely with the help of the Aristotelian defense of plot. Even so, they encounter problems. For even more important in the Spanish plays is theme. . . .

A less polemical approach might by this time have its advantages. One might ask, for example, if the various aspects of a play are running in competition. Plot is the domain of *what is done* and *what happens*. Character is the domain of *who does it* and *to whom it happens*. Must two halves of the selfsame process be rival claimants for supremacy? Again, we might ask of those who tell us that drama is made of words, not of ideas: what are words made of? Do they not, along with facts and feelings, convey ideas? I am afraid that if we say, drama is the words, drama is poetry, we shall then be forced to subdivide the kinds of words and/or poetry into as many "aspects" as we had before: any advantage is not apparent.

If our "aspects of a play" are not competitive, neither are they in all ways commensurable. The Hispanists I mentioned would have a possible way out if they could say: plot is only the chief *means* at the dramatist's disposal; his *end* is theme. And it will be appropriate to close this chapter on thought by enquiring whether thought (theme, idea) *is* the drama's true end.

More than one school of critical practice teaches that it is. The Marxist Meyerhold has written:

> Thought comes first. . . . An outstanding play is exceptional mainly in its profound ideas, i.e., it is clearly polemical—it tries to "persuade" the audience.

The doctrine is hardly inviting, stated so baldly and, as the context makes clear, bound up with other unargued assumptions—Meyerhold proposes to make of every notable play ever written propaganda for a class. Yet whoever believes that a play is there primarily to make a statement is committed to the notion of the primacy of idea. For no one who holds this view is indifferent as to *what* statement is made. Great anxiety is shown, on the contrary, that *certain* statements be made, and great satisfaction is taken in the statements found, or alleged to be found, in the masterpieces. Hence it comes about that believers in the primacy of the idea range from Marxists to some of their extreme opponents—the school of F. R. Leavis, for example, which looks for "statements" of another color and even in another place: subtly embedded in the poetry. But an unstated statement is still a statement.

If the aim of the drama is *not* to make a statement, what

is it? A recent book that takes issue with the Leavis school formulates the following counterprinciple. ". . . such a work [as a Shakespeare play] is not a statement or insight or special kind of informativeness . . . but is a momentous and energizing experience." And again: "Before it is a source of insight, great imaginative literature is a source of *power*." Thus John Holloway in his *Story of the Night*. Longinus had said as much long ago.

Such are, most probably, the two principal views of the subject. No doubt both are perennial: but does one really have to choose between them? To me it would seem that each view gets less and less true as it approaches its own pole, more and more true as it approaches the opposite pole. Hence if insight, as with Leavis, is bound up with sensibility, then we are already far from the pole at which all that matters is statement. And if experience, as with Holloway, is only momentous when it has meaning, then statements are implied in its momentousness, and we are that much closer to the pole of idea.

Drama has to do both with conveying an experience and with telling truths about it. By the same token, truth-telling is not the whole end of the drama; nor is the communication of an experience. Truth-telling—the making of statements, stating of themes, putting across of ideas —is indeed only an aspect; and there are others of comparable importance. On the other hand, the drama partakes of that *Lebensweisheit* which it is the habit of literature generally to communicate. Only a cynic or a philistine will want to dismiss as unmeaning "experience" the impression given by all the great plays of a veil lifted, the scales falling from eyes, in a word of something momentous exhibited— and *said*. But such wisdom is more than is commonly meant by thought, or idea, or theme, or statement, and as such is not a part of the play but a precipitate of the play as a whole.

And here perhaps is the most reasonable conclusion: that thought, defined as an aspect of a play, is *only* an aspect of a play, but that there is a broader definition of the term according to which it might truly stand as the aim and object of playwriting. Hebbel must have had some such broader definition in mind when he said: "In drama no character should ever utter a thought; from the thought in a play come the speeches of all the characters." Henry James, though T. S. Eliot has praised him for having a mind so fine that no idea could violate it, once said that a writer's "philosophy" was the most important thing about him. However, since James went on to equate philosophy with the way a man *feels* about life, it is clear that he too sought a broader definition of the philosophical content of literature.

I have already proposed the word wisdom instead of thought. But it, too, proves misleading. It attaches itself too readily to particular speeches where, as Hebbel noted, it was dangerous for a playwright to put it. "Freedom and Truth—these are the pillars of society." Perhaps there is wisdom in this sentence, yet if the Ibsen play from which it is taken is a wise play, its wisdom is to be found in an Action which raises doubts as to whether Freedom and Truth are the pillars of society. The wisdom of a play may well conflict, not only with the wisdom of individual speakers in it but also with the wisdom of the author's summing up. *Vision* is a better word, and gathering together the threads, we might say: a play presents a vision of life, and to the idea of vision the idea of wisdom naturally adheres. To share this vision and this wisdom— just as naturally—is not to receive information or counsel but rather to have a "momentous experience." The momentousness is to be defined partly in emotional terms: according to the play in question there accrues joy, elation, exaltation, ecstasy, or whatever. But an essential part of our conviction that such an experience is momentous derives from what we take to be the import of the play.

Finally, if part of this conviction derives from what the play means, another part derives from the mere fact *that* it means. Meaningfulness is itself momentous for human beings, as they discover, *a contrario,* whenever life has no meaning for them. All art serves as a lifebelt to rescue us from the ocean of meaninglessness—an extraordinary service to perform at any time and more than ever today when religion and philosophy prove less and less able to perform it. To be thus rescued is to rediscover our personal dignity, through which alone we can discover dignity in others, dignity in human life as such. And attendant upon our sense of human dignity is a sense of what Goethe beautifully called "the dignity of significance."

5

ENACTMENT

LITERATURE VS. THEATRE

Is A PLAY complete without performance? The question has been answered with equal vehemence in both the affirmative and the negative. The choice goes by temperamental preference: "literary" persons believe in the unaided script; "theatrical" persons believe in performance. Both are right. A good play leads a double existence, and is a complete "personality" in both its lives. When a theatrical person says a play has been misinterpreted in performance, he is certainly implying that a play is *there* and has its integrity before the interpreters touch it. As for literary persons, their concession that a play does have another life as well as that of the book is to be found, if nowhere else, in their dismissal of bits they don't like as "merely theatrical." In other words, their position really is not that the theatrical dimension doesn't exist but that they wish it didn't.

Each group is trying to make a virtue of its own *déformation professionnelle*. Theatrical people have their limitations as interpreters of literature. Literary people have theirs as interpreters of theatre. If we can avoid the blindnesses of both parties, the only real problem lies in understanding the *difference* between script-alone and script-as-performed, for any given passage may have a different import in the two different contexts. Finally, one is not forced into any choice between literature and theatre, and to know *Hamlet,* or any great play, should be to know it from stage and study, both. A fine performance will never fail to throw light on at least an aspect of the play, while even the best reading in the study will fall far short of embracing all its aspects.

The question whether one should prefer to read or to see a play is best answered pragmatically. If one can read well to oneself, one will hardly prefer to go and see a mediocre performance. But, for anyone capable of relishing theatre—and that includes more people than know it —even though the written script has its own completeness, there is no pleasure to top that of seeing a dramatic masterpiece masterfully performed. What is added means so much in such an immediate, sensuous way. If plot, characterization and dialogue give body to the theme, and transform thought into wisdom, and a view into a vision, adequate performance helps them to do so in various ways but above all by adding that final and conclusive concretion, the living actor.

Historically, of course, performance was not something added: it was that from which dramatic art grew. And, though origin and essence are not to be confused with each other, it is often easier to see an essence if we can see the phenomena as they were "in the beginning"—yes, even if this is a fictitious beginning such as Rousseau's "social contract"—or even if we take for granted that ontogeny repeats phylogeny and, when knowledge of the infancy of the race is missing, substitute what we know of the infancy of individuals. As I am about to do.

TO IMPERSONATE, TO WATCH, AND TO BE WATCHED

THE theatrical situation, reduced to a minimum, is that A impersonates B while C looks on. Such impersonation is universal among small children, and such playing of a part is not wholly distinct from the other playing that children do. All play creates a world within a world—a territory with laws of its own—and the theatre might be regarded as the most durable of the many magic palaces which infantile humanity has built. The distinction between art and life begins there.

Impersonation is only half of this little scheme. The other half is watching—or, from the viewpoint of A, being watched. Even when there is actually no spectator, an impersonator imagines that there is, often by dividing himself into two, the actor and his audience. That very histrionic object, the mirror, enables any actor to watch himself and thereby to become C, the audience. And the mirror on the wall is only one: the mirrors in the mind are many.

What is it to want to be watched? Impossible to ask such a question these days without eliciting the word: exhibitionism. To want to be watched is to be exhibitionistic. Is this merely to say: to want to be watched is to want to be watched? Not quite. "Exhibitionism" is a clinical phenomenon, and the word carries a connotation of the socially inappropriate as well as the mentally unhealthy. Which, I am afraid, only makes it the more applicable to the theatre. Wishing to be watched, sometimes and in a small way, is one thing, but wishing to become an actor is wishing to be watched all the time and in a big way. Such a wish would take a lot of justifying and even more explaining. It is bizarre, and brings to mind Thomas Mann's notion that there is a natural affinity between art and pathology.

Is the Folies-Bergère the quintessence of theatre? That depends, I think, on how one takes the Folies-Bergère. Sir Kenneth Clark has distinguished between the naked and the nude. A nude body is one that calls for no clothing; a naked body is a clothed body temporarily stripped of its clothing. Sir Kenneth's interest in the distinction lies in the fact that the arts he is professionally concerned with—painting and sculpture—deal, not with the naked, but with the nude; in fact (so far as Europe is concerned) they invented it. Not so the theatre, however. Even in places and at times which had nothing against the body, the method of the theatre has been concealment by mask and costume. True, one of the archetypal acts of the theatre is to remove this concealment. But one can only take off what is on. Or, in Sir Kenneth's terms, theatre can present the naked, but never the nude. When therefore the girls of the Folies-Bergère are made a highbrow tableau of in the likeness of classical nude paintings, in trying to be nude they succeed in being untheatrical. When, on the other hand, they take off their clothes for us, or parade around in *almost* no clothing, they become theatrical through the act or simulation of unmasking. In short, if these girls are nude, they are art; if they are naked, they are theatre. Parts of the French audience take them to be nude, or try to. The foreign tourists take them to be naked. That is because the tourists have "dirty minds." But the tourists are right. The nudity is spurious; the nakedness, genuine.

Hence, theatre has less in common with the tradition of the nude in painting than with the tradition of the striptease in "vulgar" entertainment. Theatre is shamelessly "low"; it cannot look down on the body, because it *is* the body. If you want the soul, why pay to see chorus girls? Why pay to *see* nonchorus girls? To begin to understand and accept theatrical art, we must be willing to say, yes, it's true, we *do* wish to see, and we do wish to be stimulated by seeing bodies—we decline to say "titillated" because the word "titillate" belongs to the puritan enemy of the theatre. We must be willing to aver, further, that the bodies we wish to see are not "spiritualized" as Sir Kenneth Clark says nudes are, they are "naked," their spiritual credit is nil, their appeal is "prurient." We are prying into filthy secrets: the police department and the post office can begin to shift uneasily in their shoes.

How indecent the theatre is! Yet, for our peace of mind, the indecency is in general placed at a remove: the nakedness is usually of the soul, not the body—and it is Phaedra's nakedness we see, not Gypsy Rose Lee's. For once that we see Salome remove her seven veils in Wilde's play or Strauss's opera, we see the veils removed a thousand times in other operas and plays from the individual spirit, from society, from the universe.

The problem with this is that to show the naked spirit is impossible. Only the spirit's envelope can be shown, and this is the body. And though a philosopher may represent the body as a mere shadow of a more substantial spiritual reality, and a playwright may follow him in this, our crude retort is inevitably that the shadow is itself pretty substantial. "Can spirit set to a leg? No. Or an arm? No." Platonic thoughts can be entertained in the mind, but not lived by from breakfast to lunch. And though the great nakednesses of the theatre are spiritual, the immediate reality of theatre is aggressively physical, corporeal.

The physical world is real for every artist, and is that through which even a St. John of the Cross must communicate his antiphysical philosophy. Still, literature maintains some restraint in addressing its physicalities to the mind's eye only. Even painting and sculpture maintain some restraint in that the skin tints of the one have no skin under them, and the solidities of the other have no flesh or bone. Only theatre thrusts at its audience the supreme object of sensual thoughts: the human body. And while in the theatre it will never be nude, and will seldom be naked, its clothing is the more erotic in its double function of concealing and revealing, canceling and enhancing, denying and affirming.

That clothes may be used to heighten the sexual appeal of bodies, rather than reduce it, is a familiar enough fact. The exhibitionism of the actor is not so crudely sexual. He may even make himself theatrically more interesting by being less sexual: what has more appeal than Hamlet's funereal black? At worst, an actor or actress will concentrate on secondary sexual characteristics: a sensual mouth, a soulful eye, a rich head of hair, a slim waist, a well-shaped leg. He or she exhibits the body, but not for its beauty. In this the actor is closer to the acrobat than to the artist's model, since he exhibits his body largely for what it can do. And what an actor's body can do is expressive rather than lovely, and may be expressive, indeed, in the least lovely mode, such as grotesque comedy.

Does an actor exhibit *himself?* There has been much discussion on this head. Educators usually tell students of theatre that the actor does not exhibit himself: that would be egotistic. He submerges himself in his roles: a noble example of self-discipline, if not self-sacrifice. Louis Jouvet was saying as much when he stated that to embody a role the actor disembodies himself. One knows what he meant. When Sir Laurence Olivier plays Justice Shallow, the noble Olivier face and erect body are gone. Yet the very fact that I put it this way proves that I am not looking at the performance as I would if it were played by an actor who did not have a handsome face and an erect carriage. Does this signify only that I am a gossip, unable to concentrate on the show itself? I think not. The knowledge that an acrobatic trick is difficult is not irrelevant to the experience of watching it. On the contrary. We know it is easy for many creatures to fly up and down at great speed: the interest is *only* in seeing men and women do it, because it is not easy for them to do it. To see Olivier as Shallow is to see comparable difficulties overcome, comparable laws of nature defied by human prowess. Hence we are not enjoying the role alone, but also the actor. And he, on his side, is not exhibiting the role alone, he is exhibiting his prowess, he is exhibiting himself. Nor is the self-exhibition confined to the skill with which he portrays someone we define as "so different from himself." To wear a heavy, senile make-up and hunch the shoulders would not be enough if there were not a Justice Shallow in Olivier, if Shallow were not something he might yet become, or might have become. In such roles the actor is exhibiting the many different possibilities of being that he finds in himself.

No need to say anything about actors who all too

evidently exhibit nothing but themselves. I am saying that even the actor who seems to be at the opposite pole from this is still exhibiting himself. Exceptional in Sir Laurence is the talent. Unexceptional is the original, naïve impulse that said: Watch me!

What of the pleasure of watching? In some respects, there is no difference between the theatre spectator and the "consumer" of other arts—the listener to music, the reader of novels. It might be imagined that his position is identical with that of the observer of painting, sculpture, and architecture: all are onlookers. But the phenomenon is less straightforward. If theatre is a visual art like painting, it is also a temporal art like music. The watcher is also a listener—the voyeur is also an eavesdropper.

Such words as *exhibitionist* and *voyeur*—though some will discount them as jargon—add to the purely descriptive words an implication of guilt.

> I have heard
> That guilty creatures sitting at a play
> Have by the very cunning of the scene
> Been struck so to the soul that presently
> They have proclaimed their malefactions.

Literal-minded persons will find Hamlet's ideas on crime detection somewhat far-fetched, but poetic drama deals in essences, and here Shakespeare, Hamlet, and all audiences of *Hamlet* take it that the essence of theatre is to strike guilty creatures to the soul—or, as we would say in prose cliché, to play on the guilt feelings of the audience. Seen in this way, the logic is good.

> The play's the thing
> Wherein I'll catch the conscience of the king.

* * *

—because plays *are* things wherein consciences are caught.

This makes it sound as if watching were very unpleasurable indeed—as, for King Claudius, it was. Hamlet plotted to defy the distinction between art and life, to exploit the possibility of a leap from art to life. When that happens we are no longer dealing with drama but with the destruction of its main convention. If we are not King Claudius, and have not literally killed our brother, we are also spared his reaction. Instead of calling for lights and making our exit, we stay on to "enjoy the show." Is our conscience *not* caught, then? Are our withers unwrung? It is. They are. But in art, not life. Such is the paradox of pain in drama: we do and do not suffer. We are suffering; we are also enjoying ourselves. When we watch, though we do not watch in the way we watch actual happenings, neither do we watch in the spirit of "scientific detachment" but always with some degree of emotional involvement. I am suggesting that this involvement is not an innocent one.

It would be impossible to draw the line between drama and gossip, drama and scandal, drama and the front page of the worst newspapers—which, understandably enough, claim to be dramatic. Even what is called pornography is by no means in any separate realm from the realm of the tragic and comic poets. All these things are enjoyed by human beings, and to all some measure of guilt is attached. Perhaps if one took the guilt away, the dirty picture, so called, would lose much of its appeal, and perhaps if one took from theatre the element of voyeurism, the occasion would lose much of its appeal.

Certainly that element has been on the increase in modern times. The Greek, Elizabethan, and Spanish theatres were less voyeuristic because the plays were put on in broad daylight. It is the modern age that worked out the idea of a pitch-dark auditorium. Scholars call the modern stage the peepshow stage. The corollary is that this is a theatre for Peeping Toms. It is; and the classical criticism of it is that, from the eighteenth century to Tennessee Williams, it has been so too crudely. It has been, all too often, a theatre of domestic triviality.

The pleasure of looking on is in itself an equivocal thing. It includes such delights as feeling one has committed the crime yet is able to escape the penalty because the final curtain descends and one finds "it was all a dream."

What is pornography? One element in it is that forbidden wishes are seen gratified—the punishment being escaped because the man on the "dirty picture" is not oneself. The literature that is called pornographic often has another feature: following forbidden pleasure, condign punishment. Does not Tennessee Williams' *Sweet Bird of Youth* afford us the pleasure of being a gigolo for three quarters of the evening and then in the last part giving him the punishment that exactly fits the crime? Affords *us* the pleasure but gives *him* the punishment: which is to say, affords us the pleasure, but finds us a whipping boy. This might well be called pornography. It also has a lot in common with high tragedy which from its beginnings has presented crime and its punishment, the punished protagonist being a scapegoat for the audience. Pornography is continuous with art; and the pleasure of watching is continuous with the pleasure of peeping.

SUBSTITUTIONS

SUCH is the infantile basis of theatre. When he impersonates B, A is an exhibitionist, and when C looks on, he is a voyeur. But of course A does not need B if exhibition is all he desires, for he could exhibit himself, and necessarily that is one thing he does exhibit.

B, the person impersonated, who is he? Originally, he is the little actor's father, the mother, and the siblings. Any other persons are likely to be members of the household interchangeable with a parent or a sibling. The interesting thing is that this continues to be true in adult theatre. There the persons impersonated are the work of a playwright. But the classic preoccupation of the playwright has been with the family. Comedy has often shown the family in the making. Both comedy and tragedy have often shown the family in the unmaking, and from the *Agamemnon* to *Ghosts,* from *The Mandrake* to *Candida,* have dealt with marriage and the threats to it.

It was the psychoanalysts who pointed out that the family was often still the subject even when it seemed not to be. Otto Rank, for example, maintained that *Julius Caesar* is about parricide and that Brutus, Cassius, and Marc Antony are, symbolically speaking, Caesar's sons. Such a thing cannot be directly demonstrated but it comes to seem likely if we follow a certain line of reasoning. It is a matter of those other persons in the household whom, when we are children, we take to be members of the family, the nurse who is a kind of mother, the uncle who is a kind of father, the cousin who is an older or younger brother. The fact is that we continue to enlarge our family in this way as long as we live or, putting it the other way round, we assign all our acquaintances membership in the family which we knew as children. The play of life, as each of us writes it, has a very small cast—though for each role there may be innumerable understudies. If we felt our own father to be tyrannical, the role known as Father may be played by anyone we feel to be tyrannical. If we had the coddling kind of mother, the role known as Mother may be played by anyone, even a male, who coddles us. And so on. In short we have made ourselves a list of very definite types and, far from being tenuous and nebulous as types are reputed to be, they suggest to us strong emotion and clear-cut attitude.

IDENTIFICATIONS

THERE is a peculiarity about these little systems. One does not include oneself in the cast of characters, and so it is impossible for one to identify a whole class of people with oneself. It is the other way round. Unable to see oneself at all, one gropes in the dark, one guesses, one decides one is like some other person. One does not identify others with oneself but oneself with others. Again, the family is likely to play a guiding role. A little boy is likely to identify himself with his father. In this there is another source of tragic art: oneself as the great god Daddy. Here is the root of the idea of the hero: identification with strength.

The world, I have been saying, consists of oneself and others. One makes a cast of characters out of the ensemble, and a play out of living. A tragedy can well be made out of oneself and one's identification with Father, a comedy out of one's sense of those few archetypes, "the others." Two psychological processes are involved: *substitution* of all and sundry persons for the few in one's own original background, and *identification* of oneself with someone else. To analyze any "interpersonal" situation, one might well ask: who has been substituted for whom? and: with whom am I identified?

It would be hard to overestimate the influence of the identifications we all make. Though certainly we do not become the people we model ourselves on, what we become depends upon the people we model ourselves on. This is an element in upbringing which the Victorian age understood better than ours. Identifications, at home, and later at school, are everything. Central in the dynamics of living and growing up, they are central in this so intimately human art: the drama. Even Broadway knows as much. Its reviewers know how to account for the failure of a play by its lack of anyone in the cast they can identify themselves with. Precisely in its crudity, Broadway dramaturgy is suited to illustrate an argument I am presenting in broad lines only: a Broadway cast of characters consists of the person one identifies oneself with plus the rest of one's family put there in the form most quickly recognizable, old Uncle Tom Cobley and all.

Broadway producers presuppose in their audience very little spiritual ambition. They don't expect people to identify themselves with anyone of any stature. The old melodramas were more enterprising, because there, for the space of two hours, one could make a Douglas Fairbanks of oneself. At the other pole, there is the kind of protagonist who probably *is* beyond one's reach—T. S. Eliot's Becket, for example. In *Murder in the Cathedral* Mr. Eliot put in a chorus of women for us to identify ourselves with. They are slightly better than half-witted. In this way the "high-brow" playwright reaches a conclusion not dissimilar to that of the "lowbrows"; and indeed this play achieved a certain popularity.

EMPATHY AND ALIENATION

IN CHALLENGING the traditional principles of the drama, Bertolt Brecht has in our day questioned the value of identification. The word was *Einfühlung,* translated as empathy. As used early in this century, by Vernon Lee, for example, the word empathy had to do with the mental process by which we say that a mountain rises from the plain. Since then it has come to bear one of the meanings Vernon Lee said it should not bear: more or less the literal meaning of *sich einfühlen,* "to feel oneself into." It is sympathy without the moral implication or the sentimental overtone. It is identification.

Brecht also had a word for what he saw as the theatrical alternative to empathy. This is *Verfremdung*—Alienation or Estrangement. Brecht asks that we not identify ourselves with his characters but that we stand back from them. Object is to be seen as object, with astonishment. Brecht claims to derive this latter clause from science. Most people take for granted that apples fall; Isaac Newton was astonished. In the Brechtian theatre, the playwright is to be an Isaac Newton, and make Isaac Newtons of his audience. There was really no need to go outside the drama for such an aim. Corneille would have understood it well; and something of the sort is implied in most comedy.

Brecht is perhaps overconfident in assuming that when we abandon empathy we can see "the object in itself as it really is." He reckons without the process of substitution as I have described it. And failing to notice the inescapability of identifications, he himself makes them only unconsciously. Indeed his unconscious identification with his supposed enemies becomes a source of unintended drama.

THE ADULT AND THE INFANTILE

THIS COMMENT on Brecht brings to a head my presentation of theatre as an infantile system. Brecht's objection is precisely to infantility. His Epic Theatre would be a completely adult theatre *if such a thing were possible.* As he writes in his Prospectus of the Diderot Society:

> Only in recent decades did a theatre develop which placed greater value upon a correct presentation of the world, whereby, to fit this correctness, objective, non-individual criteria should be allowed. No more did the artist feel himself bound to create "his own world" and, taking the actual world as known and unalterable, feel bound to enrich the catalogue of images which are really images of the image-makers; rather did he feel himself bound to take the world as alterable and unknown and to deliver images which give information more about the world than about him. . . . The "inner eye" needs no microscope or telescope, the outer eye needs both. For the visionary the experiences of other people are dispensable. Experiment is not in the repertoire of the seer. No, the artist who takes up the new task must, when he seeks to communicate images, deny himself the methods of hypnosis and even at need the customary empathy. . . .

In which it is taken for granted that a man "of the age of science" can become independent of the primitive side of his own nature by taking thought.

Everything in Brecht's theory of theatre—from the white light to the "presentational" acting—is dedicated to the same end: replacing a magical theatre with a scientific one, a childish theatre with an adult one. There is obviously a good deal to be said for this. What you cannot say for it, however, is that it is possible. For "growing up," so far as mental growth is concerned, is only a manner of speaking. The most mature person bristles with immaturities; the least neurotic person is still neurotic. The human race cannot reasonably be divided into two groups, the childish and the adult, because the child is not only father of the man, he is the man's Siamese twin.

The only odd thing is that an artist should not know it, since the child lives on more unabashedly in the artist than in any other class, and many artists are rather too happy about the fact. If I went back to infantile psychology in order to introduce the subject of this chapter, I did so in the interests not of simplicity but of relevance. For the theatre of grownups is much closer to the little system that children work out than the casual observer would think, the reason being, as Richard Sterba has put it, that "the pleasure of acting and looking on at a theatrical performance is a very narcissistic one, through regression to the early childhood stage of magic world creation." Brecht, who welcomed the blow to the world's narcissism that was administered by Galileo, should not have been above admitting that there are regressive and narcissistic and magical elements in all effective theatre, including of course his own. They have their negative side (immaturity is immaturity) but "becoming again like a little child" has its positive side too, and is a requirement not only of higher ethics but of higher theatre.

LATE ADOLESCENCE

LITTLE CHILDREN love to dress up and pretend to be someone else. They enjoy dolls and puppets and toy stages. They are thrilled to be taken to certain kinds of shows. And yet one would not think of saying that an infant was stage-struck. There is a characteristic age for this phenomenon: late adolescence. At some of the acting schools, where the students are mostly about seventeen, one can confront a group that is a hundred per cent stage-struck.

The word "struck," in this sense, is commonly applied only to two things: lightning and the stage. We say: that idea strikes me as true, but we don't say: I am truth-struck. The truth only dawns. It is the stage that strikes.

If it struck at puberty, an explanation would suggest itself: theatre is an extended puberty rite, the expression of the sudden onset of physical maturity. But what happens at seventeen? In the crass sense, nothing; and yet that age is one of the most interesting and crucial, for thereabouts is the meeting place of boy and man, girl and woman. It is the time when, if we were birds, we would be put out of the nest but when, since we are human, we can get ourselves sent to an acting school.

It is a time when the adolescent struggle with the parents, with home and the family, often becomes conscious and bitter. One is not really ready to be independent, to start one's own home, to be on one's own in the great world, and yet that—or something vaguer but more disruptive—is just what one would like to do. With the perennial human wish to have everything both ways, one would like to have a rebellion without facing the consequences of rebellions. One would like to go to another country and yet stay in this one. The theatre *is* another country which one can visit without leaving this one. A wonderful country! What Russia is to a non-Russian Communist, the theatre is to the stage-struck young: the place where things are right as against other places where things are all wrong. Here flourishes that emotional freedom for lack of which we, on the outside, can hardly breathe. The world outside is hard to take at the best of times and at seventeen we make one last stab at refusing to take it and escaping to the paradise of the stage.

What is it about the theatre that can exert so powerful, so overpowering, an appeal? For surely it is the violence of the reaction—comparable only to falling head over heels in love—that is the remarkable thing. Why is it only the theatre that strikes with the force of lightning?

Perhaps people who speak of the magic of the stage have unwittingly picked up a clue, though the ordinary conception of such magic would not take us far. Yes, the stage is beguiling, but we are not lightning-struck by beguilements; we are only beguiled. Freud called attention to the aspect of magic which might have a bearing here. This is magic as an expression of the illusion of omnipotence. In the great world, children often come to grief because they assume that their thoughts take effect as deeds, that thoughts can of themselves remove the obstacles to thought. The world, we say, brings them to heel. But suppose they refuse to be brought to heel? Isn't the theatre an appropriate refuge? This little world where fantasy is king? Where thoughts are indeed omnipotent?

The novel and the play both provide that emotional freedom and continuity which real life refuses to us, and the freedom which exists in the novel is, in a sense, raised to a higher power on stage. For, while in a novel, one only

165

imagines one's way into a character's feelings, in the theatre one seems to meet him in the flesh—for *there* is the actor who is playing the part—and one takes him in through one's senses. As one sits there in the dark, "dead to the world" (i.e., to one's companions) , but passing through the fourth wall into the life of the actors, one is only a step short of hallucination. And, if one is not a spectator but an actor, one may feel this even more keenly. It may well be the hallucinatory element in theatre that has irresistible appeal—at least for actors who are, literally or figuratively, in late adolescence.

WHAT THE ACTOR GIVES THE PLAYWRIGHT

SHOULD a novelist turn to playwriting, he might well feel that he has made certain sacrifices, even if he does not go all the way with Henry James, who envisaged the novelist-turned-playwright as throwing out the cargo to save the ship. However, if his plays were very well acted, such a writer might conclude that his losses had been recouped.

What does acting add to a play? Many things. Let me mention, first, one of the simplest but not least interesting: that the actors' eyes meet. This is probably not true of some of the older theatres, and some of the Oriental ones, but in our modern Western theatre it is a well-established, if not essential, feature. Though some today may think of it as a product of the Stanislavsky Method, or even of the movies, one can in fact trace it much further back. There is, for example, an eighteenth-century comment on the actress Mrs. Clive, which reads:

> Mr. Garrick complained that she disconcerted him, by not looking at him in the time of action, and neg-

166

lecting to watch the motion of the eye; a practice he was sure to observe to others. I am afraid this accusation is partly true; for Mrs. Clive would suffer her eyes to wander. . . .

Watch the acting of any intimate scene between a man and a woman—say, the last scene of *Pygmalion*. One can imagine an ancient Greek or a more recent devotee of classical Chinese theatre or Kabuki finding in our acting of *Pygmalion* a lack of formality and pattern, no special significance in where the feet are going, no special beauty in the way the body moves or stands. "Why, they're not doing anything," any of these visitors might say, "but alternately looking at each other and looking away." And this is essentially true. Acting, in such an instance, has come to concentrate itself in the eyes. And the eyes are subject to this physiological paradox: that to go on looking cancels out a look. To keep a look going, one has to interrupt it, and then look again; hence, in the various interruptions, all the looking away. A look is more dynamic as it is beginning to happen than when it actually happens; and having happened, it slows down into stony stare or sentimental gaze. As between persons, a look has its consummation when it is returned. The meeting of eyes constitutes a kind of center of human communication. The contact established is more personal than touch. What is communicated may be in doubt, but what is not in doubt is the aliveness of the lines of communication. On stage this is an aliveness of the actors, which they add to the much less directly physical life of the script. Spectators who might have difficulty with the written script have none responding physically, by empathy, to the actors' looking at each other. The stage, which renders things physically, neurologically,

sensuously, is a great instrument of legitimate populariza-
tion. Conversely, the overliterary spectator who has seized
Bernard Shaw's ideas all too readily, may not have lived
through the drama of a Shavian scene until he, too, receives
it from the actors' lips, through the actors' bodies, and
especially through the actors' eyes. Usually, when we speak
of seeing something through another's eyes, we are speaking
only of the mind's eye. In the theatre, the actors' eyes guide
us through the labyrinthine ways of the scenes; and all that
joins us to the actors' eyes is the magnetics of looking. In
the theatre, we may not be led by the nose: we *are* led by
the eyes.

If a play in the theatre should prove hallucinatory in its
vividness, it is the actor who finally has brought it to that
pitch, adding to the play, one might put it, the crowning
touch. Again, if a role is skeletal—and this I shall go into
later—it may be possible for the actor to put some flesh on
the bones. Some actors spend a lifetime filling in for
inadequate playwrights. If they are stars, one often hears
them disparagingly spoken of as mere personalities. The
disparagement is misplaced, as "mere personality," in the
sense here suggested, is exactly what the circumstances
require.

And as we have seen in the chapter on Character, a good
play may also have what novel-readers consider thin characterizations. If they do not need filling in, it is because the
play survives by its plot or by a combination of plot, style,
and theme. What the actor can contribute to a good play is
not to fill up gaps—there may not be any he could fill—but
to intensify its effects. Stanislavsky is right: it is fundamentally a matter of being able to "live" on stage. And
Stanislavsky correctly assumed that what most people do

on stage is not alive. Projection is lacking, and on stage not to project is not to live.

Pirandello points up this contrast wittily in *Six Characters* when two of the Characters speak without projecting their voices because people in real life do not project their voices. The result is that these Characters are not alive in the theatre. Now projection of the voice is a comparatively mechanical matter, and it does not follow that, if the voice is projected, the whole performance has "projection." We must take it that Pirandello here offers the part for the whole. To "live" on stage means to do more than live offstage, it means to give off life, to make it audible and visible, to make of it a projectile which is thrown out into the auditorium and reaches the back row of the balcony. "The point," says Jean Cocteau, "is not to put life onto the stage but to make the stage live."

What the actor has intensified when we out front have an "hallucination" is the illusion. Such is the acting of the tragic tradition, which in this century found its spokesman in Stanislavsky. What comic actors intensify is not the illusion but the aggression. (The comic tradition has recently been renewed by that most aggressive of playwrights—Brecht.) The comic aggression may take the form of satire and be called realistic, or it may take the form of high spirits and celebration and earn the description of fantastic. In either case the actor's fundamental contribution is not mimicry but vitality.

What indeed is that limited kind of acting which is so effectively practiced by friends of ours at parties in the way of malicious mimicry? The degree of likeness to what they mimic is a minor matter compared to the degree of wickedness with which they do it. A very little observation will suffice, provided very much fantasy and malice are superadded. Fantasy and malice are in this case the vehicles of vitality.

What acting testifies to in dramatic art is not in the first place its imitative character but its exaggerative character. The dramatist is immoderate. He likes to push his effects to the limit. The actor aids and abets him, adding powder to the bomb. The great actor resembles the great plays in that, beneath the formal calm which must be his normal aspect, he makes an immense violence felt. The impression given is that of living at great speed. And perhaps that, as Hebbel said, is just what the actor does—he lives "at speed, at unimaginable speed." Hebbel's idea is helpful for the understanding of all dramatic art. Rather than describe drama as an abridged, abbreviated form, as if something were missing from it, we should speak of it as an art in which more ground is covered in less time.

WHAT THE PLAYWRIGHT GIVES THE ACTOR

IF THE ACTOR helps the playwright by adding his presence and his vitality (not to mention his craft), the playwright helps the actor by writing, not just a character, but a role. This is perhaps the most overlooked of all the playwright's tasks, at least among students of literature. It is understood only to the extent that the differences between playwright and novelist are understood. The novelist uses artifice, but in a setting of nature—natural scenery and natural characters. The playwright uses artifice in a setting of artifice— stage roles amid stage scenery. Such are the rules of the game, the controlling conditions of this art. While the novelist has the illusion of seeing actual characters in actual settings, the playwright has to learn to visualize the actor of the character and visualize him in that most unnatural of all settings: a theatre.

A character is not a role until, to begin with, it can be put across in a few acted scenes. Any idea for a character which cannot be put across at that velocity and by that method is unsuited to dramatic art. Conversely, an idea for a character which suggests opportunities for several self-explaining and violent stage encounters can prove effective even though it be lacking in depth and complexity. This second proposition begins to explain the success of certain roles, such as that of Marguerite Gautier, which are by no means great characters. To create *dramatis personae* which are great both as roles and characters is to be, in this department at least, a great dramatist.

The matter is a subtle one and has not been sufficiently studied, partly because the full possibilities of a role are only revealed by first-rate acting, and partly because histrionic phenomena have not traditionally been found worthy of the detailed study that is lavished on many lesser subjects. Anyone can see, for example, that Goethe was a greater genius than Schiller, yet Schiller was able to write characters that were also great roles. Goethe only managed it occasionally—as with his Mephisto who saved *Faust* for the theatre.

There is a moment when we might all feel, with Etienne Souriau, that the dramatist's heroic deed is to give existence to characters. This is the moment when these characters go out on stage and demonstrate that existence—it is *the moment when the characters show themselves to be roles.* That is the eating which is the proof of the pudding. It is as if, in the theatre, the physical existence of the actor were necessary to complete the sense of the verb *to exist*. This moving, speaking incarnation of character which is an acted role is an instrument of such unique power that, for the time being at any rate, we cease to long for the vaunted advantages of other forms and arts.

Which comes first, the character or the role? We tend to think of a writer starting with a character and, if he is playwright enough, going on to make sure it is a role as well. That is because we live in a literary age. In a theatrical age, it was the other way around. The actor was there and needed lines. One handed him a role. Only when he was lucky did he get anything that deserved the name of a character. Inquiring further back in history, we find a repertoire of fixed roles which actor-writers would refurbish as effective characters. Such was the *commedia dell'arte*.

GREAT ACTING IN MELODRAMA

I HAVE REFERRED to the actor's ability to fill out the characters of mediocre plays. And what actors have done has often been not only a filling out of a role but a transformation of a play. This assertion is not subject to documentary proof, since the phenomenon is precisely that of the transformation of a document into a nondocument— a piece of theatrical art. The nearest we can come to such proof is in a careful reporting of the theatrical occasion. Despite the millions of words assigned to theatre news and so-called criticism in the press, there is a dearth of such reporting. But here is a sample, taken from Laurence Irving's monumental life of Sir Henry Irving. The play,

Louis XI by Boucicault, is a historical melodrama with unreadably stilted and vacuous dialogue. It is only when we find out what happened on stage that we get an inkling of what such a play could actually amount to.

. . . The King is seen in the solitude of his bed-chamber. Here takes place his extraordinary confession to Francois de Paule, delivered with great effect in all its blood-chilling frankness and incorrigible impenitence. And here when the holy father has retired, the monarch is suddenly frozen into abject terror by the appearance of the avenging Nemours. A terrible scene ensues—first of wild pleading for mercy, and then, when Nemours has with contempt and loathing granted the king his life, a fearful paroxysm of rage and hallucination, as the old man, suddenly young again with desperate excitement, rushes up to what he supposes to be the Duc de Nemours, and violently stabs the air until he falls fainting into the arms of those around him—a situation of great power most startlingly enacted. Great King Louis enters robed and sceptred, with death written in his countenance, and his physique reduced to the lowest stage of feebleness. . . . Long grey locks stream somewhat wildly on the king's shoulders. His countenance derives a sort of dignity, not seen before, from these changes, though such a figure can never be truly venerable—and also from the absorbing nature of the conflict which Louis wages with visibly declining powers. In this hour of extreme mental exhaustion, deepening momentarily into actual stupefaction and afterwards into coma and then into death, the extraordinary resolution and will of the king still display marvellous power. But never was there such a picture of moving prostration and animated decay. The back of a couch lost hold of for a moment, and the tottering form stumbles forward in a manner which sends a painful start through the whole audience. The sceptre drops, after being used head downwards as a staff, and is forgotten. Then the king is induced to be seated on a couch, and with extraordinary elaborated graduations of sensibility, violently interrupted by spasms of vigour, he gradually loses his consciousness. No physical detail is neglected that can help to realize a sinking of mind and body into annihilating death. The voice and articulation have the weird, half-drunken thickness of paralysis. Even the effect observable in age and sickness of drawing the retreating lips over the sunken teeth is somewhat simulated. The difficulty of carrying out such a conception of dissolution in a scene in the course of which such matters have to be dealt with as the final sentence of Nemours, and an interview with Coitier the leech, who comes from a dungeon with the rest of fetters on his wrist, at the summons of a king who sent him there, must be extreme; but Mr. Irving triumphantly surmounts it, and gives a picture of gradual and placid yet horrible death such as we believe has never been achieved before. Perhaps the greatest success of all is the still and silent impassibility into which the king sinks so absolutely that the courtiers and his son suppose it to be death. The actual death is not placid. The king struggles on his feet, and falls forward on a cushion, with his head toward the audience, as the low murmur, "the King is dead, long live the King," proclaims the close of

the long, long struggle of a mind that seemed in-
domitable with the frailties and tortures to which
humanity can be a prey, and consoled by none of the
assuagements to which the sufferings are most indebted. Such, lit up in the earlier passages by infinite comedy and artistically elevated by several tragic
episodes of the highest power, is this famous impersonation.

The possibility of good acting in a bad play is familiar.
Less familiar is the fact that acting can actually change the
genre of a piece, turning cheap melodrama, for example,
into high melodrama, even at times turning high melodrama into a kind of tragedy. An instance of the latter is
The Bells, by Leopold Lewis, as performed by Irving.
According to the original conception, the protagonist was a
villain. Irving, in part by changes in the script, but much
more by his production, turned him into a good man with
a weak spot.

More important here is the fact that acting lends itself to
certain effects not attained by any other art. That a
playwright's fantasies are mediated by actual human
beings changes the psychology of the whole communication. A Leopold Lewis may have got very little of life into
his words, but if the words come to us from the lips of Sir
Henry Irving, we confront living, breathing mankind in a
more direct way than in any mere words whatsoever. In the
theatre our contact with the actor is our primary experience. Only a person who is not at home in a theatre can
disregard the actor and, as it were, look right through him
at the author's lines. It is not enough to say that the actor is
a sort of co-author. He has certain means at his disposal
which no author can command. The least important

among these are mere audibility and visibility. What matters is presence.

What a person says in a letter is one thing; his presence in a room is another. A presence is not just seen and heard; it is sensed. One never "feels the same" when one knows someone else is present. Hence the shock if one suddenly discovers one is not alone. Now, if this is true of any presence, what of presences of unusual potency? For, obviously, people differ in the degree to which their presence imposes itself. In theatre criticism, power of presence is the chief meaning of the word *personality*.

Acting begins with the fact of such power, and becomes dynamic in the use of it. The extreme case of such use would be that an actor should literally hypnotize his audience. I haven't heard that a case was ever recorded, yet there is a *degree* of hypnotism in all acting. I would not say that acting is good to the extent that it is hypnotic, but only that it is *melodramatic* to the degree that it is hypnotic. Hypnotic acting plays a role in melodrama not unlike that of the magically hostile environment, and, while environment is the novelist's speciality, acting is the specialty of the theatre art. By its means, audiences have been able to obtain certain experiences—on the lowest estimate, certain thrills—which they could not duplicate by reading a book.

Once we see the hypnotic character of melodramatic theatre we see in a new light the fact that this theatre often actually presents cases of hypnotic and kindred states of mind. Baffling as is Richard III's scene with Lady Anne to victims of modern Naturalism, it is a characteristically hypnotic piece of melodrama. Lewis's *The Bells,* in many ways so crude, reaches its climax in a brilliant exploitation of hypnotism. The protagonist is not the hypnotist but the hypnotized. While hypnotizing his audience, Sir Henry

Irving is hypnotized by a fellow actor. We, the hypnotized spectators, identify ourselves with the hypnotized protagonist. In this example we see, not the actor's contribution as such, but its contribution to a larger pattern. Unsubtle in its dialogue, *The Bells* is extremely subtle in the relation that, given a great actor, it can establish with its audience. There is a primitive Pirandellianism in the fact that the relationship with the audience becomes part of the play itself by an analogy with the action presented on stage.

In the theatre, phenomena like Svengali or even Dracula are not eccentricities but prototypes. Though both of these characters happen to have been popular in fiction before they reached the stage, there is no comparison, in either case, between the potency of novel and acted play. Physical presence on the stage makes an essential difference here. It is not in the quiet of libraries, bedrooms, or kitchens that devotees of hypnosis or bloodsucking shriek and swoon. It is in the theatre, where such carryings-on constitute a tradition reaching back to the Greeks. And, while Irving could amuse himself heaping Pelion on Ossa by adding a story's hypnotism to his own, in general, characters like Svengali and Dracula become less and less necessary as the power of the actor himself increases. Edmund Kean could make Lord Byron faint and women give birth prematurely without such aid from the plot.

Incidentally, while his posthumous name is that of a Shakespearean actor, in his own day Kean was just as much a hero of popular melodrama. Was his procedure not precisely to infuse and inflame the Shakespearean text with his sense of the melodramatic? Which, if one is free of the vulgar prejudice against melodrama, will not seem a mistaken or paltry procedure. Time and again we witness the failure of the nonmelodramatic rendering of Shakespeare. The gain made by Granville-Barker's generation in taste and good sense and literacy was a loss in sheer theatricality. It was therefore a loss for the drama—tragic or melodramatic. In rejecting bad melodramatic acting, the twentieth century has fallen into the error of condemning melodramatic acting as such, and today the task of the actors is to rediscover and recreate a lost grandeur.

THE THEATRICAL OCCASION

WE KNOW that we do not know ourselves very well, and we sense that this makes it impossible for us to know others very well, but we never resign ourselves to either of these misfortunes. Our identifications of ourselves with others, and our attempts to create for ourselves new fathers, mothers, and siblings out of those we meet, make of our lives one long attempt to reverse the universal failure. The novel and the play offer us identifications and substitutions of the highest emotional interest, and to some of us the drama is especially attractive—not least because it concentrates on these identifications and substitutions.

I have just mentioned another reason: that a play takes place in a theatre, where the identifications and substitutions are presented as actual flesh and blood, the flesh and blood of actors. The phenomenon is complex. We can begin to understand it by looking at its own beginnings: the fact of the actor's presence on the stage and the need we feel for his company.

What is it to want company? It seems a good deal less in

moral status and emotional range than to want friendship, let alone love. And yet it is a far more insistent and elemental need. Company may indeed be what tiny children are really craving when our high-toned culture says they crave love. For a child, someone's mere presence lifts "The heavy and the weary weight/Of all this unintelligible world." It may even be very nice, from the child's standpoint, if that someone does *not* bring love but entertainment—if, for instance, he tells jokes or wears funny hats or knows a conjuring trick or two. The actor is in the first instance company, and we thank him for the pleasure of it.

But he is company of a very peculiar kind. I enjoy his company but he does not enjoy mine. He does not even know I am there. And this is agreeable to me, and partially accounts for the whole complex. In life, one is often lonely, and yet when company comes, one feels put out, "crowded." While life will never let one have anything both ways, it is the mission of art to do just that. And here one finds the theatre assuaging one's loneliness without imposing the pest of company. The actor cannot pick one out of the audience and speak to one. If that ever does happen—when, for example, a comedian picks on a spectator—this is specifically an aggression against the convention, an exception that proves the rule. Having the actors' company, it is a pleasure not to have to do anything about it, to be polite, to respond visibly, and so on. In the theatre, one does not have to be grateful, because one's gratitude has been paid off in cash beforehand, as in houses of even worse repute.

One's relations with the other members of the audience are equally ambiguous. Here one is, sitting down with total strangers to share experiences of considerable intimacy. It is rather promiscuous of one. To what was said above of voyeurism should be added that it is the voyeurism of the orgy, a collective voyeurism à la Fanny Hill. The "guilty creatures" who sit "at a play" are pooling their guilt: there is complicity among them. To do such things brings its special *Schadenfreude,* as experts have noted. Hanns Sachs, for example, refers all such experiences back to a child's way of getting another child to enter into his daydreams and share his guilt. The title of Sachs' monograph is itself enough to suggest a theory of theatre: *Gemeinsame Tagträume*—"Daydreams Held in Common."

Then there is one's relation to other members of one's own party in particular. Is it sociable to invite people to the theatre? The motive is likely to be in part sociable but can just as easily be in part antisocial. One is relieved of the responsibility, after all, not only of talking to the actors, but of talking to one's friends. Once the curtain is up, in what sense is one even still "with them"?

In what sense, indeed, is one there at all? Who, at the theatre, is related how to whom? For a couple of hours, I bask in the pleasure of my friends' company, I also relax in the pleasure of their imagined absence, while I turn my attention to a brief romance I am enjoying with —did I say actors? It is actually the characters I am experiencing, and the actors will drop their roles at eleven o'clock and become characters I do not know, handing me back to my friends who suddenly are very much "there" again. Beware of confusion! Gentlemen who rush to the stage door and insist on making the acquaintance of the leading lady may not be strong enough to face the consequences. Marry her they may (they often have), but if they believe themselves to be marrying the lady in the play, and are only interested in marrying the lady in the play, then divorce follows, and they must pursue their will-o'-the-wisp elsewhere.

One begins to feel like a ghost as one tries to figure out one's own place in this scheme of things, but how much more ghostly is the actor's experience! His temptation to love the leading lady is much greater; for one thing his chances are better, and he knows it. But he is no less prone than the spectator to confuse her with her stage roles. That is one reason why the divorce rate in the acting profession is high. Then there is the actor's relation to his audience. I have said he cannot relate himself to any of us personally, but impersonally he has a (for him) almost overwhelming relation with us. He may even have entered the acting profession from his need of this relationship. "The need to be loved," he and his psychiatrist call it. There are directors in the New York theatre who invite actors to pour out "love, *real* love" into the auditorium. The hope is that the audience will reciprocate. And it actually can respond with a warmth that has as good a claim to the word love as what the actor feels. Still, how ghostly! If we individual spectators are not the objects of this love, who is? Where in the auditorium does the amorous outpouring actually land? If the actor's role is a ghost, an audience is a ghost of a ghost. At eleven o'clock, when the actor drops his role, he stands revealed as a man, but when the audience drops *its* role, it vanishes. These people leaving the theatre are not "audience": they are Smith and Jones to whom the actor did *not* address himself.

To say that the theatrical occasion points up the problem of illusion and reality, confusing us as to which is which and where we stand in it all, would be a gross understatement. The theatrical occasion is a supreme instance of such confusion; and Pirandello is its philosopher.

PLAY, PLAY-ACTING, ACTING

THE GREATEST PART of our energy is expended in repeating what we and others have done many times before. To all appearances the aim of life is to make sure that tomorrow shall duplicate today. The same round of little duties and meals, followed by the same spell in bed! Our early education had only this kind of thing in mind. Toilet training was at first to repeat what our elders did, and later to repeat what we ourselves had begun to do. To learn language was nothing if not to repeat what the others said. To learn gesture was to repeat what the others did with their arms. So much indeed would seem to be necessary to the life process. But as if this were not enough of repetition, we add more. Repetition is a leading feature of our pleasures too. To learn a little dance is to learn a small figure which is then repeated *ad libitum*. We learn a tune in order to sing it a thousand times, not to mention that in most songs the theme is repeated even within one verse. We attach prestige to repetition. "Solemn occasions" are occasions on which oft-repeated words and music are repeated again. Ritual would not be itself if not constantly repeated. And so, if life is action, it should not seem surprising that play-acting—going through our actions again—is a universal art.

Of this art it can confidently be said that, if it became extinct, it would be re-invented again by children of two and three. Children of that age, giving up as hopeless the notion of being grownups on the full scale, become little imitation grownups and, as such, play-actors in the human comedy. This can be regarded, and often has been, as part of the educational process. We learn to grow up by pretending to be grown-up. To which some psychologists add that play-acting in children is also experimental. This means not only that we acquire (for example) a grown-up vocabulary by repeating the grown-up vocabulary but that the world of play is a workshop or laboratory for experiment by trial and error. There is no doubt a defensive side to it as well. Not having mastered the "real" world, by play-acting we construct a refuge from it, a haven whose inviolability we jealously guard.

Play, play-acting, acting: it is hard, in observing three-year-old children, to say where play leaves off and play-acting begins. Pure play would seem to belong more especially to a later age where rules are understood and adhered to. Games are a kind of abstract art, all geometry and numbers. What the three-year-olds mostly do has an element of pretending in it, and so of play-acting: there is a role and there is a drama. But it is not acting because there is no audience: it is not there to be looked at, noted, appreciated, enjoyed. Children, notoriously, are audience-conscious, they wish to be noted, appreciated, enjoyed, but what they at first exhibit to their audience is precisely not their make-believe dramas but their conquests of "reality." If the grownup is to be included in the drama he must be included as a fellow actor, not observing the fantasy, but entering into it. Only when the impulse to play-act is combined with the impulse to be watched and appreciated can a child be said to be not just play-acting but acting.

It would be a naïve psychology indeed that saw acting as a device of childhood to be later discarded. "All the world's a stage, and all the men and women merely players," or, in the words written up at the Globe Theatre: *totus mundus facit histrionem*—"all the world plays the actor." Even everyday talk concedes that grown people are often "just acting," "putting on an act," "doing a song and dance," and the Germans even say: *"Machen Sie keine Oper!"*—"Don't make an opera!" The limitation of this popular understanding of acting in everyday life is that it is marked with disapproval, applies only to hypocritical activity, and presupposes that most action is not acting. More sophisticated opinion allows that acting tends to characterize human behavior in general. Indeed to make this allowance in Anglo-Saxon countries is itself to *be* sophisticated, since our tradition in these matters is puritanic and philistine. It is for an Irishman like Shaw to tell us that the actor is the least hypocritical of men since he alone admits he is acting. It is for Irishmen like Wilde and Yeats to explain to us that our choice is not between mask and face, but between bad masks and good. And it is for the Spaniard Santayana, as provoked by Boston and Harvard, to represent, with hauteur, that the mask is the only alternative to the fig leaf, the fig leaf being "only a more ignominious mask."

> In this world [says Santayana in the *Soliloquies in England*], we must institute conventional forms of expression or else pretend that we have nothing to express.

And again:

> What . . . could be more splendidly sincere than the impulse to play in real life, to rise on the rising wave of every feeling and let it burst, if it will, into the foam of exaggeration? Life is not a means, the mind is not a slave nor a photograph: it has a right to enact a pose, to assume a panache, and to create what prodigious allegories it will for the mere sport and glory

of it. . . . To embroider upon experience is not to bear false witness against one's neighbor, but to bear true witness to oneself.

Such a philosophy, which might be traced all the way back to a passage in Plato's *Laws*, makes us see play, play-acting, and acting, not only as natural and childish, but also as a human achievement and an adult goal. If, as phenomena of childhood, they seem to clinicians merely the preparation for unplayful adulthood, the philosopher can question the value of unplayfulness—that Puritanic notion of maturity—and place at the goal of experience a renewed childhood, a second playfulness, a regained innocence. Such an idea has even as good a claim to orthodoxy as the contrary, Puritan notion (latterly adopted more, perhaps, by scientific than religious folk), for what is the traditional conception of heavenly bliss? Its image, in its familiar if vulgar form, is that of angels sitting, harp in hand, on clouds—angels playing, angels performing. Condemned, as we may see ourselves, to eat bread in the sweat of our brow, we do so only in the hope of a celestial songfest or heavenly hootenanny.

PSYCHODRAMA

To BID US, as Shaw, Wilde, Yeats, and Santayana do, find the splendid mask, or the appropriate one, is counsel of perfection. Most of us are condemned, by "life" or by ourselves, to fig leaf—or inadequate mask. We do not live well. Life is a drama; but we cannot play our role properly.

This malfunctioning, studied in the past by priest and moralist, has been the special study, in our time, of the physician. And the doctors, especially those of certain schools, have observed and accepted the human tendency to take this world as a theatre. In Freudian psychoanalysis, the therapist is assigned all the co-starring roles by the patient, who is of course the star, and a grand re-enactment of childhood scenes takes place, five acts a week for as long as neurosis, or money, or patience lasts.

One celebrated therapist, J. L. Moreno, objects to the Freudian procedure on the grounds (if I may paraphrase him) that it is not nearly theatrical enough. "The mind is a stage," one reporter on Moreno's procedure has said. Moreno finds the silent, unseen, note-taking man behind the couch too undramatic; likewise, the talkative fellow on the couch, his eyes on the ceiling, saying all the things he daren't say into anyone's face. Life is a successful piece of theatre in which people sit and stand as they will, in which dialogue is reciprocal, in which people gesticulate *at* each other, and look each other in the eye, whether from interest, affection or dislike. Living is to exist with all these means of direct personal communication working spontaneously. Neurosis, or failing to live, is to exist without such spontaneity, with fears and hates that interfere so much that (at an extreme) one either runs away from the other person or assaults him. Moreno accordingly argues that no cure can be attempted without making the patient work directly on the drama he wishes to live. How is that possible? A drama has a number of characters in it. What about the others beside the patient? Moreno appeals to the principle of theatre itself: substitution of one person for another, role playing. The therapist is assigned roles, not merely, as in Freudian procedure, in the patient's imagination, but physically, upon a stage. Auxiliary therapists take stage to fill other parts. The patient has to confront them,

186

and not in reconstructions of the past only, as in the reconstruction of crimes by the police, but in scenes arising newly and now. All this (to complete the theatrical circuit) with other patients watching—i.e., unshielded from "the others," taking place in society, in the world.

The instinctive reaction of each of us is: "*I* could never do that, I'd sink through the floor!" But it has been found that people, after a "warming up" period, can "do that," and that there is no great problem about getting people's family dramas enacted, spontaneously and vigorously, upon Dr. Moreno's "psychodramatic" stage. What therapeutic success has been attained by the method is not the question here, nor shall I go into Moreno's preference for his "real" dramas to the dramas written by playwrights. I have set down this description of what I understand psychodrama to be because it offers the most vivid evidence imaginable of the intimate link between theatre and life. Even if the therapeutic results were small, one could scarcely doubt that Moreno is "on to" something. Schopenhauer always maintained that "the drama is the most perfect reflection of human existence" and I must confess I had always read that sentence as a bit of magniloquence until it was made real for me by a reading of Moreno.

Readers for whom Moreno is an eccentric, especially if they are of a sociological turn of mind, might profit more from Erving Goffman's *The Presentation of Self in Everyday Life*. In this book, a sociologist interprets our daily conduct as an attempt to present oneself in a particular light, to "make an impression." The tendency of this approach is inevitably toward the notation of hypocrisies and the critique of what David Riesman calls "outer-directed" personality. Goffman's book is a counterblast to the public-relations handbooks with titles like *The Magic*

Power of Emotional Appeal, in one of which I found a section telling me how to make my smiles audible over the telephone. Of more value in the present context is Goffman's endorsement of Santayana on masks. In presenting our "self" to others, we do not have the pleasant and easy choice between a Real Self and a Madison Avenue False Self. There are very many possibilities, and most of us avail ourselves of a considerable number, playing different roles at different times and before different people. Similarly, when we think we are expressly *not* putting ourselves over but being discreet and self-effacing, we are putting ourselves over as discreet and self-effacing fellows. Taciturnity is inverse volubility. Silence, in company, is not a nothing, but a something, and at that a something done to others, whether in deference or defiance. One of the most far-reaching remarks of Freud is to the effect that people *will* betray themselves, will give themselves away. They wish to do this, though they think they don't, and so they willingly fail to accomplish their apparent and worldly "objective" aims in order—to "present themselves." Though it lead to the gallows, we will not deny ourselves the pleasure of saying, before the curtain is down, "Very well, inspector, yes: I *am* the demon barber of Fleet Street." Here one glimpses the connection between theatricality and the universal "compulsion to confess."

IL GIUOCO DELLE PARTI

IN LITERATURE ITSELF, the classical treatment of this theme of "drama in everyday life" is Pirandello's. He went much further than Mr. Goffman, and spoke, not just of *presenting* oneself, but of *constructing* oneself. That is the positive side of Pirandellian philosophy: Pirandello even bolstered his admiration of Mussolini with the suggestion that the Duce had excelled us all in "self-construction." But the source of the whole conception lay less in thought than in experience, and painful experience at that, so that it is the negative side of the philosophy that is active in Pirandello's art. The great question raised in his plays is: where does fact leave off and fiction begin? What is true, what is only imagined? What is life, what is drama? What is real, what is play-acting? At times an out-and-out skepticism is proposed—Gabriel Marcel calls it the most radical skepticism ever propounded—but, perforce, if Pirandello was to create plots and characters at all, this skepticism had often to be left in abeyance, so that distinctions between, say, sane and insane could retain some objective reference. It is only because the distinctions do still mean something that the paradoxes have a point. Even *Right You Are,* where at the end one is invited, at least in jest, to accept a mystical rejection of elementary logic, depends throughout on the distinction between sane and insane remaining meaningful and even clear-cut.

Still, the ending of *Right You Are* is a paean of praise to role-playing, to the theatrical view of life, for what it says is: whatever the veiled lady's lost birth certificate may have had on it, her significant identity is that of daughter to the old lady, wife to the executive secretary. She plays the role each wishes her to play. Everyone would agree that this is most feminine of her, and Pirandello is adding that he considers it most human and right. Which is an extension into ethics of Santayana's merely esthetic defense of role playing. For while Santayana is saying that to take up a role gives us *panache,* Pirandello is saying that it is morally praiseworthy. What passes for our "real" identity is something the veiled lady would only stick to out of false pride. Cordelia in *King Lear* sticks at first to her image of herself as one who does not flatter, and who has cause to be hostile to Father. Later, Cordelia melts, loses this identity, and becomes "as he would desire her," all affection and solicitude: "no cause, no cause." Pirandello's veiled lady, all love and duty, can say: "To myself I am no one."

If willingness to accept the role imposed by another can be a virtue, the determination to impose a role upon another is a vice. It is also based on unsound psychology, and its victims will say so. The most agonized of them is the Father in *Six Characters* who feels he has been hung on the peg of that single moment when he stood exposed as Lechery Incarnate before his own stepdaughter. But Pirandello's critics have generally overstressed the psychological and epistemological side, and missed the moral side. The radical skepticism does not extend to ethics. Rather, Pirandello has contrived to derive a firm ethics from the very lack of firmness all around. *Just because* all is so uncertain, including our own identities, we need consolation, we need pretexts for affection. These pretexts are the roles we play. The veiled lady is saying: "I don't know what anything is or who anyone is. I don't know who I myself am. The more reason to be willing to be anyone, assume any role, that would ease the pain in one's loved ones." Pain, love: these things are not doubted. Hence the legitimacy of a kind of categorical imperative: play any role that would reduce the pain, enlarge the area of love. Santayana's histrionism is intellectual and sanguine, Pirandello's emotional and desperate.

Drama and life have so much in common, they can easily get confused. In Pirandello's *Tonight We Improvise,* an actress feels herself disturbed by enacting a death scene: art has invaded life, a little fictional death has entered into nonfictional life, and caused a tremor, a qualm, a premonition. Simple! But not without far-reaching implications. The tremor has not (that we know of) been created in the actress we see in the theatre. The role of the actress is being played by an actress who has presumably not felt such a tremor. The paradox is stated even more forcibly in *Six Characters* where characters are offset by actors, and the point is made that actors can never attain to the reality of characters. In the show we witness, however, the characters are also played by actors. Hence the thesis of the play is refuted by the performance of the play, unless we assume that the actors are *failing* to play the characters, in which case the performance is a failure. Since we cannot believe that Pirandello intended all performances of his play to be failures, we must abide by the notion of a contradiction between the play and the idea of the play. This contradiction is not so much resolved as validated by Pirandello's view of life: we men can only play roles, we cannot just be. We can conceive of creatures who just are, but we cannot be them, we can only enact them. Hence the paradox of the six characters who just are, yet whose "being" cannot be communicated to us except through enactment. For us then, the enactment, not the thing acted, remains the ultimate term. Simulation is the only thing not simulated. Pretense is the ultimate reality.

In a sense, the possibility of a perfect performance of *Six Characters* is excluded from the start, for it would be one in which we lose the sense that the "Six" are acted parts at all. Perhaps at moments we can and do lose this sense, but we are quick, as a little time passes, to realize that this could only be because the six roles are so well—acted. We cannot forget for more than a moment that the roles are acted or we take leave of our senses. Like the man who jumps on stage to save Desdemona from Othello, we would leap forward to warn the stepdaughter that "that man there" is her stepfather. Yet, supposing the "Six" roles are superbly acted, do we not hasten to say that it is just as if six characters had walked on stage without assistance from Actors Equity? If we do, the key words are: *as if*. For only these two small words separate us from lunacy, and the play from dissolving into chaos. We get Pirandello's idea because it is *not* incarnate. He gives it to us at a remove. However powerful the illusion, we see it through a glass darkly. One might call Pirandello the last of the Platonists and say he is showing us the shadows in Plato's cave. For, just as in Plato, it is shadows or nothing, so in Pirandello it is the enactment, the improvisation, the play, or nothing. And whether or not he convinces us of his general view of things, whether indeed, as the years pass, his philosophy as such retains any interest, he has created a living image which can never die—the image of man as actor and of life as the game of role-playing, *il giuoco delle parti*.

Part Two

DIFFERENT
KINDS
OF PLAYS

6

MELODRAMA

THE BAD NAME OF MELODRAMA

SOME TIME AGO I ran into a magazine article containing this comment on Joseph Conrad:

> One word comes before long to haunt the mind of any persistent reader of Conrad's stories—the word Melodrama. Why does he do it? What has he got against life? What is the purpose of all these feuds, assassinations, revealing plottings, these fearful disasters and betrayals. . . .

Not long afterwards I met with that passage again—quoted by a critic who proffers this answer to its queries: finding it difficult either to invent or report, Conrad has to derive his narratives from other narratives. "To such a temperament," writes our critic, " 'drama' is an alternative to dramatic life." And an example is provided. It has recently

195

come to seem highly likely that the young Conrad tried to kill himself, and for what might be called prosaic reasons— "depression, bad health, and a financial mess." Instead of reporting the drab sequence of events, Conrad made out of it a melodrama of love and honor. The struggle within himself became in fiction a fight between two distinct persons.

The question why Conrad "does it" and what he "has got against life" are in greater need of explanation, surely, than his procedure. Only under the influence of a narrow and philistine Naturalism can we ask why an artist shows life at a remove and in some established genre. The transposition of an inner struggle to a duel between persons does not even need a convention to carry it: such changes are made nightly by everyone in his dreams. If one can make of one's tussles with suicidal wishes a drama of love and honor, one has given to private and chaotic material a public and recognizable form. One has made art out of fantasy and pain. One has found the link between emotion and civilized values. One has achieved universality.

All this, of course, would have been readily granted by our two critics but for the particular vehicle (form, convention) which Conrad chose: melodrama. It has a bad reputation—and that is the worst thing a word can have in the literary world just as it is the worst thing a man can have in the social world.

Where did this bad reputation come from? It is, I think, substantially the bad reputation of popular Victorian melodrama. Now it is unfair to judge anything by its weakest link, but it is not unfair to ask: how weak is its weakest link? What is the least that anyone would ask of a melodrama? As apt an answer as any is: a good cry. The contempt implied in terms like sob stuff and tear jerker is not more interesting than the very wide appeal of the thing despised.

An inquiry into melodrama—the appeal of melodrama—can legitimately start with a thought or two about tears.

IN PRAISE OF SELF-PITY

WHAT does it mean: to weep? Laughter has engaged the attention of many brains, among them some of the best. A brief search in book indexes and library catalogues calls attention to an extensive literature. Tears are a relatively unexplored ocean.

One reason why laughter has had a better press must be the obvious one: that laughter is (or is held to be) pleasant, whereas weeping is (or is held to be) unpleasant. Laughter is also something one gets a good mark for. What tired orator does not expatiate on the benefits of a sense of humor? To weep, on the other hand, is something that little boys are assiduously taught not to do. Women are greater realists: they will speak of having a good cry. The phrase points to perhaps the commonest function of tears: they are a mechanism for working off emotion—commonly, quite superficial emotion. But there are tears and tears. Crying your heart out is a matter of deep emotion. Then there are tears of joy. "Excess of sorrow laughs," says Blake, "excess of joy weeps." Shaw put it this way:

> Tears in adult life are the natural expression of happiness as laughter is at all ages the natural recognition of destruction, confusion, and ruin.

*   *   *

197

The tears shed by the audience at a Victorian melodrama come under the heading of a good cry. They might be called the poor man's catharsis, and as such have a better claim to be the main objective of popular melodrama than its notorious moral pretensions. Besides referring to superficial emotion, the phrase "having a good cry" implies feeling sorry for oneself. The pity is self-pity. But, for all its notorious demerits, self-pity has its uses. E. M. Forster even says it is the only thing that makes bearable the feeling of growing old—in other words, that it is a weapon in the struggle for existence. Self-pity is a very present help in time of trouble, and all times are times of trouble.

Once we have seen that our modern antagonism to self-pity and sentiment goes far beyond the rational objections that may be found to them, we realize that even the rational objections are in some measure mere rationalization. Attacks on false emotion often mask a fear of emotion as such. Ours is, after all, a thin-lipped, thin-blooded culture. Consider how, in the past half-century, the prestige of dry irony has risen, while that of surging emotion has fallen. This is a cultural climate in which a minor writer like Jules Laforgue can rate higher than a major one like Victor Hugo. Or think of our changed attitude to death. Would any age but this receive the death of admired persons "with quiet understatement"? We may think that Mr. Auden pours his heart out in his good poem on the death of Yeats, but just compare Mr. Auden's poem with the product of more old-fashioned culture, say, with Garcia Lorca's "Lament for the Death of Ignacio Mejias"! Would even Lorca's title be possible in English? Is lamenting something we can imagine ourselves doing? On the contrary we modernize the Greek tragedies by deleting all variants of "woe is me." If Christ and Alexander the Great came back to life, we would teach them to restrain their tears.

Once I did see death done justice to. An Italian actor came on stage to announce the death of a colleague. He did indeed lament. He shook, he wept, he produced streams of passionate rhetoric, until the audience shook, and wept, and lamented with him. Now that is self-pity, certainly. One is not sorry for a corpse; one is sorry for oneself, deprived; and in the background is the fear of one's own death. But so much the better for self-pity. The experience was had, not refused.

The point has some importance for mental health. Modern psychiatry begins with those *Studies on Hysteria* in which Freud and Breuer try to explain what happens when emotional impressions are not allowed to wear themselves out. The shock of pain craves to be relieved and released by cries and writhings and tears. Good little boys who keep still and quiet under a rain of blows may pay for their stoicism twenty years later on a therapist's couch. Their resentments, instead of being worn away by a natural process, have been hoarded in the Unconscious.

If you have dismissed tears and loud lamentation from your daily life, you might check whether they are equally absent from your dreams at night. You may be no more sentimental than the next man, and yet find you have many dreams in which you weep profusely and at the same time disport yourself like an actor in the old melodrama: throwing yourself on your knees, raising your arms plaintively to heaven, and so forth. For you, in that case, grandiose self-pity is a fact of life. As it can only be copied by the use of grandiose style, the grandiosity of melodrama would seem to be a necessity.

PITY AND FEAR

I HAVE BEEN DEFENDING melodrama in its weakest link, for certainly self-pity is only valuable up to a point in life and only tolerable up to a point on the stage. Pity for the "hero" is the less impressive half of melodrama; the other and more impressive half is fear of the villain. Pity and fear: it was Aristotle in his *Poetics* who coupled them, and tried to give an account of the total effect of tragedy in these terms. It seems an oversimplification. In tragedy, most of us now feel, more is involved. Is more involved in melodrama? Is not working on the audience's capacity for pity and fear the alpha and omega of the melodramatist's job? In his *Rhetoric,* Aristotle explains that pity and fear have an organic relation to each other. An enemy or object of terror is presupposed in both cases. If it is we who are threatened, we feel fear for ourselves; if it is others who are threatened, we feel pity for them. One might wish to carry this analysis a little further in the light of the fact that most pity is self-pity. We are identified with those others who are threatened; the pity we feel for them is pity for ourselves; and by the same token we share their fears. We pity the hero of a melodrama because he is in a fearsome situation; we share his fears; and, pitying ourselves, we pretend that we pity him. To rehearse these facts is to put together the dramatic situation of the characteristic popular melodrama: goodness beset by badness, a hero beset by a villain, heroes and heroines beset by a wicked world.

Pity represents the weaker side of melodrama, fear the stronger. Perhaps the success of a melodramatist will always depend primarily upon his power to feel and project fear. Feeling it should be easy, for fear is the element we live in. "We have nothing to fear but fear itself" is not a cheering slogan because fear itself is the most indestructible of obstacles. Therein lies the potential universality of melodrama.

Human fears are of two kinds. One belongs to the common-sense world: it is reasonable in the everyday sense to fear that one might slip on ice or that an airplane might crash. The other kind of fear—perhaps none too rationally—is called irrational. Savage superstitions, neurotic fantasies, and childhood imaginings spring to mind, and equally outside the bounds of common sense is the fear of God. Superstition and religion, neurosis and infantility are in the same boat.

Melodrama sometimes uses the "irrational" type of fear in such a direct form as that of Frankenstein's monster or Dracula. More often it lets irrational fear masquerade as the rational: we are given reasons to fear the villain, but the fear actually aroused goes beyond the reasons given. Talent in melodramatic writing is most readily seen in the writer's power to make his human villain seem superhuman, diabolical. Historically the villains in our tradition stem from the archvillain Lucifer, and a good deal of recent Shakespeare scholarship has been illustrating in detail the possible derivation of *Richard III* from the medieval Vice. The illustrations are nice to have; the principle was clear in advance. But where the villains stem from is relatively unimportant. What matters is whether a given writer can actually endow his villain with some of the original energy. We must catch a glimpse of hell flame, a whiff of the sulphur. This we do in even a comic work if the sense of horror is profound enough—as in Kleist's *The Broken Jug*. Among modern writers it must be admitted that the novelists—Melville or Emily Brontë—have been better diabolists than the playwrights. The stage villains, despite their reputation, have not been too monstrously evil. If their imprecations have seemed ludicrous, it is because the evil is not more than skin-deep. A villain shouldn't have to work too hard at villainy.

Because the drama tends to concentrate its vision in a few persons, it will tend to embody evil in a few villains, and often in a single one. This is not to say that it has no other resource. Melodramatic vision is paranoid: we are being persecuted, and we hold that all things, living and dead, are combining to persecute us. Or rather, nothing is dead. Even the landscape has come to life if only to assault us. Perhaps one might sense something of this vision behind Birnam Wood's coming to Dunsinane in *Macbeth,* even though the playwright provides soldiers to carry it. For Emily Brontë, at any rate, the Yorkshire moors and the Yorkshire weather are "the very devil"—just as much as her villain, Heathcliffe. Popular Victorian melodrama made extensive use of bad weather and dangerous landscape. High seas and deep chasms threaten to swallow our hero up. The very fact that I describe such events as "swallowing up" shows that a little of the animism rubs off, even on a critic.

It is amazing what the nineteenth-century stage could do in the presentation of raging seas, mountains, glaciers, frozen lakes, and the like, yet there were always much narrower limits than in a novel, and the playwright had to reinforce the hostility of landscape with other hostilities. "Melodramatic" artifices of plot come under this head, and particularly that notorious device: outrageous coincidence. It is often by virtue of this feature that melodrama is differentiated from tragedy, the argument being that the melodramatic procedure is too frivolous. Yet there are some particularly gross examples in the supreme tragedies, and, in general, outrageous coincidence, when not frivolously used, has no frivolous effect. It intensifies the effect of paranoia. It enlists circumstances in the enemy's ranks— as Strindberg did in real life when several little incidents conspired to deprive him of his absinthe on several successive occasions. It represents a projection of "irrational" fear.

EXAGGERATION

THE LONG ARM of coincidence is a freakish thing. Mention it and within a minute someone will use the word exaggeration. This brings us back both to the prejudice against melodrama and to the essence of melodrama itself. Like farce, this genre may be said, not to tumble into absurdity by accident, but to revel in it on purpose. To question the absurd in it is to challenge, not the conclusion, but the premise. In both genres, the writer enjoys a kind of *Narrenfreiheit*—the fool's exemption from common sense —and what he writes must be approached and judged accordingly.

We are accustomed to acknowledge only a slight degree of exaggeration in the artistic reproduction of life—just enough, we tell ourselves, to sharpen an outline. The image in our minds is of portraits in which the painter renders the appearances much as we think we have seen them ourselves, though we permit him a ten per cent deviation because he's an artist. But suppose the deviation from common sense grows much greater? Is the picture necessarily getting worse all the time? No, but for exaggerations which are no longer slight but gross, we require another criterion. A difference of degree turns into a difference of kind. Of a melodramatist whom we disapprove, we must not say: "You have exaggerated too much," but: "You have exaggerated awkwardly, mechanically." We might even have to say: "You have exaggerated too little," for in an age of Naturalism a writer's courage sometimes fails him and he tries to pass off a tame duck as a beast of the jungle.

The exaggerations will be foolish only if they are empty of feeling. Intensity of feeling justifies formal exaggeration in art, just as intensity of feeling creates the "exaggerated" forms of childhood fantasies and adult dreams. It is as children and dreamers—one might melodramatically add: as neurotics and savages too—that we enjoy melodrama. Exaggeration of what? Of the facts as seen by the sophisticated, scientific, adult mind. The primitive, neurotic, childish mind does not exaggerate its own impressions.

What is a giant? A man, eighteen feet high. An exaggeration surely? Someone has multiplied by three. What is a giant? A grownup as seen by a baby. The baby is two feet high, the grownup, six. The ratio *is* one to three. There is no exaggeration.

There is a very fine French film, *Zero for Conduct,* in which school teachers are seen through children's eyes. They seemed enormous and distorted at times because the camera has been placed near their feet. People called the result stylization. The word suggests the sophisticated, the artificial, and the adult. What was done was naïve, natural, and infantile. The word "exaggeration" can be misleading.

There is something similar to say of the "grandiosity" of melodramatic acting. That we are all ham actors in our dreams means that melodramatic acting, with its large gestures and grimaces and its declamatory style of speech, is not an exaggeration of our dreams but a duplication of them. In that respect, *melodrama is the Naturalism of the dream life.* Nor is it only to our dreams that melodramatic acting corresponds. Civilization, as I have been saying, asks us to hide our feelings and even instructs us in the art of doing so. What feelings we cannot completely conceal we reduce to mere shadows of themselves. Hence the appositeness of the movie camera: it can see those minute movements of the features which are all that is left in civilized man of corporeal expression. When it enlarges them in close-ups ten or more feet high it is achieving the old melodramatic grandiosity in its own way and without the actors' assistance.

One of the principal emotions is Fear. What does it look like?

The heart beats wildly . . . there is a deathlike pallor; the breathing is labored; the wings of the nostrils are widely dilated; there is a gasping and convulsive motion of the lips, a tremor on the hollow cheek, a gulping and catching of the throat; the uncovered and protruding eyeballs are fixed on the object of terror; or they may roll restlessly from side to side. . . . The pupils are . . . enormously dilated. All the muscles of the body may become rigid or may be thrown into convulsive movements. The hands are alternately clenched and opened, often with a twitching movement. The arms may be protruded as if to avert some dreadful danger, or may be thrown wildly over the head.

What does Hatred look like?

> . . . intense frowning; eyes wide open; display of teeth; grinding teeth and contracting jaws; opened mouth with tongue advanced; clenched fists; threatening action of arms; stamping with the feet; deep inspirations—panting; growling and various cries; automatic repetition of one word or syllable; sudden weakness and trembling of voice . . . convulsion of lips and facial muscles, of limbs and trunk; acts of violence to one's self, as biting fists or nails; sardonic laughter; bright redness of face; sudden pallor of face; extreme dilation of nostrils; standing up of hair on head. . . .

Now someone might suppose I have been quoting descriptions of melodramatic acting. We today have certainly never thought of anyone but a stage villain grinding his teeth or giving vent to fiendish hate in a sardonic laugh. Actually, the first of these quotations is from Charles Darwin's book on the emotions, and the second is from an old Italian manual on the same subject. William James used to read both passages to his classes at Harvard, and they are preserved, where I myself found them, in his *Principles of Psychology*. If these are fair accounts of emotion, then melodrama is not so much exaggerated as uninhibited.

LANGUAGE

MELODRAMATIC DIALOGUE has been the object of more mockery, perhaps, than even the plots and the characters and the acting. Naturally, vulgar melodrama is couched in vulgar rhetoric, but the joke against this rhetoric remains a poor one if the assumption is made, and it usually is, that plain, colloquial English should have been used, and not a heightened form of the language. An elevated rhetoric is a legitimate and indeed inexorable demand of melodrama. Ordinary conversation would be incongruous and anti-climactic.

In any case, the Victorian rhetoric that makes us smile was not a new thing, created by Victorian melodramatists. It was the lag-end—the rags and tatters, if you will—of something that had once been splendid. Few would call the dialogue of Victor Hugo's plays good tragic poetry. But it is good rhetoric, as is the dialogue of the German *Sturm und Drang* drama from which French Romantic drama derives. In England the postmedieval drama begins with the establishment of a melodramatic rhetoric in Marlowe's *Tamburlaine,* and melodramatic rhetoric subserved tragedy, or declined into bombast or banality, or merely served its natural purpose as the proper style of melodrama, until about 1850.

Almost exactly at that date we find the old melodramatic order confronting the new Naturalistic one in what should be a classic instance. Turgenev wrote a play about a woman and her stepdaughter both in love with the same man. This play—*A Month in the Country*—inaugurates the era of natural, unmelodramatic dialogue. Now the writing of *A Month in the Country* was possibly prompted by a play of Balzac's on the same theme, *The Stepmother,* in which some may be surprised to find the great "realist" still using the melodramatic method in general and the melodramatic rhetoric in particular. Turgenev's work ends with a quiet separation and an equally quiet departure by coach; Balzac's with poisonings, lifetime punishments, an appeal to God, and a hint of insanity:

STEPDAUGHTER. I have been told all. This woman is innocent of the crime she is accused of. Religion has made me realize that pardon cannot be obtained on high by those who do not leave it behind them here below. I took the key of her desk from Madame. I myself went in search of poison. I myself tore off this piece of paper to wrap it in; for I wanted to die.

STEPMOTHER. Oh! Pauline! take my life, take all I love . . . Oh! doctor, save her!

STEPDAUGHTER. Do you know why I come to pull you out of the abyss you are in? Because Ferdinand has just told me something which has brought me back from the tomb. He has such horror of being with you in life, that he is following me—me—into the grave, where we shall rest together, married by death.

STEPMOTHER. Ferdinand! . . . Ah! God Above! At what price am I saved?

FATHER. But, unhappy child, why are you dying? Am I not, have I ceased for one moment to be a good father? They say it is I who am guilty . . .

YOUNG MAN. Yes, general. And it is I alone who can solve the riddle for you, and make clear to you how you are guilty.

FATHER. You, Ferdinand, you to whom I offered my daughter, you who love her . . .

YOUNG MAN. My name is Ferdinand, Count of Marcandal, son of General Marcandal . . . you understand?

GENERAL. Ah! Son of a traitor, you could bring under

my roof only death and treachery! . . . Defend
yourself!

YOUNG MAN. Will you fight, General, against a dead
man?

(*He falls.*)

STEPMOTHER (*rushes to the Young Man with a cry*).
Oh! (*She recoils before the father who advances toward his daughter; then she takes out a phial, but
throws it away at once*). Oh! No, I condemn myself
to live for this poor old man! (*The father kneels beside his dead daughter.*) Doctor, what is he doing?
. . . Could he be losing his reason? . . .

FATHER (*stammering like a man who cannot find the
words*). I . . . I . . . I . . .

DOCTOR. General, what are you doing?

GENERAL. I . . . I am trying to say a prayer for my
daughter! . . .

(*The curtain falls.*) *

I have picked a passage from a great writer lest anyone
be tempted to attribute the deficiencies of such writing to
lack of talent. Another mistake would be to think that the
advantage lies in every respect with Turgenev. In art, every
advantage is also a disadvantage. The gentleness of muted
strings and the majesty of the full orchestra cannot be
presented concurrently. Turgenev and Chekhov achieved
their special effects by foregoing others. Modern persons
will tend to attribute Balzac's failure to the absurdity of
the incidents: he piles on the agony till we smile. Yet this
diagnosis cannot be correct—Shakespeare piles on as much

---

* I have translated this afresh because the only translation I could find
was far more ponderous than the French. It renders "*coupable*" as "cul-
pable," "*l'abîme où vous êtes*" as "the abyss which had engulfed you," etc.
I have left out a couple of speeches, and given the characters appellations
calculated to help those who do not know the play.

agony and we do not smile. The failure is only one of a tired rhetoric that no longer gives to the events and situations sufficient support.

ZOLA AND AFTER

So, one could say, melodrama died with Balzac's generation, and Naturalism took its place in Turgenev's generation. As such generalizations go, it is not a bad one, but as such generalizations also go, it is misleading. What actually happened was both more curious and more complex. Naturalism did become the creed of the age. Its acceptance was indeed widespread, embracing most cultured people. It is a doctrine which I find present-day American students still regarding as the law of the Medes and Persians. The curious thing is that, while our age generally is dedicated to Naturalist principles, the outstanding writers of the age are forever protesting against them. The fact of the protest, and its frequency, proves the prevalence of the principles, right enough; but, going back over the record, it is amazing how *many* writers of how *many* different schools protested. It is even enlightening to learn what some of the champions of Naturalism actually did—and actually said.

Emile Zola, for instance, who is supposed to have killed melodrama and given birth to the Naturalistic philosophy. Hear him attack melodrama:

I defy the romantics to put on a cloak and dagger drama; the medieval clanking of old iron, the secret doors, poisoned wines and all the rest of it would convince no one. Melodrama, that middle class offspring of the romantic drama, is even more dead and no one wants it any more. Its false sentimentality, its complications of stolen children, recovered documents, its brazen improbabilities, have all brought it into such scorn that our attempt to revive it would be greeted with laughter. . . .

Any wish one might feel to demonstrate the merit of plots about stolen children and recovered documents is checked by the knowledge that Zola spoke under provocation of a thousand bad works of art. And note what, in this same preface to *Thérèse Raquin,* he proposes to replace bad melodrama with:

> I made the one dark room the setting for the play so that nothing should detract from its atmosphere and sense of fate. I chose ordinary, colorless, subsidiary characters to show the banality of every-day life behind the excruciating agonies of my chief protagonists. . . .

"Banality," "colorlessness"—certainly these belong to the naturalistic conception as generally understood. But a "sense of fate"? "Excruciating agonies"? And the banality only a foil to these extremities? At this point, one remembers what had been the effect of removing "banalities" from the Victorian melodrama. It had been to reduce the spectator's anxiety by relieving him of contact with his own life. By such a reduction, melodrama was becoming ever more boring and silly. What Zola is really doing is recharging the battery of fear which had been allowed to run down. The substitution of a banal (that is, recognizable) milieu for a "romantic" (that is, unacceptable) milieu is to play on the spectator's anxieties. True, Zola regarded his view of environment as scientific, but in those days science was itself the supreme romance, and here we find him calling for a sense of fate—which is what his own depiction of environment, like Ibsen's and Strindberg's incidentally—bears witness to. Technically, Zola's accounts of the milieu differ from Melville's or Emily Brontë's. He goes through a certain rigmarole—or ritual—of sociobiology, but he arrives at similar results. He is melodramatic.

The most pointed and prolonged polemic ever conducted against melodrama is to be found in the works of Bernard Shaw, prefaces and plays alike. *The Devil's Disciple* is the obvious, crude example, but in the preface to *Saint Joan,* nearly thirty years later, Shaw is still hammering away at the same point and arguing that the merit of his new play lies in its avoidance of melodrama. Notably, he has changed the character of the historical Bishop Cauchon so that the latter will no longer remind anyone of a stage villain.

Now Shaw's Cauchon is certainly at some distance from the snarling, gloating, swaggering villain of vulgar melodrama, but, for all Shaw's propaganda against the idea of villains, is he not still a villain, and even a traditional one? It was scarcely a new idea to make the devil witty, genial, and sophisticated. Actors take to the role of Cauchon, just because, if they are experienced, they have played it many times before. One *may* smile and smile and be a villain: one often does.

If Shaw hated the morals of melodrama—the projection upon the world of our irresponsible narcissistic fantasies—he loved its manners. Maybe any man only parodies what he is secretly fond of; maybe he is envious of the parodied author's prowess; or maybe he thinks he could outdo him. In any case, Shaw did not rest content with parody. After firing salvos at melodrama, he went on to steal its ammunition. As well as illustrating the limitations of melodrama,

The Devil's Disciple exemplifies its merits, and, in the critical writings of Shaw, though we do not find the *name* of melodrama held in honor, we find the melodramatic element honored under other names: such as opera.

Unlike most opera-goers of today, Shaw enjoyed opera as a form of theatre, rather than a kind of concert, and he entered enthusiastically into just those libretti which the twentieth century has decided are so much bosh—such as the libretti of *Rigoletto* and *Il Trovatore.* Nor is this enthusiasm extracurricular: Shaw's plays themselves call for the "exaggerated," sweeping movements of operatic (that is, melodramatic) performance. At one time Shaw had to stress and reiterate this point because his stage director, Granville-Barker, leaned toward the Naturalistic use of both voice and body. A photograph survives of Shaw showing Barker a little swordplay in *Androcles and the Lion.* On the picture Barker has achieved only a "small," nervous attitude, while Shaw is striking a flamboyant pose with his feet set wide apart and his sword held high in the air. His advice to Barker about his own form of theatre in general—"Remember that it's Italian opera"—we can translate: "Play it as melodrama."

The furthest that Shaw's playwriting ever got from melodrama was, I suppose, the "pure dialogue" of the "Don Juan in Hell" scene from *Man and Superman.* The cast is made up of a hero, a heroine, a villain, and a clown, a drama quartet which is said to have become standard in the hands of the French playwright Pixerécourt a hundred years earlier. Pixerécourt is listed in the textbooks as the founder of popular melodrama.

Since *Man and Superman* (1903) we have had various modernist schools of drama and various individual departures or one-man schools. The result of action and reaction, they present themselves as battling factions of contrasting conviction, yet it is impossible to mention one innovator of the period who was not trying to reintroduce the melodramatic. German Expressionism can be interpreted as the search for a modern dress for melodrama, Brecht's Epic Theatre as an attempt to use melodrama as a vehicle for Marxist thought. Cocteau, Anouilh, and Giraudoux have put the Greek myths to melodramatic use. Of the three, the most concentratedly melodramatic is Cocteau, perhaps because fear of persecution is his strongest emotion; in his *Orpheus,* the maenads are the hostile world of all melodrama.

What of Eugene O'Neill? Some think he revived tragedy. Those who disagree have usually spoken only of a failure. But if he often failed to achieve tragedy, O'Neill succeeded as often in achieving melodrama.

What O'Neill's father had chiefly done for a living was play Edmond Dantès in the melodrama *Monte Cristo.* The young O'Neill was a rebel against Father and considered himself a rebel against *Monte Cristo.* It remains a question, though, whether the modern ideas he picked up in Greenwich Village are the backbone of his work or whether, like many rebels against Father, he was not really identified with Father. That the son of an actor should be a playwright is in itself interesting. It is as if the son wished to write the father's lines and "work" him like a marionette. However this may be, *Mourning Becomes Electra,* as it seems to many of us, fails where it is modern and intellectual, succeeds where it is Victorian melodrama.

It was the melodramatic touch that O'Neill brought to the American theatre already in the twenties, that Lillian Hellman and Clifford Odets brought to it in the thirties, and that Tennessee Williams and Arthur Miller brought in the late forties. In the nineteen fifties, one of the most striking new presences in world theatre was Eugène Ionesco. His play *The Lesson* is about a mild-seeming teacher who murders forty pupils a day. Ionesco uses Grand Guignol as a vehicle for a vision of modern life. The same is true of the leading younger playwright of the fifties in the German-language area, Friedrich Dürrenmatt....

But I would not like to spoil the point by pushing it too far. The phrase "revival of melodrama" is far from covering all that is alive in modern drama, nor would I wish to call every play *a melodrama* in which there are melodramatic elements. On the contrary, I shall later propose the label *tragi-comedy* for some plays whose melodramatic qualities have been noted here. And of course there is no reason why the same play should not be seen, now as a melodrama, now as a tragi-comedy, now as something else again, if thereby its inherent qualities are brought out. Reality in this field, as in others, is various and variable, and each perspective on it has some peculiar advantage.

THE QUINTESSENCE OF DRAMA

As MODERN PERSONS we are willy-nilly under the spell of Naturalism. However often we tell ourselves the contrary, we relapse into assuming the normal and right thing to be a subdued tone, small human beings, a milieu minutely reproduced. Indeed a tremendous amount of energy goes into keeping up this illusion of the monotonous mediocrity of everyday life: otherwise how could the genteel tradition have survived the discoveries of modern physics and the atrocities of modern behavior? I am arguing, then, up to a point, that melodrama is actually more natural than Naturalism, corresponds to reality, not least to modern reality, more closely than Naturalism. Something has been gained when a person who has seen the world in monochrome and in miniature suddenly glimpses the lurid and the gigantic. His imagination has been reawakened.

The melodramatic vision is in one sense simply normal. It corresponds to an important aspect of reality. It is the spontaneous, uninhibited way of seeing things. Naturalism is more sophisticated but Naturalism is not more natural. The dramatic sense is the melodramatic sense, as one can see from the play-acting of any child. Melodrama is not a special and marginal kind of drama, let alone an eccentric or decadent one; it is drama in its elemental form; it is the quintessence of drama. The impulse to write drama is, in the first instance, the impulse to write melodrama, and, conversely, the young person who does not wish to write melodrama, does not write drama at all, but attempts a nondramatic genre, lyric, epic, or what not. It should be clear, then, why in treating melodrama, farce, tragedy, comedy, I have put melodrama first.

In this chapter I have tried to break down a prejudice against melodrama, just as in previous chapters I tried to break down prejudices against plot and prejudices against type characters—and, *mutatis mutandis,* for the same reasons. At the same time, there has been a negative side to this chapter's argument. I have used the words "childish," "neurotic," "primitive," even the words "narcissistic" and "paranoid," and in this summing-up I have had to insert saving clauses like "up to a point" and "in a sense."

In *The Interpretation of Dreams* Freud says that neurotics, like children, "exhibit on a magnified scale feelings of love and hatred for their parents." The remark needs interpreting. What, for instance, is a nonmagnified scale of feeling, and who exhibits that? Sigmund Freud, when hating a father who humiliated himself before antisemites? Anna Freud, when dedicating her life to continuing the work of Sigmund Freud? I mean the *argumentum ad hominem* kindly; and it could be aimed at anyone. What I am saying is that any nonmagnified feelings represent an ideal standard, and what we all have are the magnified feelings of the child, the neurotic, the savage. Such feelings of course form the basis of melodrama, and are the reason for its manifold magnifications.

Though melodramatic vision is not the worst, it is also not the best. It is good "up to a point," and the point is childhood, neuroticism, primitivity. Melodrama is human but it is not mature. It is imaginative but it is not intelligent. If again, for the same of clarity, we take the most rudimentary form of melodrama, the popular Victorian variety, what do we find but the most crass of immature fantasies? The reality principle is flouted right and left, one is oneself the supreme reality, one's innocence is axiomatic, any interloper is a threat and a monster, the ending will be happy because one feels that it has to be. In an earlier chapter I said theatre corresponded to that phase of a child's life when he creates magic worlds. I meant that that is where theatre comes from, not necessarily where it remains. Melodrama belongs to this magical phase, the phase when thoughts seem omnipotent, when the distinction between *I want to* and *I can* is not clearly made, in short when the larger reality has not been given diplomatic recognition.

Am I speaking now of all melodrama or just of the vulgar melodrama of Victorian popular theatres? It is hard to draw such a line, as it is hard to draw a line between melodrama and tragedy. Rather than separate blocks, the reality seems to be a continuous scale with the crudest melodrama at one end and the highest tragedy at the other. In tragedy the reality principle is not flouted, one is not oneself the sole reality to be respected, one's guilt is axiomatic, other people may or may not be threats or monsters, the ending is usually unhappy.

Yet the idea of such a scale is misleading if it suggests that tragedy is utterly distinct from melodrama. There is a melodrama in every tragedy, just as there is a child in every adult. It is not tragedy, but Naturalism, that tries to exclude childish and melodramatic elements. William Archer, a Naturalist, defined melodrama as "illogical and sometimes irrational tragedy." The premise is clear: tragedy is logical and rational. Looking for everyday logic and reasonableness in tragedy, Archer remorselessly drew the conclusion that most of the tragedy of the past was inferior to the middle-class drawing-room drama of London around 1910. Had he been consistent he would even have included Shakespeare in the indictment.

But tragedy is not melodrama minus the madness. It is melodrama plus something. Plus what?

This question will be pursued below, following a chapter on farce, that other "lower form," which stands to comedy as melodrama to tragedy.

7

FARCE

VIOLENCE

I HAVE BEEN SPEAKING about the violence in, and of, melodrama. Farce is perhaps even more notorious for its love of violent images. And since the violence of farce and melodrama is not excluded from comedy and tragedy, it will be well to ask the question: What about violence in art? What does it signify? What does it do to us? Here is the classic statement on the subject:

> When we listen to some hero [in Homer or] on the tragic stage moaning over his sorrows in a long tirade, or to a chorus beating their breasts as they chant a lament, you know how the best of us enjoy giving ourselves up to follow the performance with eager sympathy. . . . Few I believe are capable of reflecting that to enter into another's feelings must have an effect on our own: the emotions of pity our sympathy

has strengthened will not be easy to restrain when we are suffering ourselves. . . . Does not the same principle apply to humor as well as to pathos? You are doing the same thing if, in listening at a comic performance or in ordinary life to buffooneries which you would be ashamed to indulge in yourself, you thoroughly enjoy them instead of being disgusted with their ribaldry. There is in you an impulse to play the clown, which you have held in restraint from a reasonable fear of being set down a buffoon; but now you have given it rein, and by encouraging its impudence at the theatre you may be unconsciously carried away into playing the comedian in your private life. Similar effects are produced by poetic representation of love and anger and all those desires and feelings of pleasure and pain which accompany our every action. It waters the growth of passions which should be allowed to wither away and sets them up in control, although the goodness and happiness of our lives depend on their being held in subjection.

Thus Plato in the tenth book of *The Republic*. The question has come up again and again down the centuries, not least in our own age, the age of the most extensive, as well as the most atrocious, violence that the world has ever known. In such an age, it is naturally a matter of concern to the humane that the reading matter of the mass of men (and one should now include the "viewing" matter) has no tendency to wean them from violence but, on the contrary, tends to inure them to it. And one of the glaring moral contradictions of our cultural scene is that protests are made against the presentation of healthy sensuality in good art by people who quietly accept outrageous cruelty in bad art. All this being so, it is not surprising to find a warm-hearted physician like Dr. Fredric Wertham coming out, in his book *Seduction of the Innocent,* against the violence in our so-called "comic books." And I for one had not realized how ugly and nasty-minded these books are until I read Dr. Wertham's text and examined the illustrations. Comic books are bad art, and bad humanity, and therefore meager and possibly noxious food for the minds of the young—or old.

This much could probably be accepted by any humane person, but Dr. Wertham will not rest his case there. On at least one page he indicates that artistic merit is, as it were, no excuse: the cruelties of Grimm's fairy tales are to be condemned along with those of the "comic books." Here surely we have caught the good doctor regretting that art is serious, for if art did not treat violence, it could not go to the heart of things. Without violence, there would be nothing in the world but goodness, and literature is not mainly about goodness: it is mainly about badness. When, on another page, Dr. Wertham complains of sympathy being thrown to bad characters, we realize that he is placing himself squarely in that Puritan tradition which is hostile to art as such, and whose father is Plato—or part of Plato: the part that would have thrown the poets out of his ideal republic.

The Platonists in this argument disregard the distinction between fact and fantasy. Suppose you saw one man force the head of another through the glass of a street lamp so that the latter will be gassed by the fumes. It sounds like some Nazi atrocity, and Plato would no doubt be indignant at the notion of re-enacting the incident in a work of art. Nonetheless it *was* re-enacted in Charlie Chaplin's film *Easy Street,* and in all the years no one has protested. We have all very much enjoyed seeing Mack Swain gassed and Charlie triumphant. And in general, though what we consciously remember from the Chaplin films may be Chaplin's incomparable delicacy, they are for the most part taken up with violent pursuit and violent combat. Here fantasy multiplies movements and blows by a thousand. The villain is a giant whose strength passes the limits of nature. He can bend lamp posts with his bare hands. Since the "little man's" revenges have to be more than proportionate to the provocation (as with Brecht's Pirate Jenny), he can drop a cast-iron stove on the villain's head and ram that head inside a street lamp with the gas turned on.

Another symptom of cruelty is the abstractness of the violence. Prongs of a rake in the backside are received as pin pricks. Bullets seem to pass right through people, sledge-hammer blows to produce only momentary irritation. The speeding up of movement contributes to the abstract effect. So, even more, does the silence proper to the screen of those days, many of the effects being lost when a sound track is superimposed. The cops shoot, but there is no noise. Heavy objects fall, but there is no crash. Gruesome infighting has the air of shadowboxing. All of which signifies that, in farce, as in drama, one is permitted the outrage but spared the consequence. Chaplin's delicacy of style is actually part of the pattern: he parades an air of nonchalance when acting in a manner that, in real life, would land him in Bellevue or Sing Sing.

Though Plato has shown us the importance of thought, and modern psychology has exhibited the power of fantasy, we cannot allow ourselves to be jockeyed into regarding the distinction between thought and act, fantasy and fact, as a sort of minor detail. The person who confuses the two sets of categories is not eccentric, he is insane. Conversely, it is possible for a thinker and fantasist to bank heavily on the sanity of his audience; and this is what Charlie Chaplin or any other farceur emphatically does.

Certainly, teachers and parents have to cope with the fact that in some situations children do not make a clear distinction between fantasy and reality. But they must understand that these situations do not include all the violence in drama and other fiction. Think of the tremendous violence in fairy tales, and ask yourself how many small children have actually tried to duplicate it in real life. Grimm's fairy tales do not seem to justify Dr. Wertham's fears.

For people who can distinguish between fantasy and reality certain indulgences are possible in fantasy which should not be permitted in "real life." Most notably: they can indulge in reckless violence. That extraordinary passage in *The Republic* was answered by Aristotle, though perhaps not intentionally and certainly not at length. His answer is to be found in the famous phrase about tragedy in *The Poetics:* "through pity and fear effecting the proper catharsis of these emotions." True, there is a permanent debate about the meaning of the word "catharsis," but all the debaters could agree, I think, on that solid part of the meaning that is relevant here, namely: Aristotle is rejecting the notion that tragedy might reduce us to a quivering jelly of pity and fear, and is formulating an exactly contrary conclusion: tragedy is not only an excitement but a release from excitement. It will not burst the boiler with its steam because it is precisely the safety valve. It is the exactly contrary character of Aristotle's view to Plato's that most powerfully suggests that it might be a deliberate reply. And it is this character that makes it perhaps somewhat polemical, and hard to go all the way with. One feels that the cathartic theory exaggerates. Surely not all this happens to one's emotional system during a performance of *Hamlet*? But the theory can hardly be rejected in substance unless one wishes to side with Plato, Bishop Bossuet, Dr. Wertham, and the Motion Picture Production Code.

Gilbert Murray has suggested that the idea of catharsis is easier to apply to comedy than to tragedy—easier in the sense that we agree to it more easily. There is already a certain consensus of opinion that some of our psychic violence—what our grandparents called excess animal spirits—can be worked off in laughter. It is generally agreed that a good laugh does us good, and that it does us good as a sort of emotional "work-out."

Impropriety is of the essence. As Murray put it: "Comedy . . . must . . . not be spoilt by any tiresome temperance or prudential considerations of the morrow." And again: "The anarchist and the polygamist, close-prisoned and chained in ordinary life, enjoy their release in comedy." Murray thought of comedy as continuous with orgies and fertility rites. Perhaps his doctrine implies the same error as that of the Platonists: a disregard of the difference between doing and imagining. The image of an orgy that we may get in a work of art should not be equated with the acting out of an orgy in real life; and comedy gives only a faded image of an orgy at that. Still, since the rise of Christianity, even the image of an orgy is a little more than many people bargain for. And there has been war between comedy and established religion down through the ages. The Motion Picture Production Code is but its latest embodiment. We mustn't laugh at a priest, it implies, or religion is in danger.

SCOFFING AT MARRIAGE

ABOVE ALL we must not laugh at the family and its source, the institution of marriage. If crime comics are rampant among the underprivileged young, equally rampant among the overprivileged middle-aged is a literature whose patron saint is Tartuffe. In one of those family magazines that are so moralistic as to be morally nauseating, I came across an article entitled "Don't Let Them Scoff at Marriage" in which the moral crisis of our times was confidently attributed to jokes against marriage. "The gross libel on marriage is the notion," the author wrote, "that the chase, the allure, is the goal. Marriage is seen as a dull aftermath." As a psychologist the writer should have known that even gross libels aren't made without provocation. Or if they are, they don't last for centuries and appeal to the whole human race. Obviously the human race finds more interesting what this man calls a gross libel than what he presents as the truth.

It is true, however, that the joke against marriage could be abolished if the family were the unmixed blessing that many of our contemporaries take it for. The chief of the division of Social Medicine at an important American hospital writes as follows:

The family is central to the development of humanity not only for the perpetuation of the race but because the proper psychological development of an individual can only occur within the warm circle of the nuclear family. Social and psychological studies indicate quite clearly that a strong family structure helps to

225

develop and maintain a personality free of dangerous (to self and society) characteristics.

And the author draws the conclusion that sexual deviation and juvenile delinquency can be prevented by closer, warmer family relations. "The family that prays together stays together." "Where family life stops delinquency starts."

No doubt there is some truth in all this. Unhappily there is truth in a precisely opposite proposition. The close, warm family is also the seedbed of neurosis, vice, and crime. About the same time as this article appeared, a newspaper picture caught my eye. It showed a beaming public-relations executive with his good-looking wife and three attractive children. They seemed a model American family in a model American home, and one could imagine the picture passing in triumph around the public-relations office. The caption underneath, however, reported that the mildest and most candid-looking of the boys had just killed the mother and sister and told the police that he had planned to kill the rest of the family as well. It would be comforting to think that such a shocking event could be declared irrelevant to the experience of normal folk. But it isn't, because normal folk share his wishes though they do not carry them out. An art like farce embodies such wishes: wishes to damage the family, to desecrate the household gods.

And tragedy is no different in this respect. The Greeks, who invented it, did not do so before they had created the patriarchal family and an ideology to fit it. They seem to have found the supreme virtue in the pious and loyal relation of husband to wife, of child to parent, of sibling to sibling. The subject of tragedy, over and over again, was the violation of such piety. Now what would be the worst conceivable violation of both the marital and filial pieties? Why, the double crime of Oedipus.

An entry in *The Oxford Companion to the Theatre* reads:

> The word *farce* is applied to a full-length play dealing with some absurd situation hingeing generally on extra-marital relations—hence the term *bedroom farce*. . . .

The phrase "some absurd situation hingeing . . . on extra-marital relations" suggests various tragic plots, that of *Othello*, for example. But what "situation hingeing . . . on extra-marital relations" is not full of absurdities and therefore potentially melodramatic or farcical, tragic or comic, according to the temperament, state of mind, and view of life of the witness? Outrage to family piety is certainly at the heart of farce as we know it—"hence," as our companionable book says, "the term *bedroom farce*."

It is, of course, Freud who has taught us to find such impieties in tragedy. And one of his early followers, Ludwig Jekels, applied the idea of the Oedipus complex to comedy. If tragedy, he says, shows the son paying for his rebellion against the father, comedy shows the son victorious, the father discomfited. Father and son compete for the possession of the mother, and the son wins. The element of disguise by which this naked fantasy is clothed consists very often in the son's being presented as just some young man who happens along. But many of the disguises for the theme are more elaborate. It seems to me that the modern "triangle" drama might be regarded as one of them: husband, wife, and lover being the disguise for father, mother, and son. If this were so, then the answer to the question why modern playwrights have been obsessed with adultery is that they have *not* been obsessed with adultery: they have been obsessed with incest. In Bernard Shaw's *Candida,* Morell, Candida, and Marchbanks would be the mask of a father, mother, and son. (I do not cite the evidence from Bernard Shaw's life that the three characters were indeed father [or foster-father], mother, and son [himself] to the author. That is a matter of origin. More relevant here is the possibility that Morell, Candida, and Marchbanks would still be *a* father, mother, and son for the unconscious of spectators even if we knew nothing of Shaw's life.) Such is the conversion to late nineteenth-century problem drama of the Oedipus story. In another early Shaw play, *Mrs. Warren's Profession,* the incest theme shows through, as it already had in two of the most famous plays of Shaw's playwright-father, Henrik Ibsen: namely, *Ghosts* and *Rosmersholm.* Yet for contemporaries all three of these plays seemed to be about current social problems exclusively (white slavery, hereditary syphilis, advanced ideas, etc.). For them, the incest theme remained under a veil, and when one notes what that veil was, one may begin to see social realism in a different light. By which I do not mean that the "social" content is always mere camouflage for psychological motifs but only that it can serve as such camouflage vis à vis a given public. The plays I have named are better understood today when audiences recognize the Oedipal theme at once and so take the plays to be what they are: "social" and "psychological" at the same time.

COMIC CATHARSIS

GILBERT MURRAY has spoken of the "close similarity between Aristotle and Freud," and actually Freud carried the idea of Catharsis further than any Aristotelian commentator had ever dreamt of. In the eighteen-nineties the new therapy escaped being named cathartic instead of psycho-analytic only by a hair's breadth. For Freud, jokes are fundamentally cathartic: a release, not a stimulant. This is why Freud, unlike our magazine moralists, would "let them scoff at marriage." (He would also know he could never stop them.) It is a sort of open secret, Freud says in his book on jokes, that "marriage is hardly an arrangement to satisfy the sexual demands of the husband," also that this secret is half-kept, half-told, in a million male jokes against marriage. I would add that the supreme form of the marriage joke takes a couple of hours to tell and has a cast of three characters known as *le mari, la femme, et l'amant* —"hence the term *bedroom farce.*" Just as Restoration Comedy was provoked by the Puritans and is forever dedicated to their memory, the farce of adultery throughout our Protestant-bourgeois epoch has been provoked by faithful husbands and will only end when they become unfaithful on principle.

Farce in general offers a special opportunity: shielded by delicious darkness and seated in warm security, we enjoy the privilege of being totally passive while on stage our most treasured unmentionable wishes are fulfilled before our eyes by the most violently active human beings that every sprang from the human imagination. In that application of the formula which is bedroom farce, we savor the adventure of adultery, ingeniously exaggerated in the highest degree, and all without taking the responsibility or suffering the guilt. Our wives may be with us leading the laughter.

Why do we laugh at jokes? The point of a joke can be explained, but the explanation is not funny. The intellectual content is not the essence. What counts is the experience which we call "getting" the joke or "seeing the point." This experience is a kind of shock, but, whereas shocks in general are unpleasant, this one opens a sluicegate somewhere and brings a sudden spurt or gush of pleasure. Nor is the pleasure of the laugh continuous with the mild amusement that precedes it. A joke is a purling stream most of the way, then suddenly from one of its pools rises up a veritable geyser.

The phenomenon seems less mysterious if we see it as limited to grown human beings, and grown human beings as full of anxiety and guilt. Neither supermen nor babies have a sense of humor. They don't need one. Men and women do because they have inhibited many of their strongest wishes.

How does the sense of humor go to work? Its aim is to gratify some of the forbidden wishes. But what is repressed is repressed. We cannot get at it. Our anxiety and guilt are taking care of that. Only, there are tricks for eluding anxiety and guilt, and the commonest, the least artificial, is the sense of humor. The mildly amusing preliminaries of a joke allay our fears, lower our resistance. The gratification of the forbidden wish is then slipped upon us as a surprise. Before our guilt and anxiety have time to go into action, the forbidden pleasure has been had. A source of pleasure far deeper than those directly available has been tapped. Inhibitions are momentarily lifted, repressed thoughts are admitted into consciousness, and we experience that feeling of power and pleasure, generally called elation. Here is one of the few forms of joy that can be had, so to speak, for the asking. Hence the immense contribution of humor to the survival of the species.

Hence also a paradox. Through the funny, we tap

infantile sources of pleasure, we become infants again, finding the intensest satisfaction in the smallest things, the highest ecstasy in the lowest thoughts. And yet infants themselves are without humor. But the paradox is no contradiction, for at bottom no experiences could be further apart than is the momentary return to childhood from the experience of being a child. The actual innocence of infancy is never regained but as far as pleasure is concerned there is an increment in sheer nostalgia. No little girl can love little-girlhood as Lewis Carroll did. No infant shares the grownup's enjoyment in returning, or seeming to return, to infancy. Humor has a great deal to do with the distance between the infancy returned to and the point from which the return journey is undertaken. In fact the premise that children have no sense of humor, useful at the outset, needs qualification at a later stage of the investigation. Children *develop* a sense of humor as they move away from primal innocence. They have only to hear a few of the "songs of experience," which are songs of setback, disappointment, and disillusion, and the whole-hearted cheerfulness of a baby's smile can give place on the face of a three-year-old to the aggressive smirk or the twisted, half-smile of defeat. "Innocence" is whole and single. With "experience" comes division and duality—without which there is no humor, no wit, no farce, and no comedy.

JOKES AND THE THEATRE

ONE of the key insights of both Bergson and Freud is that to make jokes is to create a theatre. Bergson says that any witticism, if articulated at all, articulates itself in scenes—

which are an inchoate comedy. Freud points out that it takes, not one or two, but three to make a joke. These are the jokester, the butt of the joke, and the listener. The trio is familiar in the form of comedian, straight man, and audience. This trio of vaudeville suggests in turn the ironist, the impostor, and the audience of the traditional comic theatre.

To say that the jokester needs a butt is only to say that he needs a joke. Does he need even a joke as much as he needs a listener? Let each of us ask himself why, at a given moment, he wishes to tell a joke. It cannot be because one wishes to be amused by it, since jokes are not amusing the second time around, and one cannot tell a joke one has not already heard. (I exclude from consideration any super-man who can invent his jokes as he goes along. He is irrelevant here because the subject I am now approaching is the comedian, who certainly does not write his lines as he goes along.) Anyhow, if one's need was to *hear* the joke one could tell it to oneself. It is inescapable that the need is not for the joke at all: it is for the audience.

Anyone who has known comedians off stage can testify, I think, that they are often men with a need of applause and appreciation that goes beyond even that of other actors. And there is a reason why men with this need—whether they are gifted humorists or not—should seek out the comedian's profession. Only the joke gets from its audience a reaction whose tenor is unmistakable and enthusiastic: laughter. The tragic actor gets no such indication, at the end of his "To be or not to be" speech, that it went over well. He will be pleased if there was silence in the house; even so he may wonder if everyone had gone to sleep. He may wonder whether his feeling that it went well is an illusion. But there is no such thing, as Ramon Fernandez puts it, as an illusion that an audience is laughing. So their laughter is peculiarly attractive to a person who needs an audience reaction every minute or two and needs to be sure that it is highly favorable. On the night when the audience does not laugh, the clown goes out and shoots himself. At least he might as well, since the one thing he has lived for is not forthcoming.

I have suggested that the comedian is the man whose need of applause is the most insistent and mistrustful. An alternative interpretation is that the comedian is the most gifted of compulsive talkers. Every cocktail party entertains many people who will not stop talking so long as they have an audience. The jokester is such a compulsive talker, it could be, who gets away with it because his talk is amusing. The burst of laughter that greets each story is a diploma stating that he has succeeded in not boring his audience. He may now be tempted to tell his stories to larger and larger groups. If he ends up on a stage talking to people he has never met, he is a professional comedian.

That what purport to be studies of comedy often turn out to be only studies of laughter is to be regretted, yet the circumstance faithfully reflects the mentality of the comedian. His wish is to capture and hold captive his audience, and he knows his wish fulfilled only when the audience laughs. Hence, though laughter may be no proper emblem for comedy, it does set the seal on jokes. For this reason entertainment merchants may be forgiven a certain hysteria on the subject, and we should receive more in sorrow than in anger the news that the television people are measuring the duration and volume of laughs with laugh meters.

If philosophers can reduce comic art to laughter, then surely the entrepreneurs can reduce laughter to the noise it makes. But in both cases, the real topic is narrowed down too much. The student of laughter should study the whole curve of which the burst of noise is but the final inch. Before people will burst out laughing they have to be prepared to burst out laughing. The only sure preparation is a particular state of expectation and sensitivity that amounts to a kind of euphoria. It can be more important than the joke itself. A stage of excitement can be reached at which people will laugh at anything. The performer may have to ask himself what they will *not* laugh at if he is to forestall chaos. He has to watch that the girls don't get the giggles and the ladies the hysterics.

In all this, the theatre stands with the art of telling jokes, not with the art of writing books. We read in solitude; and we think it remarkable if once in a while we laugh out loud. At that it is a single burst of laughter, a self-conscious, if loud, single bark. The rest of the family is sure one did it to attract attention, and asks what's so funny. And very likely one did. But when Cousin Seamus tells us his Irish jokes, we can really let go, and in ten minutes we are as "high" as any whiskey could make us. Such is the psychology of the comedian in the theatre.

In this respect, as in others, the art of farce is but joking turned theatrical—joking fully articulated as theatrical characters and scenes. It is correct to say that its aim is laughter, but this is to say no simple thing. Laughter may signify this or that, and in any case has to be most carefully prepared. Also modulated. Future students of the subject would do well to drop the individual joke and the reasons why it is funny and turn to the question: just how funny is it in particular contexts? It will be found that sometimes it is hardly funny at all, and that other times it is very funny indeed. It is a matter of how the audience was led to the point where the laugh should break out and the fun be proved.

I have been speaking of one burst of laughter with one preparation, and even in so small an event there is plenty to observe. But any farce that lasts more than a minute or two has to make the audience laugh out loud a considerable number of times. This cannot be done by just stringing along the jokes one after the other. The general elation is so much more potent than any particular punch line that one may begin to wonder: what *is* a joke? As I have said, if one succeeds very well with a first joke, the audience may get into a state of mind where anything seems funny. All one needs is a new turn of events, and a new shriek of laughter will greet it. But this state of mind will not last very long unaided. And it may not be wise to try to sustain it indefinitely lest the result be sheer exhaustion. He who organizes a whole evening of "merriment" must indeed be an organizer. Nothing could be more fatal than to stake all on making a good beginning and then to let events take their course. Which is something any good vaudeville producer always knew; and it is something every author of a farce must have in mind—or, better, in his bones.

A sidelight is provided by something Sir John Gielgud once said about producing *The Importance of Being Earnest*. It was to the effect that the director must learn to prevent the audience from laughing in too many places. Those who saw Sir John's production of the play will know what he meant. The comic temperature was raised so high, the elation of the audience was so intense, that the performance at many points could hardly continue. Wilde had written dialogue so witty that any line whatever could be the signal for renewed shrieks and whoops. The break-up of the performance—even in shrieks of merriment—is no desirable aim. What the actors had to do was the opposite of "milking" every line for the fun in it. It was to throw away a lot of the fun of individual lines for the sake of more important fun. The aim of Sir John's strategy was not merely the avoidance of riot. It was the fullest enjoyment of the occasion. Spectators are babies, and have no idea what they will like. If one lets them, they will laugh so hard that later on they can only have the hysterics or the sulks. They have to be prevented from doing violence to their own nervous systems. Laughter cannot be regular and sustained. It cannot begin *pianissimo* and then get gradually louder *ad infinitum*. Nor can it maintain the same intensity steadily like a factory siren. It is tied to our very limited respiratory and vocal system, not to mention our psychology.

If a laugh meter could measure the merit of a show, then the ideal show would be one that elicited a single uninterrupted peal of laughter which lasted from eight thirty till eleven o'clock. It would therefore consist of a play which not only could not proceed but could not begin. Actually, there is no ratio between enjoyment and the duration of audible laughter. But too little laughter is better than too much. If no comedy, however great, could make people laugh all the time, there could be a great comedy that never made them laugh at all.

How often, incidentally, does one really listen to laughter? It is quite an ugly sound. How often has one looked at people while they do it? It is not a pretty sight. And how little laughter there is on stage in a good theatre! The place for laughter is the auditorium. Perhaps one reason is that in the auditorium one does not have to see it. One sees the actors. They laugh seldom, and chiefly for negative effects. Only the other day I opened a magazine and came upon a most expressive laugh on the face of an actor. The caption told me that it was Gustav Gruendgens—as Mephistopheles.

SWEET AND BITTER SPRINGS

FREUD distinguishes two kinds of jokes, one which is innocent and harmless, and one which has a purpose, a tendency, an end in view. He distinguishes in turn two kinds of purpose: to destroy and to expose—to smash and to strip. Destructive jokes fall under such headings as sarcasm, scandal, and satire, denuding jokes under such headings as obscenity, bawdry, ribaldry.

I think the only startling thing about this classification is that it places obscenity side by side with satire. If we agree, we may take another step by observing that there is destructive force also in the joke that exposes. It is hostile either to the thing exposed or to the audience watching the exposure or both. Modifying Freud's formulation, I conclude that both the satiric and the obscene come under the heading of aggression.

We have, then, aggressive jokes and nonagressive jokes. Everyone, in fact, assumes no less, and quite widespread in our middle-class culture is a preference for the nonaggressive joke. Are we not a Christian civilization? I myself was brought up on a little hymn that went:

> Teach us delight in simple things
> And mirth that has no bitter springs.

It seemed a reasonable enough demand to make, especially since, at the time, I was not aware that mirth *ever* had bitter springs. I certainly did not know that the author of that very hymn was a man of inordinate pugnacity. (It is by Kipling.)

Some people want their jokes pleasant and harmless, and some people want their farces pleasant and harmless. Indeed it is common to interpret farce as precisely the pleasant treatment of what would otherwise have been an unpleasant subject. Here is the great theatre critic of nineteenth-century France—Sarcey—discussing the greatest farceur of nineteenth-century France:

> I had often complained that they bored us constantly with this question of adultery, which nowadays is the subject of three quarters of the plays. Why, I asked, take pleasure in painting its dark and sad sides, enlarging on the dreadful consequences which it brings with it in reality? Our fathers took the thing more lightheartedly in the theatre and even called adultery by a name which awoke in the mind only ideas of the ridiculous and a sprightly lightheartedness. . . . Chance brought it about that I met Labiche. "I was very struck," he said to me, "with your observations on adultery and on what could derive from it . . . for farce . . . I agree . . ." I had almost forgotten this conversation when I saw the title posted outside the Palais Royal. . . . It was my play: it was adultery treated lightheartedly. . . .

Anglo-Saxon opinion has been against admitting such subjects as adultery into the nonserious drama at all, and yet there is one English critic who, before Sarcey, had carried Sarcey's argument yet further. This is Charles Lamb in his once-famous essay on Restoration Comedy. In

substance, though this is not his vocabulary, he argues that
the subject matter of Restoration comedy becomes palatable if we regard the finished product as farce rather than
satire. For this is to judge leniently as in play, not harshly
as one would have to in real life.

> I could never connect those sports of a witty fancy
> in any shape with any result to be drawn from them
> to imitation in real life. They are a world of them-
> selves almost as much as fairy land. . . . The Fainalls
> and the Mirabells, the Dorimants and the Lady
> Touchwoods, in their own sphere, do not offend my
> moral sense. . . . They break through no laws, or
> conscientious restraints. They know of none. They
> have got out of Christendom into the land—what
> shall I call it?—of cuckoldry—the Utopia of gallantry,
> where pleasure is duty, and the manners perfect free-
> dom. It is altogether a speculative scene of things,
> which has no reference whatever to the world that is.

Now both Sarcey and Lamb are saying things that are
undeniably true. If adultery in the drama is becoming a
solemn bore, then certainly it would be fun to try the
farceur's approach. If parents are becoming solemn bores
in suggesting that a Restoration comedy might have an
inordinate and immoral influence on their daughters, then
certainly it is good to remind them of the distinction
between art and life, fiction and fact. But the real question
is the significance of the gaiety Sarcey speaks of, and of
what Lamb calls the sports of a witty fancy, his Utopia of
gallantry, his land of cuckoldry. Both critics assume that
they have closed the discussion once they have invoked the
twin spirits of gaiety and fantasy. Yet that is where the real

discussion begins, and that is where Freud takes it up in his monograph on jokes. Granting that jokes exist which are "innocent," Freud goes on to say that it is only the tendentious ones, the jokes with a purpose, which can make people burst out laughing. The innocent jokes don't pack that much of a punch. We do not feel them so keenly. Our receiving apparatus is not so sensitive to them. Our need for them is not so great. We crave stronger meat. We want satire. We want ribaldry. We want to attack and to expose.

To say that only the joke with a purpose can actually arouse laughter is tantamount to saying that only this type of joking is of much use in the theatre of Farce. And it seems to me that if farces are examined they will be found to contain very little "harmless" joking and very much that is "tendentious." Without aggression farce cannot function. The effects we call "farcical" dissolve and disappear.

What happens in farces? In one of Noel Coward's, a man slaps his mother-in-law's face and she falls in a swoon. Farce is the only form of art in which such an incident could normally occur.

No one ever denied that W. C. Fields' films were aggressive. Audiences became so conscious of the aggressions that they started staying away from Fields' pictures. In Charlie Chaplin's case, they said they liked him because he was less violent. He *seemed* less violent because he put the violence in the other characters. The violence was done *to* him, not *by* him, and masochistic farce always seems more gentlemanlike than sadistic. But the Tramp of Chaplin is not exclusively masochistic. He is also a sadist. One remembers what happens in *The Kid* when Charlie finds himself literally holding the baby. By all means, he is going to become a charming and sentimental foster-father, but as he sits there with his feet in the gutter he notices an open drain, and he has almost thrown the baby down it before sentiment comes again into its own. It is by touches like that—and never by sentiment alone—that Chaplin has shown himself a great comic.

> Teach us delight in complex things:
> Mirth has both sweet and bitter springs.

THE DIALECTIC OF FARCE

To the simple all things are simple. Yet farce *can* seem a simple thing, not only to the simple-minded but even to those who recognize its depth. Farce is simple, on this view, because it goes right "at" things. You knock your mother-in-law down, and no beating about the bush. One can wonder, certainly, if this is not the absolutely direct, unmediated vision, without that duality of mask and face, symbol and object, which characterizes the rest of dramatic literature.

A second way in which farce may seem simple is in its acceptance of the everyday appearances and of everyday interpretations of those appearances. It does not present the empurpled and enlarged images of melodrama. No, farce can use the ordinary unenlarged environment and ordinary down-at-heel men of the street. The trouble is that farce is simple in both these ways at once, thereby failing to be simple at all. Farce brings together the direct and wild fantasies and the everyday and drab realities. The interplay between the two is the very essence of this art—the farcical dialectic.

If behind the gaiety of farce lurks a certain gravity, it is equally true that behind the gravity lurks a great deal of gaiety. Farce can certainly present a grave appearance. Those unsmiling actors again!—or rather the unsmiling down-at-heel roles which farce offers them. Here is a point of decisive importance in performance. The amateur actor misses it, and tries to act the gaiety. The professional knows he must act the gravity and trust that the author has injected gaiety into his plot and dialogue.

Actually, to press the analysis a step further, the surface of farce is grave and gay at the same time. The gay antics of Harlequin are conducted with poker-faced gravity. Both the gaiety and the gravity are visible and are part of the style. If we go on to speak of a contrast in farce between mask and face, symbol and thing symbolized, appearance and reality, this will not be a contrast in styles but a contrast between either the gravity or the gaiety on the surface and whatever lies beneath. What do the gravity and gaiety have in common? Orderliness and mildness. What lies beneath the surface, on the other hand, is disorderly and violent. It is a double dialectic. On the surface, the contrast of gay and grave, then, secondly, the contrast of surface and beneath-the-surface. The second is a larger and even more dynamic contrast.

What farce does with this larger contrast is best seen by comparison with what comedy does. Comedy makes much of appearances: it specializes, indeed, in the *keeping up* of appearances. Unmasking in comedy will characteristically be the unmasking of a single character in a climactic scene —like that of Tartuffe. In farce, unmasking occurs all along. The favorite action of the farceur is to shatter the appearances, his favorite effect being the shock to the audience of his doing so. Bring on stage a farcical comic like Harpo Marx, and all appearances are in jeopardy. For him, all coverings exist to be stripped off, all breakables to be broken. It would be a mistake to bring him into a drawing-room comedy: he would dismantle the drawing room.

If what farce offers is the interaction of violence and something else, it follows that violence by itself is not the essence of farce. The violence of Chaplin is dramatized by a context of great gentleness. The violence of Harpo Marx is offset by something equally important to his roles: his perfectly serious performances on that most delicate of instruments, the harp.

A common mistake is to think that Charlie's and Harpo's effects are softened by the gentleness and delicacy, as if the aim were to reach a compromise between violence and sobriety. But compromises are for life, not art. The purpose of this gentleness and delicacy is to heighten, not lower, the effect of the violence, and vice versa. Dramatic art in general is an art of extremes, and farce is, as it were, an extreme case of the extreme. Farce characteristically promotes and exploits the widest possible contrasts between tone and content, surface and substance, and the minute one of the two elements in the dialectic is not present in its extreme or pure form, there is likely to be a weakening of the drama. This could be exemplified by Noel Coward's little play in which, while an extreme lightness of tone is achieved, punches are pulled (more or less literally) where a straight left to the jaw was just what was needed. In farce, we say: "I'll murder you with my bare hands," playfully, or with that mixture of the grave and gay which defines the tone as farcical, but in a degree we also have to mean it: by some flicker, at least, in word or act, it must become evident that murderous wishes exist in this world—and at this moment. If they exist in Noel Coward, he was too genteel to let his public know it. In our theatre, talents such as his drift away from farce without encountering real comedy, landing in that worst of both worlds, the sentimental "light comedy" of the West End and Broadway.

If it is dangerous to attempt a compromise between the two conflicting opposites of a dialectic, it is disastrous to accept one and forget the other. Sheer aggression is just oppressive, as many motion-picture cartoons illustrate. Sheer flippancy is just boring, as most "light comedy" illustrates. The dialectical relation is one of active conflict and development. A dialogue has to be established between the aggression and the flippancy, between hostility and lightness of heart.

MISCHIEF AS FATE

EVERY FORM of drama has its rendezvous with madness. If drama shows extreme situations, *the* extreme situation for human beings—short of death—is the point where our sanity gives out. In a very famous scene Ibsen has shown this point reached on stage; and Racine's *Andromache* had ended in much the same way as Ibsen's *Ghosts*.

Our colloquial use and abuse of words is always full of meaning, and what we mean when we say of some non-theatrical phenomenon, "It's a farce," or "It's absolutely farcical," throws light back on the theatrical phenomenon. We mean: farce is absurd; but not only that, farce is a veritable structure of absurdities. Here the operative word is *structure,* for normally we think of absurdities as amorphous. It is only in such a syndrome as paranoia that we find reason in the madness: the absurdities which we would be inclined to call stupid are connected in a way we cannot but consider the reverse of stupid. There is an ingenious and complex set of interrelationships.

I was speaking in the previous chapter of the long arm of coincidence in melodrama. It is an arm that does not get any shorter in farce. In both cases there is an acknowledgment of absurdity—and in both cases, a counterclaim to a kind of sense. A paranoiac finds a structure in coincidences, which is to say that to him they are not coincidences. The playwright incorporates coincidences in a structure, which is to say that they will not be coincidences to his audience. The melodramatist creates a sense of fatality, and, in the light of that sense, apparent coincidence reveals itself as part of a baleful pattern. And do not imagine, as William Archer did, that the tragic writer is any different. Think, rather, how the Oedipus of Sophocles has spent a lifetime just happening to be at the wrong place at the wrong time and meeting the wrong person there. Farce differs from the other genres in that its use of coincidence is accepted. People have such a low opinion of farce that they don't mind admitting it uses such a low device.

What do the coincidences of farce amount to? Not surely to a sense of fate, and yet certainly to a sense of something that *might* be called fate if only the word had less melancholy associations. In farce chance ceases to seem chance, and mischief has method in its madness. One final effect of farce is that mischief, fun, misrule seem an equivalent of fate, a force not ourselves making, neither for righteousness nor for catastrophe, but for aggression without risk.

Perhaps every type of dramatic action has to have its inevitability, including the types, such as the comic types, that seem dedicated to the opposite. The heaping up of crazy coincidences in farce creates a world in which the happily fortuitous is inevitable. And so, in a Feydeau play, the careful plan for the husband to be absent when the lover arrives is a gilt-edged guarantee that he will turn up.

What is usually said about surprises in farcical plots has to be qualified. On the surface of our minds we are surprised; but somewhere deeper down we knew all along. The convention itself creates certain expectations without which we would not have paid the price of admission. The expectation may go back before the first scene of the play to the rubric "A Farce" in the program or before that to the name "Feydeau" in the advertisements.

I have suggested that the characteristic melodramatic situations and plots derive directly from more or less paranoid fantasies—generally the fantasy of innocence surrounded by malevolence. Pity and fear are certainly aroused and possibly "abreacted"—worked through and worked off. If there is an equivalent in farce and comedy for pity and fear in melodrama and tragedy, it is sympathy and contempt. As pity is the weaker side of melodrama, sympathy is the weaker side of farce. It usually amounts to little more than mild fellow feeling with the hero and heroine. Charlie Chaplin, as an exception, was able to make more of it because he was not a juvenile lead but a character man. The character he chose—that of the Tramp—was such as to make the audience's sympathy play a very large part in the proceedings.

Innocence is probably as important to farce as to melodrama. We are as firmly identified with it. The difference is that whereas in melodrama we recoil from the enemy in fear, in farce we retaliate. If melodrama generally depends for its power on the degree of fear it can arouse, farce depends on the degree of aggression. "The comedian," says Sidney Tarachow, "is a hostile sharpshooter loudly pro-

claiming his own innocence." In this respect, the writer of
farces is a comedian. The hostility, like the terror of
melodramas, is so unqualified by any sense of justice or
truth, that it creates forms that resemble sick fantasies. The
closed structure of the Well Made Play as used by Georges
Feydeau suggests a closed mental system, a world of its own
lit by its own lurid and unnatural sun. If we were not
laughing so hard, we would find such worlds terrifying.
Their workings are as perilous as acrobatics. One touch, we
feel, and the whole thing might go spinning into space. A
Feydeau play has points in common with a highly elaborated and crazy delusion.

The masters of French farce in the nineteenth century
used incredibly elaborate plots, and it is often said of their
plays that they are "all plot." Here we have another aspect
of the madness of farce. Human life in this art form is
horribly attenuated. Life is a kind of universal milling
around, a rushing from bedroom to bedroom driven by
demons more dreadful than sensuality. The kind of farce
which is said to be "all plot" is often much more than
ingenious, it is maniacal. When one saw the actors of the
Montreal *Théâtre du nouveau monde* giving positively
spastic movements to Molière's farce characters, one said
to oneself: after all there is something spastic about farce
generally. Dryden says: "The persons and actions of a
farce are all unnatural and their manners false."

Much more is involved in the movement of the story
than we commonly realize. Why, for example, do directors
of farce always call for tempo, tempo, tempo? It is not just
because they admire business efficiency, nor is there anything to the common belief of theatre people that *fast* is
always better than *slow*. It is a question of the speeding up
of human behavior so that it becomes less than human.

Bergson might say this was one of the ways in which human behavior becomes funny by resembling the working of high-speed machines. The speeding up of movement in the typical silent-movie farces had a definite psychological and moral effect, namely, of making actions seem abstract and automatic when in life they would be concrete and subject to free will. It is a conception that bristles with menace.

Conversely, to think of a good farcical pattern of action is to think of a good pretext for rapid movement. The chase was the pride and glory of the Keystone Cops. The plot of *An Italian Straw Hat* is one long pretext for flight and pursuit. So is the plot of that homely English imitation of French farce, *Charley's Aunt*.

IN THE IMAGE OF THE APE

THE FARCEUR is a heretic: he does not believe that man was made in God's image. What are the principal images of men in farce and what do they amount to?

If one tells the story of a farce, one may well start talking of young lovers, but if instead of telling the story, one looks at what has remained in one's memory from a farce, one will not find young lovers there but two other characters: the knave and the fool. One will then find that the plot itself hinges less on what the young lovers do than on what the knave does. The knave in farce is the equivalent of the villain in melodrama. "Passions spin the plot." If the passion that spins the melodramatic plot is sheer wickedness, the passion that spins the farcical plot is that younger brother of wickedness, the spirit of mischief. Shakespeare's Puck could be the knave of a farce. He is not deep or purposive enough to be a villain. He is a trouble-maker by accident and even by nature but not always by design and never with intent to do serious damage. He is a prankster—like Harlequin.

If mischief becomes a sort of comic equivalent of fate, it is usually through the Puck, the Harlequin, the Brighella, the Scapin, the Figaro that it does so. In its simpler forms, the idea of a prankster is desperately primitive, and even in Shakespeare the pranks hover on the brink of the abysmally unfunny. (What, for example, is so fascinating about the gulling of Malvolio in *Twelfth Night?* If we didn't know the name of the author, we would dismiss it as tiresome.) On the other hand, modern names and interesting ideas should not hide from us the fact that, for example, Signor Laudisi in Pirandello's *Right You Are* is the same old prankster in sophisticated disguise.

If knaves are more influential, fools are more numerous. How many fools are there to each knave of one's acquaintance? The Romans seem to have thought the normal ratio is three to one. Their Atellan Farces had four type characters: the Blockhead, the Braggart, the Silly Old Man, and the Trickster. Only the last is a knave. The others are three different kinds of fool: the moron, defeated before he starts; the braggart, defeating himself as he goes along; and the man who has recently become a fool through senility and can remember the gay days when he was a knave and heard the chimes at midnight.

It is perhaps wrong to speak of knaves and fools separately, for what has most value to farce and comedy is their interrelationship. F. M. Cornford has shown that one of the oldest relationships in the comic drama is that between the ironical man and the impostor. These are the comedian and the straight man, one a knave, the other a fool, the fun resulting from the interaction between the two. If we say that the farcical image of man is the image of a human couple, that couple will not be the *jeune premier* and the *ingénue* but the knave and the fool, the ironist and the impostor, Sir Toby Belch and Sir Andrew Aguecheek, Jack Tanner and Octavius Robinson.

To this polarity, add a paradox. In the last analysis the knave, too, is a fool. Farce and comedy are forever demonstrating that the knave's ingenuities get him nowhere. The cleverness which seems to be capability proves in the end a rhetorical or gymnastic flourish.

The farceur does not show man as a little lower than the angels but as hardly higher than the apes. He shows us man in the mass, in the rough, in the raw, in anything but fine individual flower. If Mr. Auden is right in saying that "art can have but one subject; man as a conscious unique person," then farce is not an art. The *Oxford Companion* seems to regret that the characters of farce are stupid. But they are deliberate monuments to stupidity, disturbing reminders that God has lavished stupidity on the human race with His own unrivaled prodigality.

I have mentioned some points, and they are many, where farce and tragedy meet, but here we find them at the poles. Pascal called man a thinking reed. The metaphor embraces two characteristics: intellect and weakness. If farce shows man to be deficient in intellect, it does not show him deficient in strength or reluctant to use it. Man, says farce, may or may not be one of the more intelligent animals, he is certainly an animal, and not one of the least violent either. He may dedicate what little intelligence he possesses precisely to violence, to plotting violence, or to dreaming violence. (Mona Lisa's smile might mean that she was plotting murder, but is more likely to signify that she was dreaming murders she would never plot.)

"A Mad World, My Masters!" A play with a cast of fools
tells us that it is a world of fools we live in. If that is not
a tragic image, it is not, on the other hand, an image which
the tragic poets would find beneath them. I take from what
is perhaps the greatest of tragedies these words:

> When we are born we cry that we are come
> To this great stage of fools.

What wisdom can there be without a poignant sense of
wisdom's opposite, which is folly?

THE QUINTESSENCE OF THEATRE

WHEN we talk of Charlie Chaplin are we talking of acting
or the thing acted? Nearly all discussions of him pass im-
perceptibly from the one topic to the other, and this is as
it should be. Meyerhold said: "The idea of the actor's art,
based on the worship of the mask, gesture, and movement
is inseparably linked with the idea of farce."

If melodrama is the quintessence of drama, farce is the
quintessence of theatre. Melodrama is written. A moving
image of the world is provided by a writer. Farce is acted.
The writer's contribution seems not only absorbed but
translated. Melodrama belongs to the words and to the
spectacle; the actor must be able to speak and make a
handsome or monstrous part of the tableau. Farce concentrates itself in the actor's body, and dialogue in farce is, so
to speak, the activity of the vocal cords and the cerebral
cortex. Consider the figures in Jacques Callot's engravings,
Dances of Naples (Balli di Sfessania). One cannot imagine
them performing melodramas. They have always been
considered the very incarnation of *commedia dell'arte;* and

obviously they are the incarnation of farce. One cannot imagine melodrama being improvised. The improvised drama was pre-eminently farce. In its pride it would call itself *commedia*. But we do not hear of *tragedia dell'arte*. And so I am reversing Meyerhold's dictum and saying: the idea of farce is inseparably linked with the idea of the actor's art, the *arte* of *commedia dell'arte*.* The theatre of farce is the theatre of the human body but of that body in a state as far from the natural as the voice of Chaliapin is from my voice or yours. It is a theatre in which, though the marionettes are men, the men are supermarionettes. It is the theatre of the surrealist body.

The entertainments of the *commedia dell'arte* were Atellan Farces raised to a higher power. The fools are no longer limited to three kinds, nor the knaves to one. There is a complete human menagerie.

The celebrated types of the *commedia* have deeper roots than social manners or even society itself. In Callot's *Dances* the animal origin of the characters is clear. It has been suggested that Callot may not be giving an accurate portrait of the *commedia,* but it is likely that any deviation came from knowledge and intuition as to what the *commedia* in essence was. Aristophanes' birds represent a sophisticated use of animal fable, which could not have been sophisticated from the beginning. The characters of comedy come in time to stand for the human in the most restricted sense, the human cut off from Nature. But originally they represented human nature as part of Nature-in-general, human life as part of all life. Conversely, external nature was not external: the general forces of life

* Following Allardyce Nicoll (in his *The World of Harlequin,* Cambridge University Press, 1963, p. 26), I am assuming that the traditional interpretation of the word *"arte"* as "the acting profession" is incorrect. But that interpretation presents no threat to my thesis about farce.

were to be found in the human figures. If on the tragic side, gods merge with heroes, on the comic side the knaves and fools merge with the lower orders of spirits, as they are still doing in Shakespeare's *Midsummer Night's Dream* and *The Tempest.*

The *commedia dell'arte* petered out in the eighteenth century. The nearest thing we can see to it today is a type of theatre that is not influenced by it: the so-called Peking Opera. But there is a vestige of the *commedia* in the theatre of Eduardo De Filippo in Naples, and there have been convincing attempts to reconstruct entertainments in *commedia* style by the Piccolo Teatro di Milano.

Charlie Chaplin's silent comedies are not merely vehicles for the greatest comedian of the twentieth century, they are masterpieces of farce. And there are dozens of them. No one at the time realized what they were worth, and only, I believe, the Cinemathèque in Paris has made a systematic attempt to preserve them. Even now, if these works are spoken of as art, it is the art of film that is meant. The idea of a masterpiece *of farce* seems an unacceptable proposition, perhaps even to Mr. Chaplin himself, who in later life has aimed at forms with higher standing—not with uniformly happy results.

That the era of great farce in the motion picture runs from about 1912 to about 1927 seems to many a result of mechanical accident. The motion picture camera had just been invented, the sound track had not yet been combined with it: farce was happily suited to the silent screen. It is true that certain aspects of farce could be developed on the screen far beyond the possibilities of the stage. The screen could obviously do much more with the traditional chase and pursuit. Trick photography opened up new territory for zany behavior. Even pantomime changed. The old mimes delighted to work with imaginary props. Part of their art was to do without the actual objects. On the screen, objects—from the automobile to the alarm clock—became a vast new subject matter for farce and gave us what was in many ways a new kind of farce.

But the flowering of an art form could never be mainly the result of a mechanical invention. It happened that the invention was made toward the end of an era of great farce, one of the few. "In our day," said Nietzsche in 1870, "only the farce and the ballet may be said to thrive." He was right, but no one seems to know it. To the extent that the history of Victorian theatre and drama is taught at all in the schools, the word has been that before Shaw and Wilde there were only some shadowy and austere figures like Bulwer Lytton and Tom Robertson. That is misleading because the real glory of the Victorian stage lay in the farce, the extravaganza, and the comic opera. The great names are Gilbert and Sullivan, and the young Pinero.

As for France, there is the same contrast between what one is told and the actual situation. One is told of the serious thesis drama of the younger Dumas and Augier, drama that has seemed dated since around 1900. But there is French theatre of 1860 that is still fresh today, notably the operettas of Offenbach and the farces of Labiche. In the wake of these two geniuses of light theatre came Georges Feydeau, possibly the greatest writer of farce of any country at any time. He has not had worthy successors. The era of modern farce ended with his death in 1921—which was almost exactly the time when Chaplin began to give farce up.

Chaplin's farces, then, mark not the beginning of an era, but the end of one. The movie-makers did not follow in his footsteps. And though the farcical bits were the best parts

of the later Chaplin pictures, they were only parts—of
satire, of tragicomedy, of drama of ideas.

There is a special niche for the pictures that the Marx
Brothers made in the thirties and for those of W. C. Fields
in the same period and a little later. But whereas the early
Chaplin films had been a pure triumph, both the Marx
Brothers and Fields had an uphill battle to fight with the
times. The age of phony seriousness was upon us. There
was too much aggression in Chaplin, in Fields, in the Marx
Brothers for the age of Rodgers and Hammerstein, Norman
Vincent Peale, and Dwight D. Eisenhower.

"THE BREATH OF IMAGINARY FREEDOM"

WHILE DEFINING melodrama as savage and infantile, I have
sought also to defend it as an amusing and thrilling
emanation of a natural self which we do well not to disown.
And I follow Aristotle, rather than Plato, on the question
of violence in art, concluding that melodrama, far from
tending to make Hitlers of us, affords us, insofar as it has
any effect at all, a healthy release, a modest catharsis. Much
the same can be said of farce, except that the principal
motor of farce is not the impulse to flee (or Fear), but the
impulse to attack (or Hostility). In music, says Nietzsche,
the passions enjoy themselves. If in melodrama fear enjoys
itself, in farce hostility enjoys itself.

A generation ago people used to talk against the idea of
art as escape—they had in mind escape from social problems. Melodrama and farce are both arts of escape and
what they are running away from is not only social problems but all other forms of moral responsibility. They are
running away from the conscience and all its creations, as

at the orgies that the classical scholars have sometimes talked about. Charles Lamb called Restoration Comedies "those Saturnalia of two or three brief hours," and again we can apply Lamb's words to farce:

> I am glad for a season to take an airing beyond the diocese of the strict conscience—not to live always in the precincts of the law-courts—but now and then, for a dreamwhile or so, to imagine a world with no meddling restrictions. . . . I wear my shackles more contentedly for having respired the breath of imaginary freedom.

"Not to live always in the precincts of the law-courts." To escape the law courts, to escape the tyranny of society and public opinion, to escape also the law courts of the mind and the tyranny of the judge within each breast, the inner conscience—this sounds like an admirable prescription for the pursuit of pleasure. Then why and how do these law courts and these tyrannies get into dramatic literature? Is plain pleasure not the aim of literature? Or is there another and higher pleasure to be found "in the precincts of the law-courts," both kinds of law courts?

To ask these questions is to ask: why tragedy? Why comedy?

8

TRAGEDY

THE HIGHER FORMS

THE HIGHER FORMS—tragedy and comedy—are distinguished from the lower—melodrama and farce—by their respect for reality. "Higher," in this context, signifies adult, civilized, healthy; lower signifies childish, savage, sick. By this token, the lower forms are not excluded by the higher; they are transcended by them.

Why *should* reality be respected? asks the Peter Pan—and even the James Barrie—in each of us. The question was answered by Bernard Shaw in the only phrase of his that was ever quoted by Sigmund Freud: "to be able to choose the line of greatest advantage instead of yielding in the direction of least resistance." We *would* choose, no doubt, to be Peter Pan if it were possible, but since, instead, we grow old, since, instead, we die, the case is altered. It is altered, too, on the positive side: we wish to love and be loved in a more than childish way. We long for a range of experience beyond Peter Pan's reach.

Why should we want reality in art? Art, surely, *is* the realm of Peter Pan. There, surely, we are under no compulsion to be grown up. What is wrong with the common view that what we want in a novel or a play is pleasantness?

The usual answer is that we know reality must be faced, and we tend to congratulate ourselves on our virtue in facing it, as if we were thereby nobly sacrificing our pleasure. The thought has brought its clichés—such as "stark" or "ruthless" or "unflinching" realism, as if grim writing were to be accepted for its unattractiveness.

What about the ending of *King Lear?* Do we enjoy it? The eighteenth century boldly said, No, we don't, and substituted a happy ending. Would you or I enjoy that ending more than Shakespeare's? And, if not, why not? Why should there be pleasure where there is so much pain? This is one of the classical questions of dramatic theory, asked by Hume and Schiller in the eighteenth century. And the principal idea of Freud's *Jokes and their Relation to the Unconscious* has a bearing on it.

Reality gives pain. That is why we remove from consciousness so many of our responses to it. Reality makes us feel guilty, and so arouses anxiety. To be reminded of reality renews the guilt feelings and the anxiety. Therefore a direct reminder in art would be unwelcome: one would *not* find pleasure in the pain.

Freud's theory is that we can be *bribed* to accept a reminder of such pain. The bribe consists of a certain amount of pleasure of the harmless sort—the sort that will not touch any inner spring, that will not arouse anxiety. Once we have accepted the bribe—Freud calls it forepleasure—we are less wary. We are prepared to risk anxiety if only we can enjoy the fulfillment of some of our forbidden wishes. Such enjoyment, when a joke is told, comes out with a rush at a certain point. That is the point at which we laugh. Telling jokes is an art, and except that not all arts make us laugh, it is typical. All the arts tap normally inaccessible sources of pleasure, and, so strong are our defenses, all face a strategic problem in doing so. . . . This doctrine, which I have applied to farce, can also be applied to melodrama.

Our admiration for writers of routine Victorian melodrama may be limited, and yet their work needed finesse. Psychologically, their objective was to arouse a little anxiety without arousing too much. If they aroused none, there was no thrill. If they aroused too much, people concluded that this was no entertainment and left the theatre. One can see which elements of melodrama aroused anxiety: the hideous happenings of the plot, the terrible dangers, the wickedness of the world and of the villain. How were these things kept under control? By a remoteness and exoticism, both of geography and of style, which told the spectator: we don't mean you. It was this "far-away" quality of melodrama which Zola complained of. He was prepared to arouse a lot of anxiety. Though claiming to champion Naturalism, Zola took issue with melodrama in the way a tragic poet would: he wished to grapple with guilt even at the cost of arousing anxiety.

How can such a wish possibly be shared by us, the audience? Man by nature wishes for pleasure—or, if you choose, pleasure is that for which man by nature wishes. Should he wish for pain, it must be because he finds in it even greater pleasure: this we know from the phenomenon of masochism. A wish, in other words, can be overcome only by a stronger wish. Now popular, boy scout, Rotarian, and collegiate ethics preaches that we all naturally and simply have a greater wish for facing Reality than for accepting easy Pleasure. The speeches of statesmen imply that we fellow patriots are all by nature professional facers of Reality. And should we ever "flinch," a little rhetoric, a little moralistic blackmail, will restore the spirit of derring-do within us. "Will-power" is invoked, and will-power whispers: "If you wish to wish, then you do wish."

Students of human nature, on the other hand, tend to believe that the natural wish to know is generally thwarted by the absence of any corresponding wish to face reality, this contradiction being the source of one of the archetypal tragic conflicts, classically presented by Sophocles in his *Oedipus Rex*. We can only come to wish to face reality if we are offered special inducements. Freud, as I have been saying, specified two of these: the forepleasure that comes from beauty (the attractiveness of artistic form) and a much deeper satisfaction that comes from the tapping of deeper sources, notably, from the relief of pent-up anxieties, from the tasting of forbidden fruit.

Another path to the truth in this matter might be found in *the wish to be justified*. Tragedy and comedy are concerned, as melodrama and farce are not, with justice. This fact has immense emotional interest for the audience since one of the strongest of all our wishes is the wish, not indeed to be just, but to be justified. The insistency of this wish derives from our feeling that we are not justified. Juvenal says: "This is his first punishment, that by the verdict of his own heart no guilty man is acquitted." Each guilty man—which is to say: each man—is prepared to spend his days working for an acquittal that he himself will always refuse to concede. Franz Kafka made a life work of this singular contradiction.

The strategy of comedy is to displace our guilt upon the characters in the play. *We* are detached. *They* are, in

Brecht's word, "alienated," from us. Tragedy, on the other hand, entails perhaps the most direct, singleminded, and complete identification with guilt that is offered by any art whatsoever. The dynamics of tragic plot correspond to the urgency of our quest for innocence. The passion of tragic eloquence corresponds to the urgency of our plea for a verdict of Not Guilty. But both quest and plea are vain. They could succeed only by the flouting of justice. The tragic hero *is* guilty. Guilt is his *raison d'être*. Whereas in melodrama we identify ourselves—and how ironical *that* is!—with innocence, and live under the constant threat of other people's villainy, in tragedy we identify ourselves with guilt, and live in conflict with—well, with whom? To be identified with guilt, to be dominated by guilt feelings, is to have already decided who the culprit is: it is oneself.

One may not subscribe to Schopenhauer's theory of tragedy as a whole (as stated in the third book of his *World as Will and Idea*) but there is something profound in his belief that the crime behind all the crimes of tragic plot is the crime of being born. Also pertinent is the Christian doctrine of original sin: "I demand to be justified, but I have already conceded that I am not."

To recognize the willingness of the tragic artist to appeal strongly to guilt feelings and so arouse deep anxiety is to appreciate more vividly the easy, swift, and pleasant appeal of the nontragic—particularly the melodramatic. In tragedy, man is an angel, but also a beast; and the two wrestle. How terrible! How much nicer it would be to identify oneself with angels, and blame everything that goes wrong on devils! This is exactly what the melodramatist does. This is exactly what melodrama is for. And this is exactly why melodrama, except to unworldly folk like poets and critics, is so immensely more important than tragedy. A philosopher in his study may whisper: "The world is my idea!" but the statesman on his podium, and everyman in the street before him, thunder in reply: "No! The world is our melodrama!" Hence human history—in which in every generation we angels are challenged by devils of an opposing class, race, or nation.

Poet, critic, and philosopher confront reality and have very little immediate effect on it. The statesman and his mob run the public part of reality with the help of surrealistic fantasies in which they probably even believe: hence the monolithic sincerity which makes it possible for them to talk balderdash with a straight face. How well anybody who has lived through one of their wars remembers their reiterated declaration that our side, whichever our side was, was going to win *because we were right!* In the fantasy of villains and heroes—the fantasy of melodrama—victory for the heroes goes without saying.

How Marguerite Gautier would have complicated the life of Dumas if, being what she was, she had not only performed her beautiful deed, but had lived happily ever after! So, with the vindictive aplomb of the truly virtuous, he kills her in the last act. Whereby it is again demonstrated that the wages of sin is death and, contrariwise, that only virtue pays. The modernity of it all consists largely in the substitution of tuberculosis for the gallows.

Of course, the bottom drops out of real morality when it is equated with self-interest, and—what is more relevant here—the drama loses one of its main subjects, which is the *conflict* between ethics and self-interest. Consider, for example, the classic and indispensable instance of this conflict: Love (self-interest) versus Honor (ethics). If love is always regarded as honorable, and any dishonorable feeling for a woman is regarded as, not love, but lust, the substance of the *drama de honor* has been neatly removed like a kernel from a nut. If, as I have argued, melodrama is valid within its limits, those limits are narrow ones; and it takes tragedy to transcend them.

CHARACTER IN COMEDY AND TRAGEDY

THE DIFFERENCE between the higher and lower forms is nowhere more evident than in their characters, their image of man. If farce shows us knaves and fools, if melodrama shows us villains and heroes, what do comedy and tragedy show us? The best brief answer, I think, is that they show us these same four characters in more complex forms.

Which is not to say: in more Naturalistic forms. We are accustomed to thinking of the more serious forms as a softening or toning down of the more frivolous ones. We assume that tragedy and comedy are what we call "more real," by which we mean more plausible, more everyday, more in accord with common sense and common assumption, more respectable. But there are no grounds for assuming this. The characters of Ben Jonson and Molière are quite as extravagant as the traditional types which lay to hand. Often they have a further extravagance all their own.

Ben Jonson's most famous contribution was a precise application of the theory of "humours" to comic character. His spokesman in *Everyman Out of His Humour,* in a passage I must cite a second time, ridicules merely eccentric or foolish characters and explains:

> . . . when some one peculiar quality
> Doth so possess a man, that it doth draw

> All his affects, his spirits, and his powers,
> In their confluctions, all to run one way
> This may be truly said to be a humour.

Though Jonson did not present what modern persons would call real human beings, or "individuals, not types," he did claim after his own fashion to present the whole man. To him this means setting in motion the affects, the spirits, and the powers. Volpone is more complex than a farcical character, not by virtue of biographical detail or diagnostic analysis, but by emotional fullness. His greed is not a mannerism or a symptom but a passion.

Molière's protagonists, like Jonson's, are not just eccentrics, they are madmen. They are possessed. They have an idea, and that idea is an *idée fixe* and a fever in the blood. This fever gives the plays their special emotional texture.

In *Tartuffe,* the starting point is a couple of traditional types: knave and fool, trickster and gull, in the form of a religious hypocrite and his credulous victim. This pattern has so much strength in itself that many have never seen beyond it, and so one can read that only hypocrisy is attacked, not religion, or that to be a Tartuffe is to have no respect for religion except as a mask for machinations exclusively monetary.

In the play the pattern is complicated by Tartuffe's real lechery. Elmire is for him not simply a means to a pecuniary end. He feels the temptations of the flesh, as we suspect from the moment he overdoes his disapproval of *décolletage*. He is a less successful scoundrel on that account, but a more successful creation.

Is he a hypocrite at all? Might he not believe in religion quite sincerely and, like other religious persons, fall knowingly into sin? Certainly, he is conscious of the way he deceives people. Does he not deceive himself in a way he is not conscious of? Tartuffe has, after all, as splendid a "line of talk" as any Dickens character, and the chief purpose of a comic "line of talk" is self-deception. The words fabricate a world.

Those who think of the play *Tartuffe* as harmless to religion reckon also without Orgon. He illustrates the dangers of belief. He is an enthusiast of an unworldliness which in Molière's time was being preached by all the devout. Molière goes into some detail, lest anyone miss this point. Though Tartuffe at one stage gets carried away by lechery, he is normally a cool customer. The ferment of the play comes largely from Orgon: Molière's real target is not religious hypocrisy but religious zeal. If this were a comedy of humours, one would have to say the "humour" was fanaticism or faith. But which? In that ambiguity lies the whole scandal of this famously scandalous masterpiece. Nothing of modern Naturalistic method goes to the making of Orgon. He is left nakedly ridiculous, absurd, etc., as any New York newspaperman would remark in giving the play a bad review. But he is not simple. The implications of his character can be discovered and discussed indefinitely. This at least Orgon has in common with a "real human being"—that he is an enigma.

With complexity come ambiguities. Which is even more evident in tragedy. What happens in tragedy to melodrama's villains and heroes? The tragic hero is really heroic, while the melodramatic hero really isn't. On the other hand, while the hero of melodrama is a pillar of virtue, and therefore always does the right thing, the tragic hero at some crucial point does the wrong thing, one view of the subject being that he is "betrayed by what is false within."

The interest of melodrama, as we have seen, tends to center on the villain. It is the presence of an amusing or frightening villain, in the run-of-the-mill melodramas, that makes up for the tiresome doings and even more tiresome declarations of the heroes and heroines.

Unmixed vice interests human beings, whereas, in general, unmixed virtue does not. Which is certainly something that the better writers of melodrama have known. Shakespeare, for instance. If it is reasonable to speak of *Richard III* as melodrama, the hero of this Action—not the protagonist, but the man who represents virtue and comes to the rescue—is Richmond; and his role is rather a small one, stuck on at the end. Richmond is necessary to the melodramatic picture, but he is no more than, as it were, a dab of contrasting color in a corner of the composition.

In the melodramatic writing of Charles Dickens, the "hero" may have a larger role, but we may scarcely be aware of it, because he is characteristically the passive center of the action. Mr. Murdstone and his sister dominate any scene they enter, while David Copperfield is any and every child that such things might happen to—Dickens to whom (in some measure) they did happen, his reader, everyman. David is no tragic hero; he is not even one of the memorable characters of Dickens; but he is exactly what the context requires. Much the same can be said of the colorless young men of many stage melodramas.

As for villains, the familiar lines from George Meredith's *Modern Love* are cited in support of the view that tragedy can dispense with them:

> 'Tis morning: but no morning can restore
> What we have forfeited. I see no sin:

The wrong is mixed. In tragic life, God wot,
No villain need be! Passions spin the plot:
We are betrayed by what is false within.

Fair enough. But even this passage—not offered in the first
place as dramatic theory—does not state or imply that
tragedy cannot use villains or even that it should not. It is
not tragedy but Naturalism that is thoroughly "anti-
villain." Tragedy and melodrama are closer to each other
than either of them is to Naturalistic writing.

No dramatic critic can reject villains, since they were not
rejected by the greatest of dramatists. And if Richard III is
a villain of melodrama, Iago is a villain of tragedy. What is
the difference?

Certainly not that Iago is more natural and banal. The
difference, as I see it, has two aspects: a difference in our
attitude to them and a difference in depth. We chuckle
over Richard, though he is seldom witty. Iago is usually
witty, but if we laugh, it is "on the wrong side of our
faces": for all the banter, we take him seriously.

So much for our different attitude to the two characters.
The difference in depth is harder to describe. Let us start
from the fact that readers of novels consider Iago a flat
character because he is not mediocre, and because good
and evil do not seem evenly mixed in him, as we assume
they are in most of our acquaintance. He is not created
with those touches of idiosyncrasy which the novel has
persuaded us are the exclusive signs of real life and real
humanity. But, shedding the novelistic prejudice, we can
call him, not flat, but deep. To create Iago, Shakespeare
had to sink deep in the swamp of iniquity. The character is
molded from that clinging slime. Richard III's wickedness
is always, in some degree, "for fun"; Iago's is "for real."

And in the century of Adolf Hitler we are not as inclined as our fathers were to suppose that an extravagant, even monstrous character like this corresponds to nothing in the world outside. Actually, if one compares Iago with some of the leading Nazis, one can only conclude that he is a lot more ingratiating.

Noting the villainy of this villain, some critics attribute Othello's downfall to him. Thus interpreted, the play would be that much nearer to melodrama. There is a Shakespearean subtlety in the division of responsibility between the two men. Iago instigates; but Othello is susceptible. Remove either factor, and there is no calamity. It is in melodrama that heroes are wholly innocent, wholly whole. Hence their insubstantiality. Othello is not at one with himself. He does not see himself: he dramatizes himself. He is a man of virtue, and he is a man of charm, but his destructive passions lie too near the surface: that is Shakespeare's notion of what it is to be a black man. Iago works on Othello, and he becomes inarticulate with fury. Like Hamlet, he has the wrong virtues for the particular situation, and the wrong weaknesses. It is hard to concede Othello's faults. I think we pass rather hurriedly over the later scenes. Ours is an age of barbaric race hatred. That means it is also a time when nice people become prissily defensive—denying, for example, that Othello is a barbarian. But he is. Between them, Iago and Othello combine the vices of civilization with those of barbarism.

What we wish to deny is something larger than that. The ultimate effect of Naturalism—and modern life generally—is an effort to "naturalize" and soften tragedy and comedy as a whole. In our theatre, we have had the nice Othello of Mr. Paul Robeson and the nice Hamlet of Mr. Maurice Evans. It is a tenet of many newspaper reviewers that the

leading characters of a play should be not only "believable"
but also "likable." This makes it hard going for the old
masters, whose characters are incredible and, if not necessarily hateful, certainly deplorable, bizarre, and sick.

It might be objected that the modern theatre has done
its bit for the sick, and that the modern cast of characters
more and more resembles a list of patients in a clinic. But
this retort is not an answer. The point made about
neurotics in Broadway plays is that they are good chaps at
heart. The neuroses are there, in fact, to make them
"believable," and the heart of the matter is that they are
"likable." In *Volpone,* on the other hand, there is no one to
like, and everyone is sick, not just to the point where he
becomes believable, but far beyond it—to the point where
you are tempted to *disbelieve.* Ben Jonson's characters are
"far out." His world is a madhouse.

That, you will say, is comedy, and comedy of the
harshest kind. True. But tragedy also explores morbidity.
A story like that of *Macbeth* may at first seem that of a
banal crime committed for a banal and even sensible
reason (the wish to be top man), but before Shakespeare is
finished we have become acquainted with the utter corrup-
tion of two human beings. We see a brave soldier turned to
jelly with the act of fear. We see an apparently indestructible woman disintegrate in panic. The political assassina-
tion with which the play begins is as nothing to the murder
of MacDuff's little children later. The play is a journey to
the end of the night. Modern authors from the early
Naturalists down to the beatniks have aimed at just such an
effective morbidity, and have seldom managed it.

Of the morbidity of *Hamlet* and *Oedipus Rex* we have
perhaps heard as much in the past half-century as we can
bear, but are those two plays so exceptional? Edmund

Wilson has made something psychopathological of the festering wound of Philoctetes, also of Antigone's excessive love for her brother. . . . But when I say "morbid" I am not thinking only of such symptoms and symbols as psychoanalysts fasten on. I mean something at once more commonplace and more serious.

A slight study of the characters of tragedy and comedy will reveal that both genres explore extreme deviation from the human norm, extreme disturbance of the human balance. One would not care perhaps to call tragedy and comedy narrow, and yet their interest in human nature is distinctly specialized: they limit themselves to the extreme cases. One only has to think of Tolstoy's *War and Peace,* in which the characters are *not* notably clinical, to see this by contrast. But few great writers do not have this interest in the morbid and extreme. In Tolstoy himself one observes it grow with the years—from the tragic study of adultery in *Anna Karenina* to the hideous crimes of *The Power of Darkness* and *Resurrection.*

In the France of the classical period there reigned a "healthier" idea of tragedy—a tragedy that would be heroic in the popular sense of exhibiting doughty deeds. Only, these were deeds of the spirit. It was Corneille who liked to show his people rising to all conceivable occasions in almost *in*conceivable magnanimity. For that reason his work often strikes us as untragic.

Actually, Corneille's work is not so simple. Though it was his gift to imagine actions of almost superhuman nobility—and he did *imagine* them and not merely mouth them—he was too good a dramatic artist not to follow where an Action led him; which was sometimes into hot water. In *Horatius,* a brother finds that his sister is not overjoyed at his and his country's victory, because her betrothed was on the other side and has been killed. He takes her out and murders her. Now whether this action is, on any argument, justifiable—which of course is gone into—it is, to say the least, problematic. And the explanations in the last act do not cover the case. One cannot escape feeling that this murder was not committed for reasons but on an impulse—an impulse, ultimately, of Corneille's. Corneille "the great and good," Corneille the supremely rational—a man whose life, to judge from many of his works, seems one long romance with his own superego—had his insane moments. There was a Kleist in him after all. And where the moralist got out of hand, the dramatist showed his colors.

Of Racine it is hardly necessary to speak. True, there was a Cornelian element in him. He even developed the nobly self-sacrificing protagonist in his own way. But Berenice and Andromache are less characteristic of him than Hermione and Phaedra. Like the protagonists of Shakespeare, those of Racine are slaves of passion—in his case, slaves of a single passion, the erotic one. Lust is more degrading in Racine's plays than in Shakespeare's. Where the mad lust of Antony at least offers the solace of a dream almost as great as the dream of empire, the mad lust of Hermione and Phaedra is blank and desolating. It is simply there, and irresistible. Where Antony considers the world well lost, Phaedra has no such consolation. She regards her feeling for Hippolytus with horror. But there is nothing she can do. Animal instinct, mental disease, call it what you will, is fate in this tragedy.

Phaedra is a disastrous human being and Racine knew it. She would have made a very good villainess for the ostentatiously morbid kind of tragedy that Webster wrote. But Racine took it as his assignment to make morbidity attractive, thereby making it the more morbid. According to a contemporary account:

> . . . in a conversation Racine maintained that a good poet could get the greatest crimes excused and even inspire compassion for the criminals. As those who heard him denied that this was possible and even tried to ridicule him on the strength of so extraordinary an opinion, the irritation he felt made him resolve to attempt the tragedy of Phèdre, in which he succeeded so well in winning compassion for her misfortunes that the spectator has more pity for the criminal stepmother than for the virtuous Hippolyte.

Tragedy transcends melodrama, and many people think it does so in being more sensible. William Archer thought it "logical and rational." But actually tragedy does not discard the bizarre, macabre, and morbid elements of melodrama. It exploits them farther. In tragedy, there is even more of mental sickness, even more of destructive and monstrous passion.

DEATH IN EVERYDAY LIFE

THE popular definition of a word, like the popular understanding of a subject, always irritates the expert, but is always of great interest in itself, and usually provides an ideal starting point for study. The popular understanding of tragedy and comedy is simply that the one has an unhappy, the other a happy, ending; that one ends in death, the other in marriage, which will lead to birth; that, by consequence, the one is represented by a mourning and weeping mask, the other by a rejoicing and laughing mask.

All these propositions are full of sap and substance.

Tragedy deals with death. I was saying in a previous chapter that death presented a problem in literature in that it is something neither the writer nor his audience has experienced. Death is nonexistence, and to speak of comprehending nonexistence is to speak of taking hold of a vacuum. When we say, then, that a poet deals with death, we must mean he deals with something other than death that yet leaves an impression that it is *not* something other than death. If death itself is inscrutable, it is surrounded by facts which are not. We may not know death, but we have ideas about it, we have fantasies about it. Inscrutability itself fills the mind with very concrete content in the shape of fears and surmises: one need hardly quote Hamlet's most famous soliloquy to prove it.

Since it has been the way of human beings to assume that they understand what they do not understand, death as idea and fantasy has been busily present in the mind of man. It would be an error to think that it was reserved for funerals and poetry readings. And so, if I have made a good deal of the dramatic in everyday life, I propose now to make a comment or two on death in everyday life, not in the least meaning that people die every day, though they do, but meaning that, even when no one on the premises is dying, the thought of death is present, minute by minute, in the minds of the living.

"I die daily," says Saint Paul. We see ourselves as experiencing little deaths all the time. Lying down to sleep is a little death. Saying good-bye is a little death. In both cases, a piece of life is surrendered, and to give anything up is always to die. The person in you that is a chain-smoker dies when you give up smoking. "This losing," says Emerson,

> This losing is true dying
> This is lordly man's downlying
> This his slow but sure reclining
> Star by star his world resigning.

Now we normally think of immortality as a fantasy erected upon the solid fact of death. But, in fantasy, death may well be a deduction from the prior idea of immortality or rebirth. "Nothing arises," says Santayana, "save by the death of something else." In other words, dying is something we have to do in order to live: if death did not exist, we would have to invent it. One can think of this in relation to one's personal, neurotic problems. They are all one problem: the refusal to let go of certain habits, the refusal to die. Ideally we should be able to shed habits as a snake sheds its skin. We should be virtuosos in the art of dying. But man is the sick animal, and when we say he doesn't know how to live, we mean he doesn't know how to die. He prefers the life-in-death of severe neurosis.

If this is all analogy and metaphor, what about the actual death of the body? If the thing itself is mysterious, how far do surmises, fears, and fantasies invade our living? Tolstoy said: "If a man has learned to think, no matter what he may think about, he is always thinking of his own death." Our first reaction to this statement is to say: "But that's not true at all. Just the opposite is the case. People evade thinking of death: *that's* what they are always doing." The two statements define the same situation. Death hovers all the time, everyone senses it, but while some accept death, others push it away. To push away is not to ignore. To evade something is not to act as if it were not there. Like an outflanking movement in military strategy, an evasion is only a more indirect mode of encounter.

This is not to say it makes no difference if one evades or does not evade. On the contrary, philosophies and religions may be divided into those that do, and those that do not, take death seriously. It is the habit of some forms of Oriental mysticism to make nothing of death and hence very little of life. Life is just a bridge to eternity, death the gateway at the other side of the bridge. The word Christianity now includes so many philosophies, it is impossible to state authoritatively where Christianity stands in this or perhaps any other matter, but assuredly *some* forms of Christianity follow the Oriental pattern of unworldliness, and make little of death.

One thing can be stated with certainty. The tragic attitude is the opposite of this. The man in the street's opinion is correct: tragedy makes much of death, makes a frontal attack on it, and hence implies a certain scorn for the death-dodgers of all schools of thought—from India to Forest Lawn, Los Angeles. The opposite of tragedy is not comedy but Christian Science.

And it is not a matter only of confronting one's own death when the day comes, but of living with death in mind right now. When Rilke spoke of carrying death inside him, he did not mean he was ill. He meant he was not a death-dodger. He was able to live with death.

Just as the little deaths are preludes to rebirth, so death-facing—the facing of the one big death—is, finally, life-affirming. The point is to be able to *live* with the thought of death, not to commit suicide and *be* dead. Suicide might be a result of finding the thought of death so unbearable that the extinction of the thought in real death is sought instead. Rilke wrote a compassionate but sternly disapproving elegy on the death of a poet who had killed himself at the age of twenty. It ends with the line: *"Wer spricht von Siegen? Überstehn ist alles."*—"Who speaks of victories? To see it through is everything."

"LA OSCURA RAIZ DEL GRITO"

SOME HAVE SEEN tragedy as issuing from a wound in the hero, but, since Nietzsche, it has been commoner to find the flaw in the universe itself; or in man's relation to it; or in man's lack of relation to it. In Paul Tillich's phrase, which is in the Nietzschean tradition, "man is maladjusted to the universe." Life is "absurd," as the French existentialists have it. Camus finds human effort symbolized in the myth of Sisyphus.

To what extent we need implicate the universe I don't know. I. A. Richards once paraphrased "All's right with the world," as: "All's right with the nervous system." If that's valid, we could paraphrase "Something's wrong with the universe," as "Something's wrong with the nervous system." At bottom, these contrasting statements aren't as different as they sound. If man and the universe don't suit each other, we have our choice as to which to lay the blame on. When we complain that the universe is so big, we mean we can't fit it into our heads. When we complain that we are so little, we mean we cannot fit ourselves into the scheme of things.

In such a study as the present one, I am obviously not required to comprehend or even to cross-question the universe, and my decision is already taken as to which side of the complex to examine: namely, the self. In his poem "The Two Masks" George Meredith wrote of "disturbance in the springs of pathos," and it seems to me that the experiential or psychological side of this idea of dislocation, maladjustment, incommensurability consists in such a disturbance. The tragic poet is *disturbed* to the very root of his being, and he communicates that disturbance to us.

Another writer, P. H. Frye, has used the phrase "the tragic qualm," which is helpful, especially if we retain the full meaning of the word "qualm": "a sudden attack of illness, faintness, or pain, especially nausea," says Webster. A tragedy is not "working" if it does not communicate such qualms. The tragic transcendence will not have its full force if there is no such disturbance to transcend.

Sometimes the qualm overcomes us at the low point of the hero's fortunes. It certainly did so when Sir Laurence Olivier as Oedipus screamed his realization of his dual offense. But it is not always tied to particular moments. It can be borne in upon us with the passage of many scenes, and one might be hard put to say when it rises to full consciousness, if it ever does. Just as our physical reactions to the same stimuli vary—one man's hair rises on end while another turns pale—so the particular shade of feeling, and its timing, can vary. Probably what tragedy gets down to is one's own individual form of radically negative feeling, whatever it may be: it can even be a lack of feeling, for what happens to many when they are upset is that they anesthetize themselves, they prevent themselves from feeling. But this in itself is a great shock. The flow of thoughts and feelings stops, and there is a terrifying blank. *Stunning* is one of the many words we use flippantly which deserve to be used seriously. Akin to going blank is swooning, which used to happen quite a lot in the days of Victorian tragic acting. And one is halfway to a swoon when one goes dizzy. In a way, vertigo seems the most expressive reaction of the lot. This swift bodily response tells more about shock and confusion than words are likely to do.

In the twentieth century there has been a tendency to dehydrate tragedy and make of it an ideological scheme only, a "tragic view of life." As such it has *advocates,* and the scheme of thought reveals itself as a mere *polemic:* the idea of tragedy is being used as a stick to beat someone with. In America, that someone is usually the Liberal, who stands accused of undue rationalism and optimism, and the polemicist may be anyone from a professor of theology to an editor of *Life* magazine. In Europe, the enemy may also be the Liberal, but the polemicist is likely to be the local secretary of the Communist Party or a Marxist professor of philosophy at the Sorbonne. (Racine has been studied in the light of Pascal's tragic view of life by the Marxist critic, Lucien Goldmann.) Since the whole notion of a tragic view of life was largely the creation of Nietzsche, it is proper to recall that he did not reduce tragedy to a philosophy but was capable of observing:

> The structure of the scenes and the concrete images convey a deeper wisdom than the poet was able to put into words and concepts.

Nietzsche also said:

> The sense of the tragic increases and declines with sensuousness.

And I take comfort from his words in this study of the *life* of the drama in which, without denying the *meaning* great drama ultimately has, I start out from the drama's "low life," its points of contact with our mundane existence where this is furthest from ideology and ideals.

Garcia Lorca ends his play *Blood Wedding* with the words, *"la oscura raiz del grito"*—"the dark root of the scream." The image suggests better than abstract language what the tragic poet attempts. And where: the scream begins where words and endurance end. The tragic poet takes us there, and we do not reflect that the world is absurd: we scream. Where is the scream's dark root? The poet digs with the spade of dramatic art: it is not his thought alone but his plot, his characters, his dialogue, that give the answer. The most memorable scream in drama is the scream of the protagonist in what seems to have proved the most memorable of tragedies: *Oedipus Rex*. What is that scream's dark root? There are explanations; and each one is a theory of theatre. For the root of the scream is the root of tragedy itself.

Particularly vivid for the twentieth century is Freud's amazing explanation, which goes much further than it is commonly credited with going. For the Freudian interpretation is not a limiting one in the sense that only the special neurosis of a few is involved. That in us which responds to the Oedipus story is there all the time and is present in all. Which beautifully exemplifies the presence of the past in the present, of the tragic amid the trivial, of the ultimate amid the quotidian, of death spread through all of life.

Margaret Fuller once said that she accepted the universe, and Thomas Carlyle commented: "Gad, she'd better!" Many people seem to feel that Carlyle had the better of the exchange. But Margaret Fuller could have pointed out that the tragic poets were on her side. Carlyle's remark is after all pure cynicism. He sees man as puny, and the universe as a sort of Frederick the Great multiplied by a billion. Who cares if the common soldier "accepts" Frederick the Great? The king can shoot the soldier any time he wants to. In reasoning thus Carlyle misses the something which is everything. The king can only kill the soldier, he cannot dictate his attitude. Margaret Fuller did *not* have to accept the universe. Prometheus didn't accept it. Even Schopenhauer didn't accept it—except on condition that it become his idea.

What is it to accept the universe? Maximally, it would be a metaphysics (an acceptance of the universe through a supposed understanding of it), or a religious faith (an acceptance of the universe by making some theological assumptions about it). Such maximum acceptance is not required of the tragic poet. A minimum acceptance will do—acceptance without assumptions as to the total meaning, or as to whether there is such a meaning; acceptance, then, of the mystery of what is around one and of one's own ignorance, acceptance of the unknown.

If the tragic poet does not need metaphysics or theology to explain the mystery, neither will he allow the scientist to explain it away. While the tragic attitude is by no means hostile to reason it is hostile to that rationalism which persuades men that there *is* no mystery or that there won't be by the end of next week when all our measurements have been taken. One of Shakespeare's characters has described and deplored the viewpoint of reductive science:

> They say miracles are past; and we have our philosophical persons, to make modern and familiar, things supernatural and causeless. Hence is it that we make trifles of terrors, ensconcing ourselves into seeming knowledge, when we should submit ourselves to an unknown fear.

Here we have a bold confrontation of two opposed attitudes, one of which is familiar and easy to comprehend, the other a little strange, even incomprehensible. Making trifles of terrors is what science does, destroying belief in hobgoblins. But "submitting ourselves" to fear of the unknown? Why? Isn't fear bad? Don't we demand "free-dom from fear"? Logic would certainly tell us so. It is psy-cho-logic that might tell us otherwise. As Rilke puts it in a letter:

> He who does not at some time with definite determi-nation consent to the terrible in life or even exult in it never takes possession of the inexpressible fullness of the power of our existence but walks on the edge and sometime when the day of reckoning comes will prove to have been neither alive nor dead.

If suffering alone does not make a tragic hero, and there has to be resistance to suffering, so in us, the audience, it is not enough to shrink from terror *in* terror, we have to grasp terror by the hand. Paradoxically, as we accept terror more, we shall *be* terrified less—another possible meaning for the word Catharsis. We encounter here the strength that lies in the admission of weakness, the courage that lies in the admission of cowardice.

AWE

FEAR is not merely reduced by being accepted, it is also changed. What it changes to is best expressed by the word Awe. Absent from melodrama, awe is a characteristic mode of fear in great tragedy. Awe is fear transfigured.

"*Le silence éternel de tous ces espaces infinis m'effray-ent.*" Pascal's words, reduced to banality, say: "I am fright-ened by the silence and size of the universe." The phrasing, the diction, the rhythm are what indicate the awe to which fear rises. "The eternal silence of all those infinite spaces terrifies me." Like Margaret Fuller, Pascal accepts the universe.

Pascal (Lucien Goldmann is right) is the purest and greatest of tragic *thinkers*: an intellectual conception has put him in an intellectual panic. We do not have tragic poetry, however, until the intellectual element has been, not indeed eliminated, but fused with the sensuous. The poet must root the intellect in the sensuousness, as God did when he made each one of us. There is a fine example of tragic awe rendered poetically in the second part of Goethe's *Faust*. It is the awe of Faust himself when Mephistopheles gives him the key to the realm of the Mothers. Goethe gives the passage, to begin with, some blatantly sexual symbolism. The key expands when Faust takes hold of it, then lights up and gives off sparks. Mephistopheles tells Faust he must take it to the underworld where a tripod will show him the Mothers. To get out again, he must touch the tripod with the key.

Despite Goethe's reputation for abstractness, Faust does not speak of awe in the abstract. What happens is that, when first the Mothers are mentioned, he shudders. He shudders again when the key grows and gives off sparks. He is afraid to hear the mothers mentioned, and Mephistopheles suggests that he should call the trip off. Faust replies: No, he will not draw back from what is terrifying. Whatever the world may make him pay for the experience, he prefers to experience horror:

> *Doch im Erstarren such' ich nicht mein Heil,*
> *Das Schaudern ist der Menschheit bestes Theil;*
> *Wie auch die Welt ihm das Gefühl vertheure,*
> *Ergriffen, fühlt er tief das Ungeheure.*

The old Calvin Thomas edition in which many of us have studied *Faust* very properly suggests that *"Schaudern"* here betokens Awe. "To feel awe is the best part of being a man." That is an astonishing enough statement, so different from what parents teach us, or teachers, or even priests, but in the German it has even greater absurdity. "Shuddering is the best part of being a man." The word *"Schaudern"* has already occurred twice in the same scene. Faust *shuddered* to hear the mothers mentioned and, challenged by Mephistopheles, he now tells him that *to shudder is to be a man.* In this manner, awe becomes concrete, physiological.

"Das Schaudern ist der Menschheit bestes Theil." The line tells us something essential about tragedy. While stopping far short of either renewal or expiation, it defines an attitude with two opposing sides: the shudder itself, the tremor, the frenzy, the panic, the confusion, and, on the other hand, the acceptance of these, the feeling that one must prove equal to them, that one must not hope to escape them, that one's best hope is in the lack of such hope.

COMPASSION

SO MUCH FOR FEAR. What of pity? Although Aristotle himself obviously intends to speak quite neutrally, pity differs from fear in being not merely a reaction but a reaction for which one takes credit, a virtuous reaction. From the virtue flows a vice. Because we feel that our pity is virtuous we begin to enjoy it. Then we start to look for potential objects of our pity. These objects become our victims.

So it is that pity has a curious record in the history of civilization. It has not, in general, lost its reputation as a good thing. Yet it is suspect. And not a few thinkers have denounced it. The denunciations generally stress that most pity is self-pity. William Blake adds that it is debilitating: "Pity divides the soul and man unmans." Blake also grasps the "Marxist" aspect—that pity victimizes. "Pity would be no more/If we did not make somebody poor."

As far as the drama is concerned, one cannot ask to have pity excluded altogether: Aristotle was right to give it a legitimate place. Yet pity is unacceptable when it goes on too long. One can stand just so much of it: sentimental people are people who can stand more than that. They need further education. Tears, as Ovid noticed, are voluptuous, and the drama cannot afford too much voluptuousness. People have to stop crying so that the play can continue.

Pity is needed in a melodrama, and stays within bounds if it is properly offset by more "manly" emotions. In Greek tragedy, there is less pity than the famous phrase of Aristotle might suggest. How little pity goes to the victims in the *Agamemnon!* How marvelous the way Aeschylus manages to present what is in itself a most pitiful situation—that of Prometheus—and then lavish very little pity on him! Even in *Oedipus Rex,* how much stronger the fear, the awe, the sense of doom, than the pity we feel even for a man who puts his eyes out!

Shakespeare wrote after centuries of Christianity, and there is much more pity in his works than in those of the Greeks. Even so, there is not a great deal of mere, sweet pathos. Rather, we come upon another phenomenon, a higher kind of pity, one that is not open to the charges of the psychologists. And to be fair, in exploring such charges,

I find that some psychologists distinguish two kinds of pity, a good and a bad, one that is genuinely generous, and one that is openly or secretly self-indulgent. Ludwig Jekels wrote an important paper trying to establish both these types from exact clinical details. Now the English language has a word for the higher pity: compassion. There is a supreme instance of it in *King Lear*.

> Do not laugh at me;
> For as I am a man, I think this lady
> To be my child, Cordelia.

> And so I am, I am.

> Be your tears wet? Yes, faith. I pray weep not;
> If you have poison for me I will drink it.
> I know you do not love me; for your sisters
> Have, as I do remember, done me wrong:
> You have some cause, they have not.

> No cause, no cause.

Lear's lines are full of pity: it is Cordelia's that show her compassion and, through hers, Shakespeare's.

SHAKESPEARE TO KLEIST

COMPASSION TRANSCENDS PITY somewhat as awe transcends fear, and, like awe, seems to take tragedy to create it, whereas pity and fear are sufficient for melodrama. In all the Shakespearean tragedies fear rises to awe, and pity rises to compassion. This can hardly be said for the work of any of Shakespeare's English contemporaries. Marlowe is occasionally awesome, often fearful, seldom pitiful, and perhaps never compassionate.

Racine has a pre-eminence in French tragic drama comparable to Shakespeare's in English. While it is his pity that has been most spoken of, we should note that it almost always rises to a Shakespearean compassion. No figure in all tragedy is shown with more compassion than his Andromache, and the "scandal" of his *Phaedra* lies in the fact that compassion is felt for a villainess.

Corneille is a very great dramatist but not so richly tragic as Racine because of his lack of compassion. True, he avoids also the sentimentality of mere pity.

In the late eighteenth century, the Germans labored to create tragedy that would be neo-Shakespearean or neo-Greek or both. Schiller's *Mary Stuart* shows the limitations of the tragic pattern of destruction and renewal when the destruction is not deep and real and ugly enough. There is a warning here to all who wish to define tragedy as ennobling: one can easily make a story ennobling and thereby fail to make it tragic. *Mary Stuart* is a good play but one does not find in it an experience of chaos. That Mary has been vicious before the play opens is reported. She certainly is not vicious after the rise of the curtain. Where is the deep root of Schiller's scream? A question not to be asked—for Schiller has not screamed. That Mary should go to heaven is theologically correct; but, dramaturgically speaking, a person should not so easily get away with murder.

At the opposite pole from Schiller is his younger contemporary Kleist. Here is a poet who has no trouble getting down to the "disturbance in the springs of pathos." Here is a man who was not only fearful but positively terrorized. No one conveys a sense of vertigo better than he. His problem is to convince the audience that he is not insane.

For the danger is that we say: yes, but this is just a report on very abnormal experience, here is a psychotic who happens to be able to write. Great as must have been the temptation, Kleist is able to avoid self-pity, but there is little or no compassion in his work either. Does Aristotle wish us to understand that pity and fear must be present in equal proportions? The disproportion in Kleist is forbiddingly great: so much fear, and even awe, so little compassion, or even pity.

ANGER

BUT from the vantage point of this chapter, Kleist seems the last of the ancients. The modern drama that began in the generations after his death was preponderantly a drama of pity alone. The pitiable protagonist, or "little man," succeeded the tragic hero. The rarity of compassion, fear, and awe is acutely felt by all who know the masters of the drama.

The social dramatists tried to eke pity out with anger. Could pity and anger be to the social drama what pity and fear had been to tragedy? The formula has not proved too fruitful, though it applies to most of the more serious American plays. The author is indignant, and he shows the pitiable plight of the working class or of persecuted minorities. (The same with British drama. *Look Back in Anger* could as well be named *Look Back in Self-Pity*.) In this modern drama, it is not only the pity that palls and betrays. The anger also fails to do what is expected of it. The rage refuses to rage, and at best yields peppery repartee.

Like pity, anger suffers from natural handicaps. In art, it

is viable only in certain contexts. The Old Testament can present angry men of God who rail in magnificent poetry. They do not, however, rail in magnificent drama. Even when not self-righteous, the angry man is single-minded: for him there is no "case for the other side." A dramatist is anything but single-minded. He is of two minds—or more. He would have no need of his many voices if, like an irate prophet or Juvenalian satirist, he enjoyed listening to his own one voice. His anger has to be split up and distributed among varied characters. And, characteristically, it comes to us through the filter of comedy and farce. If "social drama" is more uniformly angry, it is also less uniformly dramatic. Much of it could be regarded as unsuccessful comedy, comedy that cannot manage a smile. In Ibsen social drama becomes truly dramatic by ceasing to be, in the usual sense, social. Nor is anger the mainspring of Ibsen's plays. It is far more important in Brecht, but in Brecht social drama turns again to comedy.

Our conclusion should perhaps be that, in the drama, anger needs to be disciplined by wit and humor; by pity it is only diluted and diffused.

THE DIALECTIC OF TRAGEDY

I HAVE BEEN SPEAKING of tragedy in terms of a disturbance and of the transcendence of that disturbance. Which is the more important: the disturbance or the transcendence? The transcendence cannot occur without the disturbance which it transcends, while the disturbance can easily exist untranscended. But this is hardly a sufficient answer. We need to ask: what is the final impact of tragedy?

E. M. W. Tillyard has suggested that there are, at

bottom, three patterns of tragic action. The first is that of suffering and endurance; the second, destruction and renewal; the third, sacrifice and expiation. An instance of each will suffice to fix each pattern in the mind. The *Prometheus* of Aeschylus is a classic instance of suffering endured. Milton's *Samson Agonistes* is a classic instance of destruction followed by renewal. Sophocles' *Oedipus Rex* is the most celebrated instance of sacrifice and expiation.

The three patterns have this in common: each consists of a duality, a negative and a positive pole, the negative elements being suffering, destruction, and sacrifice; the positive elements being endurance, renewal, and expiation. The first pattern—suffering and endurance—must be regarded as the basic one, since it is included in both the others. There is no destruction or sacrifice without suffering. There is no renewal or expiation without endurance. If we are trying to decide what is the minimum demand to make of a tragedy it is that it presents the features of the first pattern: suffering and endurance.

Now while either renewal or expiation represents a transcendence of the suffering, mere endurance does not. If there is transcendence in the Action of the Aeschylean *Prometheus,* it must have come in the later parts of the trilogy, which are lost. Conceivably the Greeks in their trilogies—which, furthermore, were followed by a comical satyr play—generally aimed at moral transcendences and so, with exceptions, such as Euripides, took the morally affirmative view of tragedy, which today seems to be the favored view. Nonetheless, it is Euripides whom Aristotle called *the most tragic* of dramatists, presumably because his stories are the most horrible and do not end in harmony. The error to guard against is that of basing an account of tragedy on one school or individual. This is just playing favorites. There *is* tragedy which ends on dissonance.

Gonzáles de Salas, a scholar of the seventeenth century, wrote in his commentary on Aristotle's *Poetics*:

> According to the Philosopher, the two principal parts of the compound plot are the Reversal and the Recognition, adding yet in another place a third, that being the Disturbance or Perturbation [*turbación*] of the spectator's spirit.

I don't know what other place in Aristotle Salas had in mind. The doctrine seems likely to be an idea of his own, calculated to accommodate tragedies of what we may call the negative type—tragedies in which the suffering, though endured, is not transcended. As modern critics have pointed out, the theory could be applied to such a play as Calderón's *Surgeon of His Honour* in which, arguably, wife-murder perturbs the spectator's spirit because it is committed in the name of honor. Here, possibly, the tragic qualm is what the whole tragedy aims at producing.

Although this instance is not uncontroversial, it is relatively simple. The dialectic of *King Lear* is much more intricate. As chief thesis and antithesis we could take these two propositions: "As flies to wanton boys are we to the gods,/They kill us for their sport." And: "The gods are just and of our pleasant vices/Make instruments to plague us." Our first inclination, as schoolboys, is to be so struck with the first proposition, and so bowled over by the horrors in the story, that we conclude: that is obviously the theme of the play. It has often been cited as such. When, however, we get to the university, we are confronted with scholars who demolish our schoolboy interpretation with erudition, professional efficiency, and a certain amount of glee. Filling in the background of Elizabethan thought, and proving beyond a doubt that England was a Christian country, even a Protestant one, they conclude that what we have here is a Christian, even a Protestant play, that justifies the ways of God to men.

One must beware of steeping authors in their time so thoroughly that they drown. Even more than he represents other people, a great poet is himself. I am not saying that Shakespeare was a man of unorthodox views and militant temperament. I think *King Lear can* be read as a justification of the gods. But even if Shakespeare came back to earth to endorse this reading, there is always an appeal from the philosophy of a play to its spirit, and there is always an appeal from an author's intentions to his works.

It is likely enough that Shakespeare saw himself as giving a Christian answer to the problem of evil. To try to give any other answer in a public theatre—this is the sort of thing historians delight to point out—would have been a fantastic proceeding. The question is: does the play, as against the one line quoted, bear this interpretation? I think the answer has to be found, not in a line here and there, but in the plot and the characters and the interrelationship of many lines. My feeling is that Shakespeare is deeply troubled by all the suffering and evil in the world, and that the play is far from embodying a quiet faith in the Christian attempt to explain and justify them. If I am right, behind the opposition of the quoted lines (an opposition of rival views) is another opposition: that between having and not having views. The validity of human understanding, Christian or otherwise, is questioned. Shakespeare has seen so much that he is staggered. All he achieves by way of affirmation is to "seize terror by the hand" and recover sufficiently from the dizziness to be able to write the play. It is a case of vertigo recollected in tranquillity.

I should have had an easier time, because no one would disagree with me, had I taken one of Racine's plays to make this point with. Except that it would not have made *this* point. Racine wrote tragedies in conscious rebellion from his Church. The Shakespeare phenomenon is more complex. What it means, I think, is that tragedy cannot be contained within any philosophy: it is not even existentialist—it is existential. What the Restoration did to Shakespeare was to accommodate him to a philosophy. The happy ending to *Lear* makes sense. Sense is *exactly* what it makes. Shakespeare's play does not make sense. Sense is exactly what it does not make: it is an image of the nonsensical life we live, the nonsensical death we die.

Only Samuel Johnson with his prodigious candor lets us know the real reasons the eighteenth century had for preferring doctored Shakespeare—Shakespeare, he says in effect, is too painful, one cannot stand it. It is clear from Johnson's remarks that neo-classic theories are but a rationalization of the fear of the anxiety which Shakespeare raised. *Lear* is a play to arouse anxiety: it pierces the armor of our ideas, and Shakespeare's, and strikes to the heart. The "disturbance" is "in the springs of pathos."

Should we generalize from this instance and say that great tragedy simply disturbs and that the disturbance is not transcended? That would be nearer the truth, in my opinion, than the dominant view of our time, namely, that tragedy is directly "positive" and "optimistic." And yet, even in *Lear*, even in *Lear* as I have just interpreted it, there is a transcendence: the transcendence implied in the power to write the play. This, I think, is the only kind of transcendence the tragic poet can promise, and it is therefore the kind that belongs to our minimum demand on his services.

Tragedy embodies an experience of chaos, and the only cosmos that the tragic poet can *guarantee* to offset it with is the cosmos of his tragedy with its integration of plot, character, dialogue, and idea. Pierre-Aimé Touchard has a splendidly simple phrase for the phenomenon tragedy. He calls it a "song of despair." The thought is an exquisite paradox because despair does not sing. If a despairing man starts to sing he is already transcending the despair. His song is the transcendence.

If it is helpful to see tragedy, for a change, as psychological rather than philosophic, and aesthetic rather than moral, one should add that the aesthetic transcendence of suffering, disorder, and meaninglessness has a moral value. It signifies courage, which one might call the tragic virtue. And there is an element of wisdom in tragedy. Giving up the universe as an insoluble riddle, even trying to get it off one's back for a while because it is an unbearable burden— there is some wisdom in this. And there is more in the acceptance of mystery. Finally, if we can learn from tragedy that we are not equipped to learn very much about anything, we thereby learn a little something about our unequipped selves.

Tragedy's truths are home truths. As Shelley said in his Preface to *The Cenci:*

> The highest moral purpose aimed at in the highest species of the drama is the teaching of the human heart, through its sympathies and antipathies, the knowledge of itself.

One need not be overawed. This high purpose is after all continuous with the childish purposes of theatre as I have tried to define them. We learn to exist by the identifications of childhood. We learn to know we exist by the sympathies and antipathies of adulthood. Self-knowledge lies at the end of a road that starts out with self-identification. The sympathies and antipathies of a tragic play define the self of the playwright, and can therefore help to define the self of any spectator who enters into them.

9

COMEDY

"I WAS ONLY JOKING!"

WHEN a person vehemently denies something that has not been affirmed, we wonder why he goes to the trouble, and we conclude that expressly what he is denying is true. It is not surprising that this form of no-that-means-yes should turn up frequently on the psychiatric couch where the patient's whole problem lies in his unwillingness to affirm what he knows is so. But in this, as in other respects, the man on the couch is only confronting a possibly acute case of a certainly universal complaint.

Now, instead of using the word no, a patient may burst out laughing. If he should also spell out in words what the laughter has said in grimaces and noise, he would say: "What you just said is fantastic! You can't be serious! I can't let you find me out like that. Please observe that not only am I nothing daunted, I am daunting you with a laughter which, as you know from your psychological researches, signifies victory and scorn!" Unfortunately, if like most American patients, this patient has done a little psychological reading himself, he knows that strenuous disclaimers are read as confessions of guilt.

Such laughter, far from being confined to clinical situations, is common in all social intercourse. Indeed we have stumbled here upon one of the basic functions of laughter generally, and of all publicly displayed gaiety, frivolity, flippancy, and so on. Even commoner than this "You can't be serious!" is: "But I was only joking!" And an interesting variant on this takes place when one's companion refuses to ignore the serious intent and one retorts: "Can't you take a joke?" conceding the point by an aggrieved and anxious tone.

We have seen that surprisingly blunt aggressions can be undertaken just because of that: "But it isn't serious"— "ma non è una cosa seria," in Pirandello's phrase—which the farce convention carries with it. But then, farce is only serious to the extent that the hostility is felt, and not to the extent of a conviction that the hostility is justified. Comedy brings with it such serious judgments that, but for the disclaimers, a comic play would invite description as a "powerful indictment" or a "shocking disclosure." This is only another way of saying what I have intimated already: that if comedy loses its frivolous tone it becomes noncomic social drama.

Comedy takes over the grave and gay manner of farce. It is the opposing element, the subterranean and eruptive element, that is different. In farce what lies beneath the surface is pure aggression, which gets no moral justification, and asks none. Aggression is common to farce and comedy, but, while in farce it is mere retaliation, in comedy it is might backed by the conviction of right. In comedy, the anger of farce is backed by the conscience.

The ethical difference brings with it quite different emotional colors. Farce offers the one simple pleasure: the pleasure of hitting one's enemy in the jaw without getting hit back. The disapproval expressed in comedy offers a wide range of emotional possibilities, corresponding to the different temperaments that do the disapproving. A man can disapprove almost without disapproving, delicately, saucily, ambiguously, like Congreve; or, like Congreve's contemporary, Jonathan Swift, he can disapprove balefully, searingly, agonizingly.

Many discussions of the comic embrace the Congreves of the art but not the Swifts. Swift, to be sure, was not a playwright, and writers of stage comedy have perhaps nearly always leaned more to Congreve's side than Swift's. Yet this could be because most of them are mediocre. When we take comedy at its admitted greatest—in Machiavelli, or Jonson, or Shakespeare, or Molière—we find the dark undercurrent at its fastest and most powerful. There is no exact terminology to deal with these phenomena, so I will choose the most everyday words and say that what we get ranges between the poles of *bitterness* and *sadness*. Bitterness we know from satire outside the drama, from Juvenal, from Swift. Among the dramatists, Machiavelli and Jonson are bitter. Molière and Shakespeare have bitterness in their repertoire, yet theirs is not predominantly a bitter comedy, it is sweetly melancholy, and at moments overwhelmingly sad.

Now all mirth, I was saying in the chapter on farce, has bitter as well as sweet springs. It is just that, in farce, the bitterness is never allowed to come flooding to the surface. The water we drink in a farce has, as it were, the merest tinge of bitterness, suggesting that there is more beneath, yes, but not destroying the sweet flavor. The violence of

W. C. Fields and Harpo Marx and Charlie Chaplin is there but we are prevented by very clear means from "taking it seriously" and linking it with the violence of Al Capone or Hitler. Nor in farce can we ever be in the mood to feel sorry for the victims. We are having too good a time doing the victimizing. Toward both the attacker and the attacked farce is as unemotional as it is unreflective. Precisely that anti-emotional attitude which Bergson attributes to the comic in general belongs, as I see it, to farce in particular. Farce, not comedy, is "unfeeling." Conversely, the bitterness and sadness that so readily come to the surface in comedy constitute our first, best evidence that in comedy feeling is not only present but abundant.

Farce affords an escape from living, a release from the pressures of today, a regression to the irresponsibility of childhood. The comic sense, as against the farcical impulse, tries to deal with living, with the pressures of today, with the responsibilities of adulthood. Its (in so many ways) dual character presupposes in the comic artist a dual equipment: on the one hand, a "lust for life," an "evolutionary appetite," an eagerness and zest in sheer being, and on the other a keen and painful awareness of the obstacles in the path, the resistances and recalcitrancies, the trials by fire and water, the dragons, forests, and caves that menace us, and the thickets and swamps in which we flounder.

Comedy has this in common with farce: in the end it decides to look the other way. But there is a difference. Comedy has in the meantime looked the right way. Comedy has seen; has taken note; and has not forgotten. Farce all takes place well to this side of despair, brashly, cockily, sophomorically. Comedy takes place on the other side of despair. It is an adult genre. What Joseph Conrad called the shadow-line has been crossed.

In farce we hit back at our oppressor and, in so doing, draw on the primitive, childish sources of pleasure. No pleasure can be purer and more unequivocal than such draughts from the primordial spring. Our experience of comedy, in being more subtle, is also more mixed. To describe and appraise it one perforce uses for purposes of comparison, not farce, but tragedy.

"LET'S NOT GO INTO THAT!"

"TRAGEDY," said Sir Philip Sidney, "openeth the greatest wounds and sheweth forth the ulcers that are covered with tissue." The metaphor conveys the directness of tragedy's relation to pain. Now the plain man's notion that comedy has no such direct relation to pain is correct. The plain man goes wrong only if he assumes that comedy has nothing to do with pain at all.

The further implication of the "I was only joking!" is: "Let's not go into that: this is a comedy!" Such an implication may be located in the comic tone as such. Byron is spelling the point out when he says: "And if I laugh at any mortal thing, 'Tis that I may not weep." "Let's not go into that" means: "That won't bear going into." Here we have a pessimism that is blacker than tragedy, for tragedy presupposes that everything can be gone into.

Going into everything—plunging into every dark abyss —tragedy brings us to the point of vertigo. Admittedly, comedy does not. The intimation of pain is there, but, in this art, appearances must be maintained, the texture must not lose its lightness. Or not for long.

In great comedy the convention of gaiety is from time to

time in danger. Some critics get quite nervous about the fact, and begin to wonder if this is really comedy any more. Mozart's *Cosi fan tutte,* for instance. That one of the ladies begins to fall in love in earnest and to sing with genuine passion has caused raised eyebrows. Isn't it a violation of comic convention? I would ask, rather: is it not one of the things that lifts *Cosi fan tutte* above the innumerable works in which convention is not violated? Anyone, after all, can refrain from violating convention.

An example from English drama—a different kind of example—is the Celia scene in *Volpone.* To see Volpone cheating rascals, to see a cheat cheating other cheats, is within the usual bounds of comedy. To see him seducing a truly virtuous wife with the help of her knave of a husband is something else again. Respecters of stability in conventions, moral and aesthetic, may disapprove, but to my mind it is just such touches that make Jonson a great writer of comedy. It is even possible that Jonson himself, priding himself on correctness of theory, would have wilted under "conventional" criticisms. Jonson's comic genius is by no means contained in his theories. There is tension within the plays between the author's conscious and always highly proper ideas and his deep sense of chaos. Such a tension is far more productive than either the ideas or the sense of chaos alone. Comedy rises through such tensions to grandeur and to greatness.

After Mozart and Ben Jonson, let me cite Molière. He has his own form of "Let's not go into that." It is this: "I'd better end this comedy fast, or it may not remain a comedy." At the end of *The Would-be Gentleman,* M. Jourdain is no longer merely eccentric or willful, he is demented. The end of the play spares us the unhappy consequences. The ending of *Tartuffe* is only slightly different. Its foundation is: "This comedy will have a tragic ending unless the king intervenes at once." Historical scholars like to remind us what a good monarchist Molière was. But he was an even better dramatist. Happy endings are always ironical (like everything that is happy in comedies), and Molière has made the irony poignant. It is only a step from here to *The Beggar's Opera* where a happy ending is openly mocked. There is a danger to comedy in such open mockery. The sticklers for strict adherence to conventions have this much right on their side: when the convention of comedy is defied beyond a certain point, comedy will give place to something else. I would only add that this is not necessarily a misfortune, and in the next chapter I shall try to show how *The Beggar's Opera* marks a step from comedy toward an equally worthy genre: tragi-comedy.

TRAGEDY AND COMEDY: SOME GENERALIZATIONS

WE conventionally consider comedy a gay and lighthearted form of art, and we regard any contrasting element as secondary, an undertone, an interruption, an exception. I am proposing, instead, to regard misery as the basis of comedy and gaiety as an ever-recurring transcendence. Seen in this way, comedy, like tragedy, is a way of trying to cope with despair, mental suffering, guilt, and anxiety. But not the same way. The tragic injunction, in the words of Stein in *Lord Jim,* is: "in the destructive element, immerse!" It is: Walk, like Rilke, with death inside you! Take terror by the hand! More prosaically put: accept the obstacles life places in your way, and confront them! Now, of course, the comic stance is comparatively opportunistic.

Its strategy is to evade and elude the enemy, rather than to tackle him. Inevitably the moralists will say that where tragedy is heroic and sublime, comedy is cowardly and frivolous—like Falstaff, its banner carrier. Serving survival better than morals, and traditionally hostile to the professional moralists, it will get better marks in biology than in religion. But since the goods it advertises are definitely pleasures, though it may lack champions, it can never lack customers.

The pleasures it peddles are, in the first instance, those of farce; for the higher forms include the lower. But, just as the satisfactions of tragedy transcend those of melodrama, so those of comedy transcend those of farce. I described in the last chapter how, in tragedy, fear turns to awe. And awe, whatever its intellectual content, if any, is an affirmative feeling, an inspired and numinous feeling, bordering upon ecstasy. The intensity and beauty of awe are in direct ratio to the quantity of horror overcome. Now it is much the same with that higher pleasure of comedy which we call joy. We can receive it only from an author in whom we sense joy's opposite. The comic dramatist's starting point is misery; the joy at his destination is a superb and thrilling transcendence. Given the misery of the human condition in general, what could be more welcome?

Tragedy is one long lament. Not restrained or elegaic but plangent and full-throated, it speaks all the pity of life and the terror. The comic poet does not speak his feelings directly but veils them, contradicts them with pranks or elegancies. It is not necessarily the feelings themselves that differ from those of tragedy, it can rather be the way they are veiled. Comedy is indirect, ironical. It says fun when it means misery. And when it lets the misery show, it is able to transcend it in joy.

All kinds of things have been said about the ending of *The Misanthrope,* but no one that I heard of ever suggested that Alceste will kill himself. He might be a more consistent character if he did. But it is tragic characters who are consistent in that way. "We are people," says Jean Anouilh's Antigone, "who ask questions right up to the end." That is just what Sophocles's Oedipus does despite Jocasta's warnings. In tragedy, but by no means in comedy, the self-preservation instinct is overruled.

At the core of any good tragedy is a profound disturbance of the human equilibrium. This is transcended, at least aesthetically, in the tragic poem itself; and such aesthetic transcendence argues a kind of courage. It is not so clear that each comedy reflects a particular experience of this kind. One cannot tell, because even if the experience were there, comedy would shield it from sight. What one can tell is that the comic writer knows about such things in his bones.

The tragic poet writes from a sense of crisis. It would never be hard to believe of any tragedy that it sprang from a particular crisis in the life of its author. The comic poet is less apt to write out of a particular crisis than from that steady ache of misery which in human life is even more common than crisis and so a more insistent problem. When we get up tomorrow morning, we may well be able to do without our tragic awareness for an hour or two but we shall desperately need our sense of the comic.

Tragedy says, with the Book of Common Prayer: "In the midst of life we are in death." The paradox of this sentiment is that, as it sinks in, the sense of life, of living, is renewed. And the man who truly feels that "the readiness is all" attains a rare serenity, not only in dying but in living. Comedy says, "In the midst of death we are in life."

303

Whatever the hazards of air travel, we continue to plan for the morrow. We are not often in the mood of the tragic hero just before his end, when he has attained to a complete stillness of the will. "The readiness is all" is a noble sentiment but the exact reverse of it also has its human point.

I warmed both hands before the fire of life,

(so William Lyon Phelps parodied Landor):

It fades and I'm not ready to depart.

The desire to live is not merely love of living. It is also greed. Comedy deals with the itch to own the material world. Hence its interest in gluttons who imbibe part of this world, and misers who hoard another part. And from *devouring* and *clutching,* human nature makes a swift leap to *grabbing.* In how many comic plots there is theft or the intention of theft! If men did not wish to break the tenth commandment, comic plotting, as we know it, could never have come into being.

It is possible that in my discussion of "Death in Everyday Life" I gave tragedy too benign an image. This would be the time to add that very often the subject of tragedy is not dying but killing. Tragic stories from *Agamemnon* to *Macbeth,* and from *The Duchess of Malfi* to *Penthesilea,* embody the impulse to kill. People who express surprise at the piles of corpses on the tragic stage are asking tragedy to reflect their actions, and they have not committed murder; but tragedy reflects their souls, and in their souls they *have* committed murder. Modern psychology, with its intensive study of daily living, daily imagining, has had no trouble demonstrating the ubiquity of murderous wishes. A human being, in sober fact, needs very little provocation to wish his neighbor dead. The joke behind the joke in the colloquial use of "Drop dead!" is that the phrase means exactly what it says. Children of three are also taken to be joking when they tell a parent they wish he or she were dead. The joke is on the parent, and it is gallows-humor at that.

Comedy is very often about theft, exactly as tragedy is very often about murder. Just as the tragic poets present few scenes of dying or being dead but many (on stage or off) of killing, so comedy has fewer scenes of possession than of expropriation (or the plan to expropriate). There is a technical reason in both cases: it is of the nature of dramatic art to show, not states of being, but what people do to people. Death is a state, possession is a state, murder and theft are what people do to people. But there is a nontechnical reason for the technical reason—as in art there always is. Drama, the art of the extreme, seeks out the ultimate act that corresponds to ultimate fact. In the tragic world, if death is the ultimate fact, the infliction of death is the ultimate act. In the comic world, if possession is the ultimate fact, dispossession is the ultimate act. The motor forces are hatred and greed respectively.

To steal is to falsify, for it is to forge, as it were, a title to ownership. The greed we find in comedy is an offshoot of the spirit of falsehood and mendacity. St. John's gospel speaks of Satan as both "the father of lies" and "a murderer from the beginning," and this is to say that the mischief in both comedy and tragedy is the very Devil and, conversely, that Satan has a great traditional genre to report each of his two favorite pastimes. "And of these two diabolical manifestations," a recent theological commentator adds, "it is arguable that falsity is the more essentially Satanic." It is arguable, as we have seen, that comedy is a blacker art than tragedy.

The other face of the greed in comedy is tenacity, by which men survive. It is hard to survive. The tragic hero, at the last, can attain to the readiness and ripeness that are all. The rest of us, first and last, cling to existence and on our deathbeds will regret only, as Fontenelle did on his in 1757, that it is so "difficult to be." "*Je sens une difficulté d'être,*" he said, "I am finding it difficult to be." It is a difficulty, like death itself, that permeates all of life.

> In the last analysis [as Jean Cocteau put it], everything can be taken care of except the difficulty of being: the difficulty of being cannot be taken care of.

In the last analysis, it cannot. This comedy knows, and acknowledges in sadness or cynicism. And yet we do not live only in the last analysis, but serially, in analyses first, second, and third. Though in the last analysis, no priest and no physician can stop us from dying, it may be a comfort to have both of them on call until finally we are dead. The comic sense tries to cope with the daily, hourly, inescapable difficulty of being. For if everyday life has an undercurrent or cross-current of the tragic, the main current is material for comedy.

Yet, if comedy begins in the kitchen and the bedroom, it can walk out under the stars. It can attain to grandeur. If this is not generally admitted, it is only because any comedy that has grandeur is immediately stamped as Not a Comedy. (Someone should make an anthology of the various fine works that have been called Not a Comedy, Not a Tragedy, and Not a Play. It would be one of the Hundred Great Books.) A comedy that achieves grandeur is also said to be veering toward tragedy. There is seldom any plausibility to the attribution. If any of these comedies were subtitled A Tragedy it would be said to be toppling toward Comedy.

Molière's *Don Juan* is an example. There is something marvelously lofty and mysterious about it. One would be at a loss to name any tragedy with an atmosphere of this type. The weighty world of tragedy is created the direct way: with weighty words to which in the theatre is added weighty acting. The world of Molière's *Don Juan* is created by the traditional dialectic of farce and comedy, that is, indirectly, with the weight only suggested, what is actually said and acted kept studiously flippant.

To think of Molière's *Don Juan* is to think of Mozart's *Don Giovanni*. Mozart also used the comic dialectic: it exactly corresponded to his own mentality, as it had to Molière's. Mozart early attached himself to the tradition of great comic theatre: he had completed a setting of a Goldoni play at the age of twelve. *La finta semplice* is musical farce. His development from there to *Cosí fan tutte* and *Don Giovanni* is not a progress toward tragedy. It is a progress from farce to comedy. What grows is his power to suggest the immensity of what lies underneath. But the comic surface is resolutely and scintillatingly maintained. To call *Don Giovanni* tragic makes no sense. We are in no way encouraged to identify ourselves with the Don's guilt. So far is such an attitude from Mozart that he can show the death of the Don (as Jonson shows us Volpone punished) without winning sympathy for him. The work is called tragic only by those who refuse to consider the possibility that such immensity and terror might be within the scope of comedy.

Though there are so many differences between tragedy

and comedy, it is news as old as Plato that the two have something in common. Scholars are not agreed as to how to take the passage in the *Symposium* in which this point is made but, thinking for ourselves, and with so much drama to think about which Plato did not know, we can see that the two genres stand together in very many ways. For example, they stand in contrast to an art such as music which glories in the direct expression of affirmative sentiments like the feeling of triumph. Tragedy and comedy are alike negative arts in that they characteristically reach positive statement by inference from negative situations. "In stories like this," says the Gardener in Giraudoux's *Electra,* "the people won't stop killing and biting each other to tell you the one aim of life is to love."

Surprising though it may be, the ego takes as much punishment in comedy as in tragedy, even if it is the pretensions of knaves and fools that are cut down, and not the rashness of a hero. Both tragedy and comedy demonstrate, with plots and characters that provide horribly conclusive evidence, that life is not worth living; and yet they finally convey such a sense of the majesty of our sufferings or the poignancy of our follies that, lo and behold! the enterprise seems worth having been a part of. Both tragedy and comedy are about human weakness, but both, in the end, testify to human strength. In tragedy one is glad to be identified with a hero, whatever his flaw or his fate. In comedy, even if one cannot identify oneself with anybody on stage, one has a hero to identify with, nonetheless: the author. One is proud to be lent the spectacles of Jonson or Molière.

Like tragedy, comedy can achieve a transcendence over misery, an aesthetic transcendence (of art over life) , and a transcending emotion (awe in tragedy, joy in comedy) .

Both tragedy and comedy amount to an affirmation made irrationally—that is, in defiance of the stated facts—like religious affirmation. Unlike the church, however, the theatre claims no metaphysical status for such affirmations.

Finally, tragedy and comedy have the same heuristic intent: self-knowledge. What tragedy achieves in this line by its incredibly direct rendering of sympathies and antipathies, comedy achieves by indirection, duality, irony. As Northrop Frye says, comedy is "designed, not to condemn evil, but to ridicule a lack of self-knowledge." To condemn evil would be direct, single, unironic, and therefore uncomic. To spend one's life condemning evil has all too often been to lack self-knowledge and to fail to see this. The classic condemners of evil are the Pharisees. And the Pharisees, then and now, cannot make use of comedy; they can only be made use of by it.

Molière, says Fernandez, "teaches us the unspeakably difficult art of seeing ourselves in spite of ourselves." We are mistaken about our own identities: comedy makes of mistaken identity a classic subject. And if "to be mistaken about" is a passive phenomenon, it has its active counterpart. We are not only mistaken in ourselves but the cause that mistakes are in other men. Deceiving ourselves, we deceive our fellows. Now the art of comedy is an undeceiving, an emancipation from error, an unmasking, an art, if you will, of denouement or "untying." But a knot cannot be untied without first having been tied. A denouement comes at the end: through most of the play we have in fact been fooled. Thus, by a truly comic paradox, the playwright who exposes our trickery does so by outtricking us. In that respect, he is his own chief knave, and has made of us, his audience, his principal fool. The bag of tricks of this prince of knaves is—the art of comedy.

AS YOU LIKE IT

I HOPE the foregoing generalizations are clear, but, if they are, they must also be too simple, too definite, and too schematic to correspond to all the facts. Categories, as Bernard Berenson put it, are only a compromise with chaos. And having used them, we do well to renew contact with the chaos and ask what damage a particular compromise has done.

The history of the arts if full of discrepancies between theory and practice, nomenclature and fact. For example, the word comedy is generally used—and not only by the amateur—in a sense too narrow to cover all comedies. In his essay on laughter, Henri Bergson's performance is one to hold any intelligent reader spellbound, but when one puts down the book one realizes that this dazzling piece of theory leaves no room in comic writing for Shakespeare.

And this is due to no peculiar limitation of the great French philosopher. It is due to the fact that the way we all discuss comedy grows out of one tradition of comedy and covers the case of that tradition alone. Since this is the classical or Latin tradition, coming down from Greek New Comedy through Plautus and Terence to Machiavelli and Ben Jonson and Molière, it has some application to comic writers of all schools. Even Shakespeare made an adaptation from Plautus. Yet by this time perhaps anyone but a Frenchman would admit that a kind of comedy has come into being that differs almost as much from Latin comedy as either kind of comedy differs from tragedy. *A Midsummer Night's Dream*, for example, differs from *The Alchemist* as much as either differs from *Hamlet*.

Writing of each genre *en bloc*, as I am, I would have

been content to go on writing of comedy *en bloc,* except for the excessive degree of distortion entailed. It is not that a conventional list of types (comedy of manners, of humours, of character) is needed to illuminate the life of comedy, but that to speak of Shakespeare and Molière, Jonson and Mozart, in one breath, as I have just done, leaves an impression of a single tradition and a single method. All minor categories and subtler distinctions aside, it seems to me that the history of comedy bears witness to two traditions, two methods of quite contrary tendency.

A hint of the divergence has already been provided in my discussion of jokes. Following Freud, I distinguished two kinds of jokes, the harmless and the purposive. Only the purposive or tendentious joke, it was remarked, had enough violence in it to be useful in farce. This kind of joke is at the root, not only of farce, but of comedy in the Latin tradition. The harmless joke is rooted in sympathy, the purposive joke in scorn. The main or Latin tradition of comedy is scornful comedy. Its weapon is ridicule. But sympathy, if not of much use in farce, can be abundantly used in comedy. When it is at the heart of comedy, we have comedy of a radically un-Latin sort—such as Shakespeare's or Mozart's.

This idea can be elaborated by recourse to the old distinction between wit and humor. Making use of this distinction we must probably define all comedy before the Elizabethans, and most French comedy afterwards, as comedy of wit. (Nervous about the word *humeur,* the French resort to the English word *humour* to describe that evidently un-French thing.) The tradition of humor is the tradition of Shakespeare and Cervantes, Sterne and Jean-Paul Richter, Dickens and Charlie Chaplin, Manzoni and Pirandello, Gogol and Chekhov and Sholem Aleichem.

Pirandello clarifies the old distinction in his essay, "Humor," when he remarks that if you see an old woman with dyed hair and too much make-up, and she strikes you as ridiculous, you have only to go on thinking about her to find her sad. "Humor" in writing is to include both these elements, where "wit" would rest content with the first. Wit and humor are therefore not simple opposites, since humor includes wit. Still, a comedy that is rooted in humor may well emerge so different from a comedy rooted in wit that generalizations about comedy will not be equally true of both.

For example, my own definition of comic dialectic. The main dynamic contrast, as I have presented it, is between a frivolous manner and a grim meaning. The tone says: life is fun. The undertone suggests that life is a catastrophe. The extreme instance is the kind of comedy in which the final curtain has to fall to save us from a veritable cataclysm.

Now though this formula may apply to particular scenes in Shakespearean comedy, and to early plays like *A Comedy of Errors* and *The Taming of the Shrew,* it does not cover any of his mature comedies as a whole. In *Twelfth Night,* for instance, the brio of Latin comedy is not in evidence during most of the play. The tone of most of the scenes is not flippant or frivolous or skittish or clever or elegant. The atmosphere is not even, in the everyday sense, "comic." It is that of "romance" in the old sense—a tale of wonder and misadventure. The misadventures are on the grand scale, the scale of the "terrible." Yet—and this is the contrast on which the play is based—a happy ending is somehow implicit from the beginning. A very curious blend: something close to tragedy is counteracted by a kind of magic or hocus-pocus of comedy-with-a-happy-ending. A surface of the "terrible" conceals beneath it a kind of cosmic beneficence, a metaphysically guaranteed good luck. Such is the "contrary tendency" in our second tradition of comedy, which reveals itself as a kind of inversion of the first: for grim statements in a gay style are substituted benign statements in a style not without solemnity.

The two kinds of comedy would seem to have different ends in view. In the logic of the first is a shock effect in the shape of a revelation of what is horrible. This kind of play seems to drive inward toward the forbidding truth. Its "happy ending" is purely ironical. In the logic of the second kind of comedy is an effect of enchantment in the shape of an apparent realization of our fondest hopes—that is, our hopes for love and happiness. Its happy ending is not only not ironical, it is, in effect, spread through the play; when it finally supervenes, it is a fitting culmination. "I was only joking" and "Let's not go into that" give place to "As you like it."

What does such an ending mean? Does it offer comforting truth to offset the grimmer truth of witty comedy? Comfortable, philistine critics will wish to think so. It is the tendency of this "romantic" comedy to create a "romantic" atmosphere in which the possibility of happiness and love arises—but whether as illusion or reality remains forever uncertain. The signature of this kind of comedy is a loveliness which can be "reality itself" or the "veil of illusion"—as you will. Here the Shakespearean "what you will" touches the Pirandellian "as you wish me" and "it is so if it seems so to you." Love dissolves in the cosmic mystery of illusion and reality.

> A great while ago the world begun
> With a hey ho, the wind and the rain,

> But that's all one, our play is done,
> And we'll strive to please you every day.

We'll strive to please you. Our play will be exactly as you like it. As for its meaning (illusion? reality?), we have pleased you, and you shall please yourselves. The world of our play shall be as you like it; also the world outside our play. . . . Thus, with a pun on the verb *to like,* is "solved" the ultimate problem of metaphysics.

Mozart often worked from plays and libretti in the Latin tradition but his own contribution was of the Shakespearean sort. Beaumarchais' *Marriage of Figaro* ends with the kind of improbability which we are to recognize as such and take ironically. "In real life," we are to go home saying, "things couldn't be patched up this way: Almaviva was a wolf and would continue so." In the Mozart opera, the patching-up is preceded by a different work, different, most of all, in that the "romantic" feelings of the characters have been made fully real to the audience, as in a Shakespeare comedy. Thus it is that the lovely notes Mozart has set to the Count's request to be forgiven, and to the Countess's accession to the request, can come as a true, unironical climax. Life is seen here, not through the eyes of the worldly, witty, Gallic Beaumarchais, but through those of a spiritual and humorous Austrian. In Mozart's *Marriage of Figaro,* as in *Twelfth Night,* love and happiness have their reality in art, while the question of their reality in life is left in uncynical abeyance.

Two kinds of comedy, one that moves toward unresolved discord, one that moves just as irresistibly toward complete concord: give to either of these a little more tragic an emphasis, and we shall get tragi-comedy. Suppose, for instance, after the discord of the first kind of comedy, more scenes were added, and the earlier scenes were then adjusted to these extra ones. A play like *Celestina* would result. Or suppose the kind of comedy that ends in true concord were proceeded by misadventures of a more malignant sort, as in *The Winter's Tale*.

Both these things shall be supposed in the next chapter.

10

TRAGI-COMEDY

TRAGEDY: AVERTED AND TRANSCENDED

THE WORD *tragi-comedy* can be traced back to ancient Rome but does not seem to have been in general use until the Renaissance. The best definition of it in its earlier forms is, perhaps, Susanne Langer's: "averted tragedy." Renaissance Italians spoke of "tragedy with a happy ending," and they also invented and perfected pastoral tragi-comedy, which is quasi-tragedy with a happy ending implicit, as in romantic comedy, from the very beginning.

It would not seem that in the era of the Renaissance and the Baroque, the tragi-comic was thought of as an inferior, bastard genre. A rigid separation of tragedy from comedy was not made in England and Spain until later, and even in France, the country that championed this separation, it was not made till well on in the seventeenth century: normal before that was tragi-comedy and a form so free it has been called *drame libre*. And not long after the rigid separation had become the established pattern throughout Europe, revolt began where resistance to the pattern had gone most against the grain: England. Every history of the drama gives 1731 as a landmark because it is the year of George Lillo's play, *George Barnwell, The London Merchant.* The notation is a valid one, even though *George Barnwell* is a bad play which spawned other bad plays. Artistic history is not made by artistic masterpieces alone. Old-fashioned in many ways even in 1731, Lillo's work founded a new nontragic, noncomic genre. Lillo influenced Diderot and Lessing, and through them the theatre of the whole Western world.

But even Diderot's plays were bad; and Lessing's had most distinction when they were least in Lillo's vein. The eighteenth-century blend of tragedy and comedy made a choice of the worst from both worlds. In the new "middle genre"—*comédie larmoyante* or *tragédie bourgeoise*—comedy lost its breadth and tragedy its depth. The search for "middle ground" was an avoidance of more significant ground. The new genre followed the feebler strain of eighteenth-century thought toward an excessive optimism about human nature. If men are "good-natured"—if they are "men of sentiment," "men of feeling"—then where are tragedy and comedy, that take their dynamics from human destructiveness? If the "middle genre" were the whole of eighteenth-century drama, one could say that dramatic literature had lost itself on a false trail, and the "middle genre" might have proved the end of drama as an art that could take the measure of man.

But history is more complex than history books, and Ibsen's "modern drama" is not a simple development out of Lillo's "bourgeois tragedy." Somewhere, a reversal of direction took place. A middle genre that came into existence to reflect and flatter the unheroic life of the shopkeeper proved later a weapon to be used against him. In order to be a weapon of *any* kind it had first to be re-made. Comedy with tears instead of laughter was comedy without comedy. Tragedy in which irreconcilable conflict is excluded *ex hypothesi* is tragedy without tragedy. To call the result tragi-comic has therefore no logic. Valid tragi-comedy would come about only if the dramatists could bring back into this middle genre precisely what had been withheld from it. And indeed Ibsen, while on the one hand modern, represents, on the other, a return to much that is traditionally comic and traditionally tragic. His very view of human nature nicely balances the classical and the modern. It is modern in that he tends to see the destructive elements as specifically a neurosis. It is classical in that this neurosis is no small thing, no mere nomenclature to which the phenomenon is neatly reduced; it is as large as sin and can be related—poetically, dramatically—to the traditional sense of destiny. *The Wild Duck* may be regarded as a culminating point, if one is watching Ibsen win back the tragic and comic territory in order to create his own special kingdom of tragi-comedy. And if in that respect this play looks back to the two previous centuries, it has also proved to be the most "forward-looking" of plays, containing, as it does, the seeds of Pirandello's work and Eugene O'Neill's.

This much literary history is perhaps needed to introduce the subject of the present chapter, which is not, of course, the history of tragi-comedy but its life in our minds and hearts. I propose to ignore its—for us—less alive, less lively forms, such as Renaissance pastoral or eighteenth-century middle genre, and concentrate on what seem to be the two most successful kinds of tragi-comedy. The first is a

kind of "tragedy with a happy ending" which is not
"tragedy averted" but "tragedy transcended." The theme
here is conflict resolved, and the example I shall take is the
resolution of revenge through forgiveness. The finest examples of this tragi-comedy are to be found, perhaps,
among Shakespeare's so-called "problem plays" and "last
romances." But it was not one poet's personal experiment.
Goethe's *Iphigenia in Tauris* is another attempt of this
sort. So is Kleist's *Prince of Homburg,* which Kleist calls a
Schauspiel (Play) —the alternative to *Trauerspiel* (Tragedy) and *Lustspiel* (Comedy) . Goethe's *Faust* itself can be
regarded as one of the mightiest achievements in this line,
and its hopeful ending is not to be written off as shallow
optimism, much less as a facile exploitation of religious
orthodoxy. (The right target for these criticisms would be
Zorrilla's *Don Juan Tenorio.*)

The other kind of tragi-comedy that invites discussion is
"comedy with an unhappy ending." If "tragedy with a
happy ending" can be seen as a development from tragedies
like *King Lear* in which the beginnings of forgiveness and
reconciliation are suggested, "comedy with an unhappy
ending" can be seen as a development from Moliéresque
comedies which end "unconvincingly" with a *deus ex
machina.* The latter is essentially a nineteenth- and
twentieth-century kind of tragi-comedy (though earlier
examples exist, such as *The Celestina*) . Ibsen's *Wild Duck*
is perhaps *the* classic of the genre. Bernard Shaw's conception of the "unpleasant" play is in this vein, though his
own plays bearing that label are far more comic than
tragic. *Saint Joan,* not *Mrs. Warren's Profession,* is Shaw's
great *tragi*-comedy; *Enrico IV* and *Six Characters* are
Pirandello's. Chekhov's full-length plays are all tragi-
comedies of this stamp, and I would read Chekhov's

insistence that *The Cherry Orchard* is a comedy as but a
stage-direction to Stanislavsky and others advising them
not to overlook the strongly comic elements. It is *comedy*
with an unhappy ending. Brecht's *A Man's a Man* and
Mahagonny are tragi-comic in this way. So are Chaplin's
Monsieur Verdoux * and Beckett's *Waiting for Godot* and
Ionesco's *The Chairs*.

REVENGE, JUSTICE, FORGIVENESS

I HAVE WRITTEN of melodrama largely in terms of fear, but
this is to overlook what happens to the villain. We punish
him—that is to say, we wreak a revenge upon him. And it is
unlikely that we resist admitting as much. Everyone admits
at least that melodrama and farce are full of revenges. But
some draw the line at tragedy and comedy. (Such a term as
Revenge Tragedy seems to say that most tragedy is *not*
concerned with revenge.) And others conceive of revenge
as something that belongs rather to literature than to life.
Needed at this stage in my argument is the admission that
life itself is pervaded by the fact or the imagination of
revenge. To try to establish this point I shall permit myself
a digression.

Is it unusual to see life, and to live life, as nothing but a
series of revenges? Very early on, we can acquire the feeling
of having been wronged; we can then spend the rest of our
time on earth trying to get our own back. We can begin by
punishing our siblings. In adolescence, if not before, we

* *The Great Dictator* would be another example if Chaplin had given
it the unhappy ending it needs (both historically and artistically) instead
of the happy ending that it actually has. Nor is this happy ending the
ironical one of a *Tartuffe* and hence truly comic. It represents the victory
of ideology over both truth and fiction and, as such, is neither tragi-comic
nor comic.

can punish our parents. In our twenties, we can accept marriage as a device for the continuation of punishment till death us do part. Divorce is shunned by some people, no doubt because it permits an interruption of punishment, and welcomed by others, no doubt because it permits remarriage and the resumption of punishment with renewed relentlessness. Education until recently permitted the punishment of pupils by teachers; now it permits of the punishment of teachers by pupils. Under both systems, younger children are punished by older. The products of education compose what we call human society. Human society is designed for punishment on a grander scale, by poverty, by strikes, by law courts, by concentration camps and prisons, by the noose, the axe, the gas chamber, and the electric chair, by war. That is stating the position in the broadest terms. We meet it day in day out in the narrowest terms. The tone of voice of a New York bus driver bespeaks a life solemnly dedicated to the proposition that one must get one's own back at all costs, every hour of every day, and in relation to every human being one encounters. Since a bus driver encounters half a dozen persons a minute, he can amass a number of victims beyond the wildest hopes of any villain of melodrama. And beyond the hopes, also, of the New York taxi-driver—who accordingly deals out more punishment per customer.

Getting one's own back, taking revenge, inflicting punishment for real or, more often, imagined wrongs—this has good title to be considered the principle activity of the species *Homo sapiens*. So much may be obvious. Somewhat less so is the circumstance that the idea of revenge is not nearly as welcome to mankind as the reality. Though taking revenge may be what we chiefly do, it is also what we chiefly deplore. We always have to pretend that our revenges are not revenges but equitable punishment. Not that even punishment is quite reputable but it almost becomes so when it is believed to be deserved. Hence justice, as we know it, whether in private life or in the law courts, is pure fraud, mere rationalization of vindictiveness. In his *Revolutionist's Handbook* Bernard Shaw left this message for lawyers:

> When a man wants to murder a tiger he calls it sport; when the tiger wants to murder him he calls it ferocity. The distinction between Crime and Justice is no greater.

To say that justice as we know it is a fraud is to say that it is not justice, but it is not to say that true justice has played no part at all in human proceedings. I am willing to postulate not only a passion for revenge, but also a passion for justice, the misfortune for the world being that the passion for justice does not show itself either as insistently or as powerfully. Though measures making for justice are not unknown to history, the societies we know are all radically unjust. Much the same could be said about the individual realm, with the happy difference that here acts of justice are more numerous. Many people, indifferent to justice in the great world, attach importance to it in their family and their personal circle of acquaintance.

Perhaps this, too, is obvious but there is another circumstance that invites attention. Although there has been so little of justice in human affairs, and nothing approaching a just society has ever been seen on earth, the imagination of mankind has been able to figure forth, and the conscience of mankind has been able to accept, a yet loftier idea. This is forgiveness.

Mutual forgiveness of each vice
Such are the gates of paradise.

Blake is telling us in these precious lines what it could be
most valuable for human beings to know. But in fact the
gates of paradise remain closed because we are unable to
act on such knowledge. *How should we practice forgiveness, when we have not even managed to practice justice?*
Yet the idea of forgiveness is instructive if only in reminding us that justice will never be enough.

Better than revenge, justice is itself quite primitive. It is
the principle expressed in the *lex talionis,* a Latin phrase of
which the best translation into English is W. S. Gilbert's
"to make the punishment fit the crime." A man has stolen
one hundred dollars: when caught, he will be fined one
hundred dollars. Such is the famous "eye for an eye"
principle in the Old Testament. Brought up in Christian
schools, I was always told the principle was one of pure
revenge. That is probably just a slander on Judaism, but
I'll give my teachers the benefit of the doubt, and assume
they may have dimly sensed there was something dubious
about justice itself. To be forever matching offenses with
equivalent punishments is no good way to spend one's
time, much less is it a good way for God to spend eternity.
A truly superior being would utter the word Forgiveness
with an immense sigh, not only of love, but of relief, so
much effort would he be saving himself at the adding
machine. And He did utter that word as early as the Book
of Leviticus (XVIII, 19) : "Thou shalt not hate thy brother
in thy heart. . . . Thou shalt not take vengeance. . . .
Thou shalt love thy neighbor as thyself."

Whether or not I am right in all this, I must hope that

my digression—now over—has made vivid to the reader the fact that, if revenge is so prominent in dramatic literature, life itself will show why. Leviticus is still ahead of the human race, which, in the theatre as elsewhere, is ever on the lookout for revenges. What, after all, are plays about? Action and reaction. A slaps B's face, and B slaps A's face back. The root idea of plot is nothing more than tit for tat: injury and retaliation. In farce, as we have seen, that idea is given free rein, and is defensible on the grounds that at the least it is harmless, since it takes place in what anyone but a madman can recognize as pure fantasy, and that at the most it might be useful, since it effects a catharsis and works some of our aggressions out of our system.

We have found the value of melodrama to reside in candid acceptance of fantasies and full-bodied feelings, especially fantasies and feelings of fear. The moment has now come to pursue the melodramatic plot through to the end. In all conventional melodrama the villain we fear so much is finally punished. The lily-white hero and heroine get their own back, and, therefore, so do we, the audience. Images of fear are canceled by images of exquisite vengeance. Seldom is this admitted. As in life, so in melodrama, we pretend our revenges are equitable punishments. I have described melodrama as neurotic. It is a neurotic habit to collect injustices, taking for granted that injustice is something that others do to me and that what *I* bestow upon *them* is deserved punishment. Melodrama reflects this little scheme. If the avengers of the Victorian melodramatic stage at first seem remote, wrapped as they are in an alien rhetoric and an outmoded type of storytelling, they remain symbols of what goes on daily in the lives of millions.

To proceed to tragedy and comedy is to proceed from the crude revenges of farce and the fake justice of melodrama to justice itself, the *lex talionis.* Volpone and Mosca must be arraigned and found guilty and sentenced. Portia, in *The Merchant of Venice,* preaches forgiveness but does not practice it. She has the Duke figure exactly what is the equivalent of a pound of flesh measured in what is dearest to Shylock, namely, property.

> For half thy wealth it is Antonio's;
> The other half comes to the general state.

To which Shylock with perfect good sense answers:

> You take my house when you do take the prop
> That doth sustain my house; you take my life
> When you do take the means by which I live.

Such is comedy.

How meticulous the tragic poets also are with their weights and measures! "Life for life, eye for eye, tooth for tooth" reads the famous passage in the Book of Exodus, and the "life for life" idea is taken up by the playwrights as a principle at once ethical and aesthetic: ethical because it expresses the idea of the *lex talionis,* aesthetic because it corresponds to the dramatic tit for tat. A life is taken at the beginning of a story; restitution is made for it at the end with another life. Since Duncan's life is taken in Act Two, Macbeth's, not will, but *must* be taken in Act Five. *Othello* represents but a slight variation on the pattern. Desdemona's life is not taken till near the end, but it has been threatened ever since the plot got under way, and once forfeited, it must be paid for in the same coin: Othello must die.

One cannot understand the extent to which the dramatists depart from what happens in "real life" until one has noticed their inordinate respect for the *lex talionis*. Consider, for instance, the idea of Poetic Justice. It represents an extension of the *lex talionis* from the field of crime into that of virtue. Not only are the bad punished, the good are rewarded, the quantities again being meticulously measured on the scales of justice. There is nothing in Poetic Justice to stop a man writing a great play, and a distinguished scholar has recently argued that it is presupposed in all the great Spanish drama.

The modern dramatists, on the other hand, have objected to Poetic Justice, and have delighted to let the malefactor go unpunished. This, however, does not mean that they care less about justice, and have rejected the *lex talionis*. By showing justice outraged, they hope to outrage the audience, and fan the passion for justice into flame. The old approach was conservative. In Lope de Vega's *Fuente Ovejuna,* justice was imposed by God and the King. The play has been modernized in the Soviet Union by simple omission of the ending. What the play then comes to mean is that justice will be done when the people take over. Understood in this way, justice can easily deteriorate into mere revenge, and drama into melodrama. Marxist fighters, like other fighters, are all too eager to match the enemy's atrocities with their own, and when men *enjoy* carrying out the *lex talionis,* something has been added to justice: namely, cruelty.

Jesus said: "Father, forgive them for they know not what they do." With the capitalistic oppressors in mind, Bertolt Brecht once posted up on a stage the words: "They do know what they do." He had a point; but it is unlikely that anyone would be able to implement it except vindictively.

The Elizabethans tried to forestall this danger. They invoked the passage from Paul's Epistle to the Romans in which the apostle said that revenge was not for us to take, but should be left to God. " 'Vengeance is mine, I will repay,' saith the Lord." So far, so good. But in this world God's vengeance must find a human instrument. And then how are we to know if a given avenger *is* God's instrument? It is even harder to tell if a man is God's instrument than if his motive is a passion for justice. And why does Paul use the word vengeance? What business has God with vengeance? Is there not something dubious in Paul's attitude? Is there not something dubious in the world's attitude? No one professes belief in revenge; everyone agrees that justice is preferable; and the highest teaching invites us to that transcendence of justice which is forgiveness.

It is vain to expect the drama—or any art—to stand far above the culture it belongs to. If the culture practices revenge, tempering it occasionally with a little justice, it is to be expected that that is exactly what its drama will do. This in turn explains why a really radical thinker like Tolstoy may come to reject most of literature with most of society. He did stand above his culture. On the high pinnacle he judged from, literature seemed barbaric, like the men who wrote it, and the men they wrote it for. Tolstoy included in this general indictment his own masterworks. And why not? They show the dialectics of life as it is lived, the tit for tat, the battledore and shuttlecock, of ordinary action and reaction. Ideals are present, just as they always are, but people fail to put them into practice, just as they always do. And anyhow they are only ideals of justice; they fall hopelessly short of the limitless forgiveness of Christ.

Shelley takes a position far less defensible than Tolstoy's. He believes that we should practice forgiveness in life, while retaining justice and revenge in literature. Let me again quote his Preface to *The Cenci*. He is talking about Beatrice, his heroine:

> . . . the fit return to make to the most enormous injuries is kindness and forbearance, and a resolution to convert the injurer from his dark passions by peace and love. Revenge, retaliation, atonement, are pernicious mistakes. If Beatrice had thought in this manner she would have been wiser and better; but she would never have been a tragic character: the few whom such an exhibition would have interested could never have been sufficiently interested for a dramatic purpose, from the want of finding sympathy in their interest among the mass who surround them. It is the restless and anatomizing casuistry with which men seek the justification of Beatrice, yet feel that she has done what needs justification; it is in the superstitious horror with which they contemplate alike her wrongs and their revenge that the dramatic character of what she did and suffered consists.

Now it is true that the drama deals more readily with badness than with goodness, with failure than with success. So does literature in general. The best character in *Paradise Lost* is Satan. The *Inferno* makes better reading than the *Paradiso*. Literature stops far this side of paradise and deals with the world, the flesh, and the devil. . . . But what Shelley overlooks in this passage is that literature reflects human interests, reflects life. If reality were suddenly changed in the way he proposes, the result would be that, with equal suddenness, literature would be all forgiveness too. Revenge appeals to the dramatists because they are masters of reality, and not ideologues.

Shelley takes forgiveness and love to be inherently

undramatic. He sees only the final state of beatitude, reached possibly by a forgiving saint in a supreme moment, and therefore overlooks the fact that forgiveness is achieved with difficulty; and that there is a drama in the difficulty, the conflict, through which it is achieved. Forgiveness is an alternate reaction to revenge, and can be understood—functionally speaking—as revenge is understood. Here is an account of revenge from *Studies on Hysteria* by Freud and Breuer:

> The instinct of revenge, which is so powerful in the natural man and is disguised rather than repressed by civilization, is nothing whatever but the excitation of a reflex that has not been released. To defend oneself against injury in a fight and, in so doing, to injure one's opponent is the adequate and preformed psychical reflex. If it has been carried out insufficiently or not at all, it is constantly released again by recollection, and the "instinct of revenge" comes into being as an irrational volitional impulse. . . .

By not taking revenge, one develops the habit and mentality of revenge. Freud and Breuer envisage no third possibility, but there is one. It is to react, using the same energy in the spirit of forgiveness. That too would be an "adequate psychical reflex." In view of his interest in nonviolent resistance, it is curious that Shelley did not think so. His point of view in the passage quoted is pretty much that of juvenile philistinism today, according to which turning the other cheek is "sissy." We have had Gandhi and Martin Luther King to demonstrate the contrary. Vengefulness is nothing if not a sign of diffidence, and forgiveness, far from being a sort of natural emanation of mere mildness, has to be fought through to in an arduous process beside which hitting back is child's play.

Machiavelli was right: in public life, things like forgiveness do not exist. Imagine a candidate for the United States Senate proposing to forgive anybody, any group or nation whatsoever! Yet forgiveness sometimes enters into private life. Why? Is it not largely because each of us, weary from orgies of revenge, yearns to be forgiven? Our very existence seems to demand not only *justification* but *forgiveness*. If the human interest in forgiveness can be attributed to no nobler source, it can be attributed to this natural or existential need. We wish—we need—to be forgiven. We are sometimes able to forgive others, if for no better reason than that we wish and need to be forgiven. "And forgive us our trespasses as we forgive those that trespass against us." We cannot come directly to Blake's conclusion ("Mutual forgiveness of each vice/Such are the gates of paradise") but we may come to it indirectly by realizing, with Juvenal, that "by the verdict of his own heart no guilty man is acquitted."

A thorny subject! In *Hamlet* do we not find Shakespeare himself entangled in the ambiguities of justice and revenge? The story seems basically pagan, even to the extent of accepting revenge as legitimate, yet the culture suggested by the Shakespearean poetry is unmistakably that of Elizabethan England, and there are many references in the play to Christian belief. I remember wondering as a child how it could be Hamlet's duty to take revenge when the Bible says that revenge is wrong. Later on, I was told what St. Paul wrote to the Romans—"Vengeance is mine," saith the Lord—but I must confess that for Hamlet it seemed to provide too neat an alibi. Does Hamlet ever really seem the instrument of St. Paul's God even when he kills his uncle?

If that is Shakespeare's point, he made it badly. (Curious how many logical arguments about *Hamlet* make quite a bad play of it!) There is an unresolved ambiguity here which is not that of the play alone, or even of its author: it is the ambiguity of a whole civilization—a civilization that has never made up its mind but has always had a double, nay, a triple, standard: preaching forgiveness, while believing in justice, while practicing revenge.

In the *Oresteia*, Aeschylus described the transcendence of revenge by justice, and we re-enact this transcendence as we see his trilogy. Though Shakespeare began with revenge plays—which, as I have been using the terms, should mostly be called justice plays—he went on to show the transcendence of justice by mercy. No one has missed this motif in the "last romances." Prospero, instead of dealing out punishments to his enemies, forgives them (except for Caliban). Hermione, instead of getting her own back on Leontes, is reconciled with him. Even in *King Lear*, the motif is present. The play is not a demonstration that the "gods are just," for what happens is not deserved punishment. The gods may not kill us for their sport. They may kill us without even knowing it. Or there may be no gods. If there is a morally positive element in the play, and I think there is, its most lovely—and I would add: not least dramatic—manifestation is Cordelia's forgiveness of her father. It is the purified love of these two that gives the ending its moral beauty.

Cordelia herself stood in need of forgiveness. In the opening scene, she is not only right, she is rigid. She is insistent on her rightness and unwilling to make use of any of her resources except her rightness. When she returns from France we see a different woman. The ice has melted.

331

Her attention is no longer focused on her own rightness. Her forgiveness is so deep, it is absorbed by her love, and requires no statement. The very need for it can be denied:

> I know you do not love me; for your sisters
> Have, as I do remember, done me wrong:
> You have some cause, they have not.

> No cause, no cause.

We are right to speak of the beauty of these lines in which there is no separable beauty of word or phrase. It is the beauty of a moral attitude that overcomes us, embedded as it is in character and action. Forgiveness and reconciliation are not here the static, inert goodness that Shelley feared. They are worked through to, fought through to, suffered through to. Neither justice nor revenge was ever more dramatic.

This is just an aspect of *Lear,* but there is one Shakespeare play—aside from the last romances—that is all about forgiveness. This is *Measure for Measure. Lex talionis* is the subject proposed in the title of the play and repeated at the opening of the last scene in which it will finally be repudiated and transcended:

> The very mercy of the law cries out
> Most audible, even from his proper tongue,
> 'An Angelo for Claudio, death for death!'
> Haste still pays haste, and leisure answers leisure,
> Like doth quit like, and Measure still for Measure.

Claudio is not dead. The God of this play is not one who lets a Claudio die so that the death of an Angelo can follow. Not God but Angelo is here the champion of the *lex talionis.* Early in the play Isabella advises him to forgive,

332

since he will need to be forgiven. None of us is good enough to wish justice handed out to him:

> How would you be
> If He which is the top of judgment should
> But judge you as you are? O! think on that
> And mercy then will breathe within your lips
> Like a man new made.

Such is the main point of this play and its place in the main Action.

But the play has a double or dialectical Action, of which the second and antithetical part is often overlooked. In the last scene, Isabella is asked to practice all she preaches: to take the Christian message so much to heart that she will plead for mercy, not for her brother, whom she supposes dead, but for her enemy, whom she thinks her brother's killer. Every law except the law of sheer forgiveness speaks against such a plea:

> Should she kneel down in mercy of this fact
> Her brother's ghost his pavèd bed would break
> And take her hence in horror.

How can she do it? She is not the kneeling kind. Her virtue is of the unbending sort, like Cordelia's. The answer to the question is written out in the Action of the play as a whole. In the beginning, she could not have done it; in the end, she can. As with Cordelia, the ice melts. The bristling virgin becomes the compassionate woman. Guilty of a rigidity that could have been as fatal as Angelo's, she, like him, learns a lesson in forgiveness—a lesson, of course, not in ethical theory, but in human, emotional practice. The existential fact is what is rendered. It is what dramatic art is there to render.

DESPAIR, HOPE

THE other most significant kind of tragi-comic play, in my opinion, is comedy with a tragic sequel. In choosing this formulation, I am thinking of Schopenhauer's comment on comedy: "It has to hurry to lower the curtain in the moment of joy [*im Zeitpunkt der Freude*] so that we don't see what comes afterwards." The dictum covers some comedies more satisfactorily than others, but it is perhaps true of all to this extent, that there is irony in happy endings as such. We always understand that "it ain't necessarily so," even, on occasion, that it couldn't possibly be so. But, in the circumstances, anything save a happy ending would be impolite, just as it would be churlish in real life to mention to a bride and groom how marriages actually turn out. The idea of "happy ever after" is a legal fiction, a civilized convention, a courtly pretense.

To the extent that a whole comedy has a fairy-tale atmosphere, the happy ending can also be rendered with naïve childlike faith. There is nothing cynical about the happy endings of Shakespeare's romantic comedies, but the noncynicism is childlike: we are not asked to apply the formula to marriages outside the world of the play. In less "romantic" comedy, there is the more definite implication of: "But this is what does *not* happen in life." When we read the last act of *Volpone*, we know we are seeing life, not as it is, but as it ought to be. Art is normative, and leads Ben Jonson to this form of happy ending: the punishment of the wicked.

It is to certain Molière comedies that Schopenhauer's view emphatically applies, for it is characteristic of Molière to bring his dramatic situation to the brink of disaster. That the turnabouts which then give him his happy ending are unconvincing will be held against him only by those with no feeling for comic convention in general and the convention of the happy ending in particular, while those who argue that the ending of, say, *Tartuffe is* convincing, in intending to give Molière a helping hand, are taking the ground from under his feet. The whole point, surely, is that we must not be convinced. Certainly, it is splendid to live under Louis XIV, when so many abuses are corrected, but he could not really be all over town in this fashion and, even if he could, comedy is universal, and most places and times have no Sun King to shine on them. Consequently, most Tartuffes have nothing between them and success, their story will end unhappily for the good, and villainy will be triumphant. Such a story would hardly make for pure comedy, yet the materials remain the comic ones. Tragi-comedy would be the apt label.

To call this kind of play a comedy with a tragic sequel is a suggestive rather than descriptive account of it, for if a dramatist were to remove the denouement of a Tartuffe play, and substitute a catastrophe, he would then find that Schopenhauer's remark was only true on broad lines and that, as to a hundred particulars, he would have to work back and back into his play, making changes. In the *Tartuffe* of Molière, for all its summer lightnings, the tone assures us reliably enough that a solution will be found in some fashion, however unconvincing. The "new" play would require a new tone. What was before but a cross-current is now a flood: the whole play will become, in a degree, macabre. A critic might well describe this comedy with an unhappy ending as a tragedy made with comic materials. (Susanne Langer does.) It is only natural that a balancing of the tragic (A) with the comic (B) should be definable alternately as A modified by B, or as B modified by A.

The comedy with a tragic sequel—or tragedy with a comic substructure—probably could not have come into its own until the rise of Naturalism with its insistence that happy endings do not occur in real life. Naturalism in its purer forms yields a ponderously documentary form of drama, but in a less pure, yet more valid, form lends itself to comedy—of a new kind. In other words, though the objection to the happy ending is invalid as theory, still, special effects can be got with the *un*happy ending, and it will not be the first time that bad theory has abetted good practice. Henry Becque's *The Vultures* has often been regarded as one of the most purely documentary plays ever written, yet it is as if Becque drew a wiry line around each of these Naturalistic genre pictures. This line makes a comment, and a comic one. We realize that the play is not written in the spirit of detachment but of loathing. And yet the action rolls downhill all the way. No happy ending: it is comedy with a tragic sequel.

Gay, in his *Beggar's Opera,* has reached a stage halfway between Molière and Becque. He still uses the happy ending, but it is no longer a smiling convention in which irony lurks beneath the flowers. There are no flowers. What had been a merely implicit recognition becomes the explicit dramatic point: this kind of ending is absurd and should be subjected to ridicule. Brecht, in his *Threepenny Opera,* is merely rubbing the point in even harder when he has Peachum say: "But in real life their end is miserable, and when you kick a man he kicks you back again."

Gay, Becque, and Brecht are giving us "the modern

note," that note of the inexorably hideous and relentlessly sordid which, for so long, earnest young people have defended against earnest older people who want their art noble, lovely, and wholesome, if not also genteel and "nice." The debate is *so* old that by now the roles are sometimes reversed, and the middle-aged find themselves championing Henry Miller and William Burroughs to young people who would find the heroic and sublime both more surprising and more impressive. In this case it is time to tell the young how much more the "modern movement" meant in its day than the defense of outspokenness in sex.

An editorial in *Life* magazine may exhort us to write tragedies, but it may be hard for us to comply—because we live in the age of *Life* magazine. Before deploring the scurrility in Miller or Burroughs, it would be well to ask what it consists of and why it exists. For a hundred years now, literature has made a mission of something that has been tagged with labels like "brutal frankness," "ruthless exposure," "unsparing realism." A section of the public has been shocked—how many times over!—and another section has been glad they were shocked. The discussion, being in the first instance a journalistic one, centered on sex and the mentioning of the unmentionable. That is why we are slow to realize that sex was the least of it, and that the plea for "liberalism" in morals was extraneous. The essence was *a vision of the world as an unmitigated horror.* True, many of the writers concerned would have hastened to explain they only intended to say that such and such *parts* of the world were an unmitigated horror. The point is that these were the parts they wrote about. The operative vision in their work is a vision of horror. The philosophy of the movement is Schopenhauer and early Nietzsche:

337

contrariety is at the heart of the universe. The motto of the movement is: Hell is a city much like Seville. From Shaw's *John Bull's Other Island* to Brecht's *Mahagonny* we are told—no: shown—that hell is the place we are already in.

Now this vision can be interpreted in various ways, and greeted with any shade of approval or disapproval, but neither its existence nor its importance can be denied, and even the most indignant disapprover must grant to the movement that carried the vision its characteristic achievements. If Beauty in the classic sense was allowed to die, a *terrible* beauty was born. If the Noble and Heroic were excluded *ex hypothesi,* the ignoble and unheroic revealed a wider range and a deeper humanity than they could ever have been thought capable of. If a limit was placed on the definition of Truth, and time-honored Higher Truths were ignored or even mocked, the dedication to the "lower" truths was informed with intelligence and passion: if the boundaries had been narrowed at the upper end, they were vastly extended at the lower. Finally, the champions of Tragedy (Beauty, Nobility, Heroism and Higher Truth) should be told that, in Karl Jaspers' words, "tragedy is not enough." Tragedy itself has limits: indeed it excludes most of the experience of most men. The transfer of attention from a Wallenstein to a Mother Courage can be defended, not only on Marxist, but also on Christian and, in the least political sense, democratic grounds. But defending "modernism" as a viewpoint is easy. It is harder, and more important, to realize what the essentially modern *vision* was like, and what it was capable of in the way of art.

It is the informing vision of those who continued to write what we must probably call tragedies, although they lack Beauty, Nobility, Heroism, and Higher Truth, namely, plays in the tradition of Ibsen and Strindberg. The line from Schopenhauer to O'Neill's *Long Day's Journey into Night* is a continuous one. Modern tragedies are all journeys into night. (O'Neill's title was itself suggested by that of a novel of similar tendency.) A modern tragedy is all that Schiller's *Mary Stuart* is not: its movement is simply and steadily down to defeat. Schiller's era ended, and the modern one began when Büchner wrote *Danton's Death*. A hundred years later, the same "movement" or "rhythm" is to be found in Eisenstein's modern tragedy of a film, *Strike*. (This splendid film was banned by Stalin precisely because it is a tragedy, modern tragedy being "pessimistic" and "negative.")

Perhaps in the light of all these facts, we can see that the modern hostility to Happy Endings entailed much more than a failure to understand that such endings had been a convention. The Unhappy Ending now became the programmatic vehicle of a vision that was a passionate possession. Tragi-comedy as "tragedy with a *happy* ending" would in this epoch be relegated to the theatre of vulgar melodrama. Tragedy with an "inwardly happy" ending (*Mary Stuart* was only the extreme case) would also seem sentimental, wish-fulfilling. The new vision knows no half-measures. It is nothing if not black, stark, implacable. If the old tragedy had been a song of despair, the new seemed to aspire to express despair without any singing. Only Hilda Wangel's "harps in the air"—an hallucination—remain to remind us of the heroic music that was. If in the old tragedy despair, as I have suggested, was transcended by beauty, in the new it can be transcended only by truth. And if a transcendence by beauty argues an unflinching courage, transcendence by truth argues a courage just as unflinching in the face of a world even more comfortless. And the new vision penetrates comedy as well as tragedy. We pass from *The Beggar's Opera* to *The Threepenny Opera,* and from Molière to Henry Becque. The French speak of *comédie rosse,* having in mind a particular group of tragi-comic plays, but the truth is that comedy now, when serious, tends in general towards the tragi-comic.

The lifework of Leo Tolstoy himself affords an excellent example of modernity in tragi-comedy, what it is, and how it comes to be so. This is his unfinished masterpiece, *The Light That Shines in the Darkness.* (It is perhaps a token of the deep uncertainties underlying modern drama that some of the greatest attempts remain torsos: Kleist's *Robert Guiscard,* Hoelderlin's *Empedocles,* Büchner's *Woyzeck,* Alban Berg's *Lulu.*) The substructure of Tolstoy's play is the tragedy of a great and idealistic man who is misunderstood. "The light shineth in the darkness, and the darkness comprehendeth it not." It would, one conjectures, have been a "modern" tragedy, running steadily downhill to despair and death, but Tolstoy turned his critical searchlight on himself; and the Biblical phrase becomes a more and more cruel irony: the light is no light. "At least we could feel sorry for Tolstoy's protagonist," a playwright in the tradition of the older theatre could say. But this escape Tolstoy cuts off. The modern vision is found here in the mercilessness of a great artist and moralist toward himself. And the last straw is, not that he is bad and wrong, but that he is repellent, ludicrous, funny. Finished, this play would have been one of the greatest comedies-with-an-unhappy-ending.

Of recent years plays on this tragi-comic pattern have been written by the dramatists "of the Absurd." At this stage, the term tragi-comedy often gives place to tragi-farce. The new term * reminds us of a truth once stated by Stark Young: that tragedy has more in common with farce than with either *drame* or the higher forms of comedy. I have spoken of the drama as an art of extremes and of farce as an extreme case of the extreme. Tragedy is another. At the Grand Guignol one often wasn't sure which way to take a play: it could be Jacobean tragic horror, it could be farcical nonsense—the difference lies not in the materials themselves but only in interpretation. Similarly, it is but a step from a frivolous farce of Courteline's, such as *These Cornfields,* to a tale of serious horror like Ionesco's *The Lesson.*

Because "the Absurd" has needed a lot of explaining, at least to the English and American public, it has come to be identified with the explanations, and many think of Ionesco as a philosophical dramatist. His plays are referred back to their background, and he gets the credit for all the thought of the Existentialist line of philosophers from Kierkegaard down. Of course, it is historically correct to derive the modern despair, pessimism, anguish, in part from a sense of the loss of faith—Nietzsche's "God is dead." It is quite another question whether an individual play-wright really has the genius to put all that into one little play, and it is another question still whether the plays depend on "all that" for their appeal.

What *is* the appeal of the tragi-comedy we are discussing? Even before literature was stripped of Beauty, Heroism, Nobility, and Higher Truth, the question was debated why men take pleasure in painful objects. One answer, at that time, was obviously that Beauty, Heroism, Nobility,

* New *as* a term. The phrase "tragic farce" (*tragische Farce*) is found in Schopenhauer.

and Higher Truth made them palatable, but what is the answer nowadays? Modern tragi-comedy is usually defended on the grounds of fidelity to fact—its lower truth is still true. Even so, the appeal of truth per se is rather limited. Though we have seen sheer duplication of fact to be at the basis of the drama, a basis is not an art any more than a foundation is a building. Duplication is not generally enough. If a given set of duplications does make an appeal to human beings the question would be: why? What is special about this particular set of duplications?

We have found that comedy takes over the extraordinary aggressiveness of farce. Tragi-comedy takes it over from comedy. But whereas the seriousness of comedy often tends to qualify the violence of the aggression—conquering or interrupting, if not actually softening, it—the seriousness of tragi-comedy tends to underline and even increase it. Where romantic comedy says: these aggressions can be transcended, and realistic comedy says: these aggressions will be punished, tragi-comedy of the school here under consideration says: these aggressions can neither be transcended nor brought to heel, they are human nature, they are life, they rule the world. The peculiar, unparalleled ruthlessness of the genre suggests a wrestling match with no holds barred. If the comedian is indeed a "hostile sharpshooter proclaiming his innocence," this kind of tragi-comic drama is one long shooting match. In its implacable aggressivity, it naturally holds a special attraction for those who are implacably aggressive.

Or to those who are implacably opposed to aggression? They, to be sure, are the ostensible audience. The appeal is to conscience. I would not mock such an appeal; on the contrary. I would only point out that the conscience is not an organ of enjoyment: it has no taste buds. Consequently what "appeals" to the conscience must appeal to something else besides. And we must not take affront if the something else is something the conscience disapproves of. Art critics who point to the sadistic streak in Francisco Goya are not necessarily malicious reactionaries, resolved to debunk Goya the social critic. The question for a candid psychology is: would it have been possible for Goya to recreate so vividly the cruelty of others, had he not been able to find a like cruelty in his own breast? Once this question has been answered in the negative, it is but a step to the admission that the admirer of Goya's paintings enjoys his share of the cruelty.

Is Goya's protest against cruelty swallowed up in enjoyment of cruelty? Life is not so simple. The proclamation of innocence remains just as important as the hostile sharp-shooting. Whenever the cry of *J'accuse!* goes up—and in modern art it is forever going up—the presumed innocence of the accuser must be given as much weight as the presumed guilt of the accused. Even so, if it is the pleasure mechanism we are watching, rather than the rights and wrongs, we have to recognize the immense emotional attractiveness of innocence, both genuine and spurious. Nor are the pleasures of "passive" innocence independent of those of active aggression. In proportion to the vehemence with which I make an accusation, I draw upon my own accumulated stores of guilt, and spatter the accused with them. I then feel lighter, freer, happier. I have entered into the joy of the prosecutor, the policeman, the informer, and the professional patriot.

The moral dangers inherent in opting for innocence are obvious. Any cheap pornographer these days can persuade himself he stands alongside Flaubert, Baudelaire, and Zola, nobly battling censorship and dirty-mindedness. But this is only to say that, just as guilt feelings are no proof of actual guilt, so innocence feelings are no proof of actual innocence. Such facts of the moral life are not really compromising to morality. If it is a shock to discover a sadistic ingredient in a protest against sadism, we still need not be stunned into confusing Goya with the pornographers. In Goya, the enjoyment of cruelty is in the end swallowed up in the protest against cruelty, not the other way around. Which is why "the good and the just" can sincerely deny that the enjoyment of cruelty is present at all. They underestimate Goya, who is bigger for being "contradictory." Art is made from such contradictions and, conversely, a Goya who was free of the sadistic lusts he depicted would have produced art that was so much the less passionate and cogent. Art that is rightly condemned as "mere propaganda" is often just such a virtuous display of moral disapproval: "superior," simplistic, one-sided, gutless. . . . While by all means conscience should win the final victory, it should not win it too easily, and above all it should not be without an enemy to defeat, because the pleasure we demand from art derives only in a small degree from conscience itself and far more from the enemy—and of course from the battle.

The extreme virulence of modern tragi-comedy—like that of a Goya in painting—is not easy to account for. Yet most observers would concede that, in modern times, a peculiar vehemence of attack is called for both by the conditions which provoke it and the torpor of the public that is addressed. "Black" tragi-comedy not only gives a somber account of the world, it also gives the public a shaking. *Modern art is upsetting*—and for a reason: for the double reason I have just given.

Do people enjoy being shaken and upset? The question

is part of the larger one: is there pleasure in pain? To which the answer is: on certain terms, yes. Nor are the terms necessarily those of masochism. Being shaken by a tragi-comedy of Ibsen or Chekhov is a pleasure, because it is a shaking into life. True, a great deal may be taken away from life by what these writers show: when Graham Wallas saw *The Wild Duck,* "the bottom dropped out of the universe" for him. Still, the universe's loss was his gain. The play was a revelation. Scales had fallen from his eyes. Suddenly he could see, could live. Need one labor the point that such an experience does have an appeal?

As for the comic element, its function is the exact opposite of comic relief, since it makes the tragic darkness grow still darker. The Polish critic Jan Kott has written of *King Lear* as grotesque buffoonery in the manner of Beckett's *Endgame,* and what he calls a grotesque is, in my terminology, a tragi-comedy of the modern kind—a "comedy with a tragic ending." On the other hand, this gigantic and many-sided masterpiece has an element of reconciliation in it—not through faith, but through forgiveness—which brings it close to the other kind of tragi-comedy, "tragedy with a happy ending." Itself a tragedy, perhaps the greatest of tragedies, *King Lear* contains the seeds of both kinds of tragi-comedy. For clear-cut instances of tragedy intensified, instead of lightened, by comedy, modern drama would be the obvious place to look. Ibsen's use of Hjalmar Ekdal is the classical instance; but his use of Pastor Manders, in *Ghosts,* is not in principle different. And, as we have seen, it is by an element of the ridiculous that the protagonist of Tolstoy's tragi-comedy becomes strongly terrible instead of weakly pathetic.

What is the appeal of this humor in which humor seems thus denatured? To the extent that it adds aggression to aggression, such humor reinforces the already considerable attraction which modern tragi-comedy holds for unusually aggressive persons, and tragi-comedies at this Brechtian extreme do provide, among other things, an equivalent in the imagination to sado-masochistic whipping and beating. However, the words "in imagination" introduce a whole other dimension, for the imagination at work in these plays is a large one, and the targets are broadly significant. Kierkegaard, God, and the universe *are* implicated, whether or not a particular play does them justice.

Perhaps we have no real clue to the meaning of the special aggressiveness of this kind of tragi-comedy until we hear in it the note of exasperation. This has everything to do with humor, for humor contains an admission of failure. "Nothing to be done." Humor is a shrug of the shoulders, an accommodation to things as they are. Gallows humor is an accommodation to the gallows, to a world that is full of gallows. Does one have to go back to Swift and Juvenal to be reminded that a furious desire to accuse, arraign, punish, and reform can consort with a passionate conviction that accusation, arraignment, punishment, and reform do not work? Swift and Juvenal are tragi-comic writers.

That we can see the protagonist of Tolstoy's play as ludicrous makes the "criticism of life" more devastating without suggesting that anything can be done about it. That this picture of the ludicrous is actually pushed beyond that into the funny and (in a dark way) amusing makes the point that *nothing* can be done about it: "this is how things are."

What happens when an artist is both comic and a reformer? An illustration—doubly relevant because it is obviously intended as tragi-comedy—is Charlie Chaplin's

The Great Dictator. The "play" ends with an appeal to the audience to do something about Hitler, but this appeal is no more organically related to the tragi-comedy than the moralistic appeals to law and order which used to be added to gangster films like *Scarface.* One should perhaps regard the ending as Chaplin's attempt to restore to art the *deus ex machina*—an appeal to the *vox populi* being the modern equivalent. The film as a whole depends on humor. There is a joke—there is a tragi-comedy—in the very act of Chaplin mimicking Hitler. It is the joke of the little boy who stands behind the orator's platform mimicking him. It has to be a little boy, or there is no joke: essential is the contrast between real power and pretended power. Power is ridiculed, no doubt; and it can stand it. But also pointed up is the powerlessness of the mimic.

Even if the appeal to the audience were not left to the end, the tragi-comedy itself could not be integrated with the reformist intention. Such tragi-comedy does not move toward a changing of the world. It is itself an adjustment to the world, a way of living *with* Hitler. It is the humor of the small men who have thumbed their noses at the "great" for millennia, and thus expressed, and exhausted, their revolutionary urge. The expression "grin and bear it" says all. It is grinning that enables us to bear it. Gallows humor, again: such humor is not an outlet for aggression to no purpose. The purpose is survival: the easing of the burden of existence to the point that it may be borne. Of course, there are several sides to the phenomenon. Humor in a concentration camp will not help you to get out. It contributes to making you accept staying in. But by so doing, it may help you keep body and soul together against the day when getting out is possible. . . .

It may be helpful to apply some of this reasoning to

Waiting for Godot. Everyone will agree that this might, in some broad sense, be called a tragic play, and also that in its procedure from line to line, and section to section, it is comic. There is the big tragedy of man in a disvalued world, an incomprehensible and threatening world, a world either godless or having a God who leaves much to be desired; and there is the little comedy of a couple of bums amusing themselves and us with music-hall patter. *Waiting for Godot* can also, without stretching a point, be called a "comedy with an unhappy ending." Its substructure is the story of two men waiting for a third who will solve their problems. At the end of Balzac's play *Mercadet,* a certain Godeau arrives with money to solve everyone's problems; and at the end of Beckett's play the God of the Old or New Testament could arrive to solve everyone's problems. That would be a happy ending indeed. That "Godot" does *not* come is what makes the play a parable of life as seen by modern man.

People talk of Beckett's despair, and how should they not? It is the "modern" despair—despair unrelieved by any last-act *deus ex machina,* a harrowing despair beyond the familiar despairs, further gone into moral paralysis, a despair that needs neither a catastrophe to point it up, nor a climactic speech to sum it up, because it is *there,* insistently, obsessively, monomaniacally. It hangs in the air. You need only walk into a theatre where *Godot* is playing, and the ghastly despondency will cut into you like an icy wind. That people reject Beckett, provided they do not do so flippantly, may be very proper, and a compliment to his power as an artist. Goethe rejected Kleist, and as a man, if not as a critic, may have been wise to do so in rather a hurry, for there was something in Kleist that Goethe might well not have been able to bear. In Beckett, the despairing element is so weighty and oppressive it could easily prove dangerous—for anyone who is already in danger.

In danger, that is, of total collapse. We speak of despair as if it were a clear-cut and absolute thing. On Wednesday one felt despair, and on Thursday one did not. In actuality it is a hovering, free-floating thing. It is here, and it is there. It resembles London fog, visible all around, and yet not visible in one's own immediate vicinity, though it pierce one's clothes and rack one's throat. Despair is often most active when most hidden. It uses anaesthetics: when one is numb and feels nothing, one may be most under its influence. One can look back on things one has done and say: "I must have been in despair," and there is terror in the thought of having been in such a state of soul and not having known it. "Most people lead lives of quiet desperation," says Thoreau. How true that is, and how far from what is taught in school! Our school teachers lead lives of quiet desperation—one of the quietest and nicest of mine one day walked out and killed himself—but they teach us that they don't. The head office of all the educational systems in the world is on Madison Avenue.

Despair is around all the time but one can never be sure if "this time it is real" because reality is as mysterious, fluid, uncertain, and many-leveled as despair itself. All despairs are real, and it is right, when they happen, to sound the alarm, but there is only one despair that is "really real," ultimate, and a hundred per cent, and that is the despair that precipitates collapse into psychosis, serious physical illness, or suicide. At that stage, a man does not write a poem, novel, or play expressing despair.

He does not write *Waiting for Godot*. He falls ill or he falls under a bus or he falls into a state of "quiet desperation" so complete that he cannot put pen to paper. Very likely Samuel Beckett sometimes falls into such a state (I speak theoretically, not with personal knowledge) but the existence of his works—several novels, several plays—is proof that he has from time to time fallen out of it. Artistic activity is itself a transcendence of despair, and for unusually despairing artists that is no doubt chiefly what art is: a therapy, a faith. A work of art is organized and rational, a victory of the human in the highest sense of the term: it has dignity. Though it well may be imbued with despair ("He who has never despaired," says Goethe, "has no need to have lived"), and may easily be *about* despair (*Hamlet* opens with a young man wishing he was dead), a work of art is itself a sign that despair is not at the wheel but that a man is.

If Beckett's despair can make the despair of other writers seem "literary," then either he has tapped a deeper despair than theirs or he has expressed an equally deep despair much more vividly. In either case, he got rid of the despair, if only for the time being, *by* expressing it. And so this "more despairing" person is actually a less despairing person than many a miserable fellow who never expressed anything but collapsed into idiocy or suicide.

Of course, the non-despairing element of *Godot* is not to be attributed exclusively to the work's existence as an ordered whole. Even gallows humor is humor: though it springs from despair, and conveys despair, it also springs from joy and conveys joy. Playfulness is playfulness, and in *Godot* Beckett is sometimes playful to the point of being zany and even zestful. There are definite interruptions of the baleful mood, spurts of invaluable frivolity. And all is left in suspense at the conclusion. For this play is tragicomic in yet another respect: if the conclusion is not the happy one of Godot's arrival, neither is it the unhappiest one imaginable—discovering that Godot does not exist or will never come. He may exist and he may come. A door is open. The suicide tree is not used. No,

> in this immense confusion one thing . . . is clear. We are waiting for Godot to come . . . or for night to fall. . . . We are not saints but we have kept our appointment. How many people can boast as much?

A play could be even more somber than this, as Beckett has proved in some of his subsequent plays, but the main question remains—on Beckett's tragi-comedies and other people's—why is the deadly analysis pushed so very far, why is the relentlessness as relentless as *this,* why is the pessimism so deep, the despair so devastating, what satisfaction can we possibly derive from such dissatisfaction? I find a clue to the answer in the observation often made by middle-brow critics to the effect that we have in work like this of Beckett's a perverse countersentimentality, counteroptimism, counterfaith. The insinuation is that the modernists mechanically invert the philistine, middle-class attitudes. There would be some shrewdness in not fighting this accusation but in saying: "Granted, and what then?" It is indeed "middle-class ideology" that has been found wanting. More than that, all ideals have become suspect, all values thoroughly disvalued. In our time, if the man of letters (read: man of mind and conscience) hears himself uttering the big affirmations he has to ask himself if in seeking his salvation he has not got himself well and truly damned. Now when the affirmations are suspect, negations may be more honorable. In these circumstances, the negative attains the force of the positive.

The last ideal to go is hope, for none of the others can live on unsupported by it. And so in this time of *tabula rasa,* to hope or not to hope, that is the question. We have been swindled so many times that life itself is now most characteristically pictured as the Great Swindle. Comedy, especially modern tragi-comedy, sees life as such, but just as there is despair and despair, so there is belief and belief. One shouts that something terrible is about to happen in the hope that everyone will then stop it from happening. Call this cunning, call it superstition, it is very human.

Goethe once said that defining a person was dangerous as it tends to hold and limit him to the definition: until that is done a man is what he is becoming, and cannot be summed up as being what at any passing moment he is. But sometimes, one must retort, the definition, in its unjust violence and its comedic scorn, can act as shock treatment. Catch a man stealing, and call him a thief. The label generalizes unfairly. But it may serve a purpose. And comedy, for its part, has never been fair. It is not fair to shout: the house is burning down! when you see flames at a window. It is *pessimistic* to shout that a house is burning down when the only evidence you have is fire at one window. But it may save lives. And much of the celebrated pessimism of modern literature is of this kind. Such negativism does not feed on itself: it is fed by the ardency of a desire for something positive.

At the root of the infinite and poignant despairs of modern literature—and, in particular, of the tragi-comic works I am discussing—is hope. And in this situation hope reveals itself not as an idea one is "interested in," or an ideal one is "prepared to die for," but as a humble, indispensable fact of existence—like, say, metabolism. If one had truly lost hope, one would not be on hand to say so. Oddly enough, it is a writer's despair that needs proving, not his hope. And perhaps such proof has become more a point of honor in modern times than might be desired. That is because we live surrounded with the false hopes raised by charlatans and timeservers and feel the need to dissociate ourselves from them.

All art is a challenge to despair, and the type of tragi-comedy I am describing has addressed itself to the peculiarly harrowing, withering despairs of our epoch. Whatever one may say of it, one cannot say it does not get down to the bedrock. The vision is as negative as that of such modern tragedies as the *Nibelung's Ring,* or *Rosmersholm,* or *The Father,* or *Long Day's Journey into Night.* The humor which diverts it into tragi-comedy only deepens the horror, and turns the sublime toward the grotesque. It also deepens the "defeatism" with a smile of acceptance. One would perhaps not have believed in advance that any art could be as negative. But precisely in this it is reassuring. Nothing less drastic would have given us any comfort, for we would not have believed it, any more than we believe bishops and politicians. Real hope can be found only through real despair—short of the latter's being so "real," so utter, that it swallows us up. *"Was mich nicht umbringt, macht mich stärker,"* as Nietzsche says: "what does not slay me makes me stronger." The appeal of that comedy which is infused with gloom and ends badly, that tragedy which is shot through with a comedy that only makes the outlook still bleaker, is that it holds out to us the only kind of hope we are in a position to accept. And if this is not the hope of a Heaven in which we would live forever, it is not the less precious, perhaps, being the hope without which we cannot live from day to day.

REFERENCES

I HAVE DELIBERATELY left the body of this book unburdened with scholarly apparatus: rather than invite my reader to stop and read something else, I wanted to induce him to read my own pages uninterruptedly. But some of my references are relatively recondite, and some readers may welcome more bibliographical guidance to these than the text itself affords.

CHAPTER 1

PAGE 5 Brasillach, Robert: *Pierre Corneille*. Paris: Fayard, 1938.

8 Muir, Edwin: *The Structure of the Novel*. London: The Hogarth Press, 1928.

15 Moulton, Richard: *Shakespeare as a Dramatic Artist*. Oxford: The Clarendon Press, 1885; New York: Dover Publications, 1965 (reissue).

15 Touchard, Pierre-Aimé: *Dionysos*. Paris: Aubier, 1938.

16 Gouhier, Henri: *Le Théâtre et l'existence*. Paris: Aubier, 1952.

20 Barzun, Jacques: *The Energies of Art*. New York: Harpers, 1956.

23 Fernandez, Ramon: *La Vie de Molière*. Paris: Gallimard, 1929. (Translated as *Molière, the Man Seen Through the Plays*. New York: Hill and Wang, 1958) .

CHAPTER 2

40 Bullough, Edward: *Aesthetics*. Stanford, California: Stanford University Press, 1957.

46 Knight, G. Wilson: *The Wheel of Fire*. Oxford: Oxford University Press, 1930; revised and enlarged edition London: Methuen & Co., 1949; New York: Meridian

50 Books, 1962 (reissue).

P. 55 Galsworthy, John: "Some Platitudes Concerning Drama," *The Inn of Tranquillity*, 1921, but current in *Playwrights on Playwriting*, edited by Toby Cole. New York: Hill and Wang, 1960.

60 Ferenczi, Sandor: *Final Contributions to the Problems and Methods of Psychoanalysis*. London, Hogarth Press, 1955.

61 Constant, Benjamin: "Quelques Refléxions sur la tragédie de Wallstein et sur le théâtre allemand" (an essay originally published as preface to Constant's adaptation of *Wallenstein*).

61 Souriau, Etienne: *Les 200,000 situations dramatiques*. Paris: Flammarion, 1950. (My quotation from Souriau's admirable volume is an "unfair" one in the sense that I ignore its original context for my own purposes.)

64 Moreno, J. L. This author's ideas have been stated in a number of volumes, either in German or English, beginning with *Einladung zu einer Begegnung* (1914) and coming down to the third edition of *Psychodrama*, Volume One, Beacon House, Beacon, New York, 1964.

CHAPTER 3

73 Peacock, Ronald: *The Poet in the Theatre*. New York; Harcourt, Brace, 1946; Hill and Wang, 1960 (reissue).

78 Brasillach, Robert: *op. cit.*

90 Harding, D. W.: "Aspects of the Poetry of Isaac Rosenberg," Scrutiny, Volume III, Number 4. (The relevant passage has been quoted more than once, e.g. in *The Importance of Scrutiny*, edited by Eric Bentley, pp. 216–217. New York: George W. Stewart, 1948).

CHAPTER 4

105 A Man of Brilliant Intellect. George Jean Nathan, in an essay originally published in the American Mercury, December 1925, but now more easily accessible in *The World of George Jean Nathan*, edited by Charles Angoff. New York: Knopf, 1952.

P. 144 Meyerhold, V.: "On Ideology and Technology in the Theatre," International Theatre, Number 2, Moscow, 1934.

CHAPTER 5

151 Clark, Sir Kenneth: *The Nude.* New York: Bollingen, 1956; Doubleday Anchor, 1959 (reissue).

161 Lee, Vernon: *The Beautiful.* Cambridge: Cambridge University Press, 1913.

163 Sterba, Richard: "The Significance of Theatrical Performance," Psychoanalytic Quarterly, 1939.

166 Eighteenth-Century Comment. Davies, Thomas; Memoirs of the Life of David Garrick Esq. London: 1780.

171 Souriau, Etienne: *op. cit.*

186 The Mind Is A Stage. "The mind is a stage: adjusting mental problems in a spontaneity theater" is the title of an article by Gardner Murphy in Forum, May, 1937.

189 Marcel, Gabriel: "Une oeuvre capitale du théâtre à Strasbourg," L'Alsace Française, 3 mai, 1924.

CHAPTER 6

195 On Conrad. The two articles mentioned are: "The Short Stories," by Tom Hopkinson, The London Magazine, November 1957, and "London Letter," by V. S. Pritchett, The New York Times Book Review, January 12, 1958.

218 Archer, William: *About the Theatre.* London: Allen & Unwin, 1886.

CHAPTER 7

224 Murray, Gilbert: *The Classical Tradition in Poetry.* Cambridge, Mass.: Harvard University Press, 1927; New York: Vintage Books, 1957 (reissue).

225 Family Magazines. Better Homes and Gardens, August 1957. The writer is Howard Whitman.

225 Chief of the Division. George Silver of Montefiore Hospital, writing in The Nation, May 25, 1957.

P. 228   Murray, Gilbert: *op. cit.*

232   Fernandez, Ramon, *op. cit.*

238   Sarcey, Francisque: *Quarante Ans de théâtre.* Paris: Bibliothèque des Annales (Volume 4) , 1901.

246   Tarachow, Sidney: "Remarks on the Comic Process and Beauty," Psychoanalytic Quarterly, 1949.

249   Cornford, F. M.: *The Origins of Attic Comedy.* London: Edward Arnold, 1914; New York: Doubleday Anchor, 1961 (reissue) .

251   Meyerhold, V. in "Farce" a chapter from his book *On the Theatre* (1913) . Quotation is from Nora Beeson's translation, two chapters of which have appeared in The Tulane Drama Review, Volume 4, Numbers 1 and 4.

CHAPTER 8

272   Contemporary Account. Attributed to Madame de la Fayette, though first found in print in *Anecdotes dramatiques,* by Abbé de la Porte, Paris 1775. The English translation cited is from Eugène Vinaver's superb study *Racine and Poetic Tragedy.* Manchester, England: Manchester University Press, 1955; New York: Hill and Wang, 1959 (reissue) .

276   Richards, I.A., *Principles of Literary Criticism.* London: Kegan Paul, Trench, Trubner & Co., Ltd., 1924; New York: Harvest Books, 1961 (reissue).

277   Frye, P. H.: *Romance and Tragedy.* Boston: Marshall Jones Company, 1922; Lincoln, Nebraska: University of Nebraska Press, 1961 (reissue) .

278   Goldmann, Lucien: *Le dieu caché.* Paris: Gallimard, 1956. A translation is published by Humanities Press, New York, 1964, called *The Hidden God.*

285   Jekels, Ludwig: "The Psychology of Pity," *Selected Papers.* New York: International Universities Press, 1952.

288   Tillyard, E. M. W.: *Shakespeare's Problem Plays.* Toronto: University of Toronto Press, 1949.

CHAPTER 9

P. 293 Touchard, Pierre-Aime: *op. cit.*

305 Theological Commentator. Charles Moeller in the Introduction to *Satan* (New York: Sheed and Ward, 1952, reprinted in part as *The Devil* by Walter Farrell, Bernard Leeming and others, New York: Sheed and Ward, 1957).

309 Frye, Northrop: "The Argument of Comedy," *English Institute Essays*, New York: Columbia University Press, 1948.

309 Fernandez, Ramon, *op. cit.*

CHAPTER 10

326 Distinguished Scholar. Professor A. A. Parker in "The Approach to the Spanish Drama of the Golden Age," The Tulane Drama Review, Volume 4, Number 1.

345 Kott, Jan: "King Lear or End Game," Polish Perspectives, March 1961, a chapter from Professor Kott's book on Shakespeare, published in English translation by Doubleday and Company, New York, as *Shakespeare Our Contemporary* (1964).

359

ACKNOWLEDGMENTS

THIS BOOK has grown out of the Charles Eliot Norton Lectures which I delivered at Harvard University in the course of the academic year 1960–61. I wish to acknowledge the generosity of the Norton Committee in inviting me to Cambridge, and especially of McGeorge Bundy who sent the invitation and Mr. and Mrs. Perry Miller who thereafter looked after all my needs.

Special thanks are also due to the Harvard University Press which had proprietary rights to the publication of the lectures but handsomely forewent them at the request of Atheneum and myself.

My thanks to the Guggenheim Foundation are tinged with embarrassment, since they gave me a fellowship to write this particular book some fifteen years ago.

If Harvard provided the particular occasion for me to write out a first draft of my book, Columbia University presided over the several drafts that preceded the first one, and the one or two that followed it: it is through Columbia that I have been working on and with drama since 1952.

Also behind the book is the experience of professional dramatic criticism; I would like to express my gratitude to The New Republic, which I served from 1952 to 1956.

My rather mixed experiences in the world of professional entertainment leave me indebted in the positive sense to too large a number of people to name here; and indebted in a negative sense to an equally large number whom it is a pleasure not to name; yet lessons in How Not To Do It are lessons still.

In my chapter on farce I have made use of sentences,

and even paragraphs, out of an essay of mine that was published by Hill and Wang as the introduction to the anthology *Let's Get a Divorce!* My thanks to Lawrence Hill and Arthur Wang.

As for my debts to authors, many of them are explicitly labeled in the text. But quotations are not planned as letters of thanks, and one may quote the most cherished author least because one has absorbed his thought so well one considers it one's own: I apologize to any whose imaginary friendship I have rewarded with such real churlishness. As a token amends to all authors in this category, I should like to name four books I read with special avidity while this book was being written but which somehow are never cited in it: William Barrett's *Irrational Man,* Ernst Cassirer's *Essay on Man,* Martin Grotjahn's *Beyond Laughter,* and Simon Lesser's *Fiction and the Unconscious.*

The passage I quote from González de Salas was specially translated for me by William C. McCrary. I had been guided to the Spanish original by Everett W. Hesse.

Dr. Manfred George corrected my view of the *lex talionis.*

This ms, like others of mine, was typed by the efficient Miss Violet Serwin, and I have Miss Anne Stern to thank for being in effect a research assistant as well as a secretary. The index was made by David Beams.

The Pacifica Foundation let me have tape-recordings of the Lectures, as broadcast by their three radio stations, by the Harvard University Station, and by wgbh-Boston and wftm-Chicago. Listening to them proved another lesson in How Not To Do It: I decided the book should *not* be presented in lecture form, nor should it stay close to what these particular lectures said.

Everyone at Atheneum was solicitous and friendly far beyond either the call of duty or the customs of publishers. I naturally feel a special gratitude to my friend Harry Ford, who has been helping me in an editorial capacity since 1945.

My closest companion during the years of work on this book was my wife Joanne. And that is to say I could not possibly estimate either the kind or the quantity of her influence on it or me. I only know that her presence, with that of our children, was the greatest of my blessings.

E. B.

Winter 1963–1964

INDEX

ERIC BENTLEY

Born in England in 1916, Eric Bentley was subsequently a scholarship boy at Bolton School. From there he went to Oxford University on a history scholarship. After graduation at Oxford, a fellowship took him to Yale where he got a doctorate in comparative literature. He has taught at universities in the West, the South, and the Mid-West; was Charles Eliot Norton Professor of Poetry at Harvard; and today is Brander Matthews Professor of Dramatic Literature at Columbia. Eric Bentley has led a double life. If one half was passed in the groves of academe, the other was spent in the jungles of Times Square and Greenwich Village. As adaptor of plays by Pirandello, Brecht, and others, he became a well-known writer for the theatre. In addition he wrote *on* theatre as dramatic critic of The New Republic, and the reviews he wrote still command a large audience as collected in the paperback volumes *The Dramatic Event* and *What is Theatre?*. Another book—*In Search of Theater*—gave an account of the European theatres as well, and incidentally was a choice of The Readers' Subscription book club. Eric Bentley's name is a byword as editor of such play-collections, "standard" and "adventurous" at the same time, as *The Modern Theatre* and *The Classic Theatre*. His work on behalf of Bertolt Brecht has recently been extended into the field of recording, the album *Bentley on Brecht* being perhaps the best introduction to its subject in English. Aside from collections of reviews and other "occasional" pieces, *The Life of the Drama* is Eric Bentley's first book since 1947, which marked the publication date of his influential *Bernard Shaw*.

Atheneum Paperbacks

LITERATURE AND THE ARTS

Atheneum Paperbacks

THE WORLDS OF NATURE AND MAN

LIFE SCIENCES AND ANTHROPOLOGY